THOMAS DE QUINCEY

Texts in English Literature

THOMAS
DE
QUINCEY

Edited by
BONAMY DOBRÉE

SCHOCKEN BOOKS   NEW YORK

Contents

CONTENTS

Bibliographical Note

Apart from the first two parts of the *Confessions* published as a book in 1822, De Quincey produced nothing in volume form except his novels, *Walladmor* (1825) and *Klosterheim* (1832). All his work appeared in journals, chiefly *The London Magazine* (1821–5); *Blackwood's Magazine* (1826–8); *Tait's Magazine* (1833–41, 1845–8, 1851); *Hogg's Instructor* (1850–3); and *Titan* (1856–7). In 1853 he began to gather his works together in a collective edition, in the process altering and greatly enlarging his *Confessions*. His *Autobiography*, justly so named by Masson, originally appeared as a succession of 'Autobiographical Sketches'.

The main editions are:

De Quincey's Writings, ed. J. T. Fields, 20 vols., becoming 22, Boston 1851–59. Reprinted as Author's Library Edition, Boston 1878.

Selections Grave and Gay from the Writings Published and Unpublished by Thomas de Quincey, ed. Hogg, 14 vols., Edinburgh 1853–60. This is De Quincey's selection. It was reissued with a few modifications as *De Quincey's Works*, 15 vols., becoming 17, Edinburgh 1862–71.

The Works of Thomas De Quincey, ed. David Masson, 14 vols., London and Edinburgh 1889–90. The standard edition.

The Posthumous Works of Thomas De Quincey, ed. A. H. Japp, 2 vols., 1891.

The Diary of Thomas De Quincey for 1803, ed. H. A. Eaton, 1927.

De Quincey's letters have never been collected: many are quoted from manuscript sources; but a considerable number are printed in:

Thomas De Quincey to Wordsworth: A Biography of a Relationship, by J. E. Jordan, Cambridge 1960.

Unpublished Letters of Thomas De Quincey and Elizabeth Barrett Browning, ed. S. Musgrave, Auckland 1954.

The chief biographies are:

Thomas De Quincey: His Life and Writings, by H. A. Page (pseudonym for A. H. Japp), 2 vols., 1877, revised and enlarged 1890.

De Quincey, by David Masson, English Men of Letters Series, 1881.

BIBLIOGRAPHICAL NOTE

Thomas De Quincey, by H. A. Eaton, Oxford 1936. This is the best of many
biographies and studies, and contains a full bibliography.

Recommended for preliminary reading is *Thomas De Quincey* by
Hugh Sykes Davies, in the 'Writers and their Work' series
(Longmans, 1963), which also contains a useful brief bibliography.

Chronological Table of De Quincey's Life

1785	Born, 15 August, at Manchester
1791	His father dies. The family soon moves to Bath
1795	Goes to Bath Grammar School
1800	Visit to Ireland with Lord Westport
1801	Manchester Grammar School
1802	Runs away from school. Leads a nomadic life, on a small allowance, chiefly in Wales, then goes to London. Meets Ann
1804	Worcester College, Oxford. Begins to take opium while there
1807	Leaves Oxford before taking final examinations
1808	Goes to see Wordsworth at Grasmere. Stays to live at Dove Cottage
1814	Pays intermittent visits to Edinburgh
1816	Marries Westmorland country girl. Begins to contribute to *Blackwood's Magazine* and the *Quarterly Review*
1819	Edits *Westmorland Gazette*
1821	Goes to London. Meets Hazlitt, Lamb and others. *The Confessions of an English Opium-Eater* begins to appear in the *London Magazine*. Now launched on his literary career
1825	Returns to Grasmere
1828	Goes to Edinburgh, where his wife and family join him in 1830
1837	His wife dies
1840	Goes with his daughters to a cottage at Lasswade, near Edinburgh. Begins to get harried for debt. Hides about in Edinburgh, and finally goes back there
1859	Dies 8 December

INTRODUCTION

Thomas Quincey (the 'De' was his own addition), born in 1785—the same year as Thomas Love Peacock—was a decade or more younger than the great figures of the time: Wordsworth (1770), Scott (1771), Coleridge (1772), Landor and Lamb (1775), Hazlitt (1778); and about a decade before the second sprouting with Shelley (1792) and Keats (1795). He therefore doesn't 'belong'. As a result he is more individual, eccentric if you like, than any of the people of that great seminal period, of which the characteristic was not any 'romantic' theory but a marked individuality. He could worship his seniors, Wordsworth and Coleridge—though in due course with certain reservations—and feel detached from his juniors, even from Byron, who was only three years younger than himself. But with all of them he shared that great independence of thought and feeling that makes them valuable. Nothing is more misleading than to regard the 'Romantics' as a group, standing for something easily earmarked or labelled. Each is *sui generis*, and De Quincey had a genius of such wide scope as to make him speak directly to us now, provided always that we are prepared to understand, and enjoy, a voice so different from those that we usually hear. In some ways he saw more penetratingly than his coevals, and had a sensibility, especially as regards the music of words, that makes him unique.

The most autobiographical of writers, he was deeply penetrative of himself even from an early age. Thus at 18 he could write on 1 May in the *Diary* that he kept in 1803: 'A few days ago (I think during the course of last week) I became fully convinced that one leading trait in my mental character . . . is *Facility of impression*.' In the *Confessions* he notes: 'My life has been on the whole the life of a philosopher; from my birth I was made an intellectual creature, and intellectual in the highest sense my pursuits and pleasures have been.' But (as we all realize), 'some stimulus is necessary, and it remains to enquire *what*? And this I answer', he wrote, 'that I am firmly persuaded that there is none but a deep interest in these exhaustless and most lofty subjects of *human life*

I

and *human nature.* . . .' Thus he was, as can be gathered, an admirable conversationalist, always giving his company their full allowance of speech, unlike Coleridge, whose idea of conversation was to do all the talking himself. But beyond these characteristics, and perhaps the most important, was his insistence on the need for solitude, which at one time he sought 'in a morbid excess'. 'No man', he tells us in *Suspiria*, 'ever will unfold the capacities of his own intellect who does not at least checker his life with solitude.' To these pointers as to his nature must be added the importance he gave to dreams (nurtured by an addiction to opium which he never entirely threw off), as throwing 'dark reflections from eternities below all life', together with an ability to remember his dreams so vividly as to make them a part of his daily being.

The way his life shaped itself—it can hardly be said that he shaped his life—gives some clue as to the manner of his writing. In his 1803 *Diary* he wrote: 'I have always intended, of course, that *poems* should form the cornerstone of my fame', and he drew out an elaborate list of the poems he intended to write, which included three dramas which were to be 'poetic and pathetic'. In his late twenties he was ambitious to bring about 'a great revolution in the intellectual condition of the world', especially in philosophy, education, and mathematics. None of these schemes came to anything, nor did the idea he had in 1819, after reading Ricardo, of writing a *Prolegomena to All Future Systems of Political Economy*. The only literary work in which he was at all engaged until he was 36 was, in 1809, seeing through the press Wordsworth's *Convention of Cintra*.

But towards 1820, having dissipated his small fortune in buying books, and making generous gifts to those in want, including £300 to Coleridge; and having married in 1816 the country girl who had already borne him a child (his marriage certainly helped him largely to conquer the opium habit), he had incurred responsibilities which made it imperative for him to earn a living. His first task was the editing in 1818-19 of the *Westmorland Gazette*—Wordsworth had helped him to get the post—in which he warmly espoused the Tory cause, or hoped to. But he was in no way cut out to be a journalist; he always wanted to write about what attracted him, not what would interest his readers. How should the countryfolk care for the articles he was eager to write on Coleridge, Kant, or the planet Uranus? Beyond this he had schemes for writing in the great Edinburgh magazines, *Blackwood's* and the *Quarterly*, and to try to arrange this he dashed from Grasmere to Edinburgh, but without result. In 1821 he flitted to London, and in September there appeared in the *London Magazine* the first part of the *Confessions of an English Opium-Eater*, the second part coming out in October. The promised third part was never written. The first two appeared in book form in the next year.

The *Confessions*, though in the first place published anonymously, immediately made him famous, and set him upon his career of writing for the journals. His biography cannot be gone into here, and the indications given above are merely to help explain the kind of writer he was, producing essays for the great magazines. He was not really fitted for this sort of work, even on the generous scale of those days, any more than he was for fulfilling his task on the *Westmorland Gazette*. He was always an indisciplined writer: in conformity with his life he did not so much form his articles as let them form themselves. One can contrast him with that admirable critical essayist, Hazlitt. De Quincey was a far deeper thinker, and a more subtle person altogether; yet he is in many ways less satisfactory as a writer, except in his many outstanding passages, because he will so seldom stick to the point. He flies off at a tangent, putting in enormous parentheses, two or three pages long. For example, in his *Autobiography*, just because as a boy he had a casual meeting with George III, he gives us not only a kind of essay on that monarch, fascinating in itself, but adds what you might call a coda, a brilliant one, on the nature of kingship in a modern society. But if his habit of darting all over the place can sometimes be infuriating, one finds, after living with De Quincey for a little, that this is part of the charm of a complex personality who does not see things in isolation, but realizes how one thing has a bearing on another. It is no use to expect conciseness from him, though he often produces a strikingly compact sentence, sometimes almost an epigram.

Moreover, it is often in his digressions that he gives us his most valuable utterances, philosophic, psychological, or critical, and they sometimes come as a delightful surprise. Who would expect to find one of his most notable passages on prose in the essay 'On the Philosophy of Herodotus' (see p. 174)? Again, it is in his essay on Richter that you will

3

find an illuminating passage analysing the genius Shakespeare showed in devising Mistress Quickly's account of the death of Falstaff; and later in the same essay, distinctions between wit and humour, one of them being:

> that whilst wit is a purely intellectual thing, into every act of the humourous mood there is an influx of the *moral* nature: rays, direct or refracted, from the will and the affections, from the disposition and the temperament, enter into all humour; and thence it is, that humour is of a diffusive quality, pervading an entire course of thoughts; whilst wit . . . is always punctually concentrated within the circle of a few words.

Which may bring us to De Quincey's own sense of humour.

He had something of what we normally call a sense of humour, as we see from some of the anecdotes he tells, as in the account of his early adventures with his brother (see p. 18, *seq.*), or of when at Oxford he committed the solecism of appearing in hall without a waistcoat. But his own characteristic curious sense of humour is one of the oddest things about him. It seems in a way to have been an escape from horror, and we can approach this—making what may seem a De Quinceyan digression—through his essay 'On the Knocking at the Gate in *Macbeth*' (see p. 80). In this famous piece of criticism, written in 1823, he tells us that in—

> such a murder as a poet will condescend to, there must be raging some great storm of passion—jealousy, ambition, vengeance, hatred—which will create a hell within him; and into that hell we are to look.

To pass from this to 'On Murder Considered as one of the Fine Arts', of 1827, is to enter an altogether different atmosphere. Saintsbury writing of De Quincey said that, 'The humour of such things as the once famous *On Murder* has gone out of fashion.' But then this treatise, to call it so, is not by any means just rather gruesome play, a bit of quiet macabre fun. There is a great deal of very solid moral reflection behind it; murder is horrible, but there is an inescapable fascination in it. Saintsbury seems to have forgotten that in 1890 Wilde published his 'Pen, Pencil and Poison' about the murderer Wainewright, whom De Quincey had met at Charles Lamb's dinner table; and to look to-day at the average bookstall one would suppose that murder stories were the main light literature, even the nourishment, of the great reading public.

But to the thing itself. A large part of the first section is included in this volume (see p. 84) and it is worth while to make some comments on it. It begins with the 'Advertisement of a Man Morbidly Virtuous', after which delicately satiric phrase, added to by telling us that there was once at Brighton a short-lived Society for the Suppression of Virtue, he goes on to say that the paper which follows was read to the Society of Connoisseurs in Murder. This is given further point in view of a notorious, nationally exciting case of murder by a man called Williams, by this being called 'The Williams Lecture', as though it might be the annual Warton Lecture at the British Academy, or the Reith Lectures on the wireless. For Williams, we are told, like Æschylus, Milton, and Michelangelo, 'has carried his art to a point of colossal sublimity', a statement followed by a touch which seems to be merely artless fooling (a pretty reference to the Preface to *Lyrical Ballads*), but which begins to get under the skin: Williams, 'as Mr. Wordsworth observes, has in a manner, "created the taste by which he is to be enjoyed".' The lecture then goes on to distinguish between morality and art (remarkable if we remember that this was before Ruskin, and the Art for Art's sake reaction against him). Murder is, of course, 'an improper line of conduct, highly improper. . . . But what then? Everything in the world has two handles. Murder, for instance, may be laid hold of by its moral handle (as it generally is in the pulpit, and at the Old Bailey): and *that*, I confess, is its weak side: or it may also be treated *aesthetically*, as the Germans call it—that is, in relation to good taste.'[1] No more need be said here about this extraordinary performance: it illustrates what Professor David Daiches has said about De Quincey's 'sense of the disturbing relation between the ordinary, quotidian events of experience and the violent, or grotesque, or strange [being] illustrated with considerable virtuosity in his essay "On the Knocking at the Gate in *Macbeth*", and with a mocking philosophic humour in "Murder Considered as one of the Fine Arts".' The moral purpose of the essay, assuming De Quincey to have felt a sustained moral purpose while writing it, might well be summed up by, 'Clear your *mind* of cant.'

We may return to the 'Knocking at the Gate' essay for another

[1] This seems to have been the first appearance of the word 'aesthetic' in English. See the admirable chapter on De Quincey by Dr Ian Jack in *The Oxford History of English Literature*, Vol. X, 1815–1832.

purpose. The opening passage brings us directly to what could well be considered the core of De Quincey. It is an imaginative core, and through it he comes to his deep interest in psychology, his own and that of others, which strikes a curiously modern note. He has been asking himself why the knocking at the gate has always had such a tremendous effect upon him. In due course he comes to his explanation, but to begin with he shows us the road he started off on to arrive at his solution, and in doing so makes a tremendous generalization:

> Here I pause for one moment, to exhort the reader never to pay attention to his understanding, when it stands in opposition to any other faculty of his mind. The mere understanding, however useful and indispensable, is the meanest faculty in the human mind, and the most to be distrusted: and yet the great majority of people trust to nothing else, which may do for ordinary life, but not for philosophical purposes.

And then, at the end of the essay, he tells us that the works of Shakespeare, like the phenomena of nature, 'are to be studied with entire submission of our own faculties'. The last phrase is the essential one. Something has to come through to us, not through our intellects alone but through the whole of our being, including what we rather crudely call the subconscious. This was a new precision given to the idea of the 'unconscious' touched upon by Prior and Pope about a century earlier. In this De Quincey went a good deal further than the mass of writers of his day, probing more curiously into psychology. As he said in the opening paragraph of his 'On Wordsworth's Poetry' (a paragraph not included here): 'In the sense of absolute and philosophic criticism, we have little or none: for before *that* can exist, we must have a good psychology; whereas, at present, we have none at all.'

Such a view leads to further development, or at least ramifications. Talking of Pope he says (see p. 191):

> Poetry, or any one of the fine arts (all of which speak alike through the genial nature of man and his excited sensibilities), can teach only as nature teaches, as forests teach, as the sea teaches, viz. by deep impulses, by hieroglyphic suggestion. Their teaching is not direct or explicit, but lurking, implicit, masked in deep incarnations.

And later he says that, 'To address the *insulated* understanding is to lay aside Prospero's robe of poetry.' How does he himself apply this admirable theory? He is not a poet—in the sense of one who writes verse—so what has he to do with Prospero's robe of poetry? But perhaps Prospero also has a robe of prose, and what De Quincey has to say about this is admirably stated in the passage on prose in the essay 'On the Philosophy of Herodotus', already referred to, in which he says that, 'Each mode of composition is a great art; well executed is the highest and most difficult of arts.' But literature can be art only under certain conditions, and here we come to a principle complementary to those enunciated above, namely the distinction between the literature of *knowledge* and the literature of *power* (see p. 181). 'The function of the first is—to *teach*; the function of the second is—to *move*.' The first is not literature at all; a proposition supported by one of those rare epigrammatic passages where he writes: 'What do you learn from "Paradise Lost"? Nothing at all. What do you learn from a cookery book? Something new—something that you did not know before, in every paragraph.'

Thus it is in those portions of his work where he teaches by hieroglyphic suggestion that he best illustrates how prose can be a great art. Not that he fails to show considerable artistry in realms he inhabits with other writers. He can describe the physical world—an indication is given in the extract included from 'The English Mail Coach' (see p. 103) where he exhibits a magnificent power of imparting a sense of speed, as he does also in the passage from 'The Spanish Military Nun' (see p. 116), and superbly in 'Dream Fugue' (see p. 72). He can give the sense of crowds and action in 'The Revolt of the Tartars', for which room could not be found here. He can communicate the feeling of childhood and adolescence, as is plain from some of the portions of the 'Autobiography' printed in this volume: he can at times argue and debate. But where he excels, beyond all comparison, is in describing those parts of his experience which he considered the most important, the most solid glimpses into the nature of things, namely dreams and visions, as in 'Suspiria'—those late additions to the *Confessions* and for which he claimed the *Confessions* were written—and 'Dream Fugue'. The individuality of his utterance, the extra-ordinary music he can compel from the harmony of prose is unrivalled, even among such masters of deliberately musical prose as Sir Thomas Browne or Walter Pater. It is tempting to try to analyse a passage.

We may take a paragraph of the 'Levana' portion of 'Suspiria' (for a larger extract, see p. 68). He has been dreaming of the Three Sorrows who talk with Levana, though they do not use language so much as symbols which De Quincey put into words.

> The second sister is called Mater Suspiriorum, Our Lady of Sighs. She never scales the clouds, nor walks abroad, upon the winds. She wears no diadem. And her eyes, if they were ever seen, would be neither sweet nor subtle; no man could read their story; they would be filled with perishing dreams, and with wrecks of forgotten delirium. But she raises not her eyes; her head, on which sits a dilapidated turban, droops for ever, for ever fastens on the dust. She weeps not. She groans not. But she sighs inaudibly at intervals. Her sister, Madonna, is oftentimes stormy and frantic, raging in the highest against heaven, and demanding back her darlings. But Our Lady of Sighs never clamours, never defies, dreams not of rebellious aspirations. She is humble to abjectness. Hers is the meekness that belongs to the hopeless. Murmur she may, but it is in her sleep. Whisper she may, but it is to herself in the twilight. Mutter she does at times, but it is in solitary places that are desolate as she is desolate, in ruined cities, and when the sun has gone down to his rest.

That would seem to be perfect of its kind, emotive, 'hieroglyphic' prose, working on the reader by suggestion. Above all, it is musical prose. There is a beautiful modulation of vowel sounds, of length of sentence, of pace within the sentence. Again the attack of the sentence is never too often repeated, and he beautifully varies what might be called 'the threesome' which characterizes so much English prose. 'She weeps not. She groans not. But she sighs inaudibly at intervals.' Again, she 'never clamours, never defies ...', but De Quincey does not go on with 'never dreams ...' but writes, 'dreams not of rebellious aspirations'. Listen also to the distribution of stresses at the end of certain phrases, giving a conclusive sound which the Roman orators sought after and is often to be met with in our literature. There is great power in such dactylic effects as in: 'and with wrecks of forgotten delirium' or 'and when the sun has gone down to his rest'. But the whole passage must be read to experience the enchantment of the sounds that haunt the memory.

The pleasures to be got from De Quincey are enormously varied, and it might be as well to say here on what principle—not too rigidly applied—the present selection has been made. De Quincey's range is almost fabulously wide; to read all that he wrote is an education in itself: but he is at his best when talking about his own experiences, either of his own introverted self, or describing his acquaintances, who were the most distinguished figures of the older side of his generation. It cannot be said that he is notable, though as a rule he is interesting, in his treatment of more general subjects—the philosophy of Kant, which he found fascinating, but which repelled him by what he felt to be a too strong anti-Christian bias; the economics of Ricardo, Malthus's *Essay on Population*, ancient history, or astronomy. In short, his realm was the literature of power, not the literature of knowledge. Thus in spite of his delicate critical sensibilities his formal pieces lack his peculiar quality, even when he is writing on Shakespeare, Milton, or Pope; though even there, every now and again, where his addiction to digression serves him well, he produces, as will be seen, some notable paragraphs.

Nobody can make a selection from De Quincey to satisfy any other person acquainted with his work; he cannot satisfy even himself. There are many portions the present writer would have wished to include, as, for instance, the first part of 'The English Mail Coach', with its vivid picture of the road system of his day before railways were introduced, its postal system, and the way news was carried over the countryside—a part, moreover, which contains one of his most amusing divagations, an anecdote about the Emperor of China! It seemed a pity to exclude so much of his description of his life in London, especially his portraits of Lamb and Hazlitt. Everywhere there are gems of wisdom, or humour, or description, too deeply embedded for easy extraction; but it seemed preferable to give large stretches, illustrating the movements of his mind, rather than to prize out a number of small, detached jewels. An attempt has been made to present the man in his totality (though perhaps passing too lightly over his many miseries), and therefore the selection begins with a large autobiographical section, which of necessity includes his dreams. The text is from Masson's edition (see Bibliography), except for two letters which reinforce biographical passages. This section is followed by some famous pieces, then by large portions of his descriptions of Coleridge and the Wordsworths, succeeded by some critical dicta or assessments concluding with a few pieces which might be called generalizations. Altogether omitted are the two novels, *Walladmor* and *Klosterheim*, for which kind of writing De Quincey had but little talent ('The Spanish Military Nun' is in a different category), as well as his excursions into politics, which have little value at the present day, even for the historian. It is hoped that the selection is representative enough to compel the reader to a wider and more detailed acquaintance with so markedly individual, original, and imaginatively stimulating a writer.

Life and Dreams

Life

Early Life

The earliest incidents in my life which left stings in my memory so as to be remembered at this day were two, and both before I could have completed my second year; namely, first, a remarkable dream of terrific grandeur about a favourite nurse, which is interesting to myself for this reason—that it demonstrates my dreaming tendencies to have been constitutional, and not dependent upon laudanum[1]; and, secondly, the fact of having connected a profound sense of pathos with the reappearance, very early in the spring, of some crocuses. This I mention as inexplicable; for such annual resurrections of plants and flowers affect us only as memorials, or suggestions of some higher change, and therefore in connection with the idea of death; yet of death I could, at that time, have had no experience whatever.

This, however, I was speedily to acquire. My two eldest sisters—eldest of three *then* living, and also elder than myself—were summoned to an early death. The first who died was Jane, about two years older than myself. She was three and a half, I one and a half, more or less by some trifle that I do not recollect. But death was then scarcely intelligible to me, and I could not so properly be said to suffer sorrow as a sad perplexity. There was another death in the house about the same time—viz., of a maternal grandmother; but, as she had come to us for the express purpose of dying in her daughter's society, and from illness had lived perfectly secluded, our nursery circle knew her but little, and were certainly more affected by the death (which I witnessed) of a beautiful bird—viz., a kingfisher, which had been injured by an accident. With my sister Jane's death (though otherwise, as I have said, less sorrowful than perplexing) there was, however, connected an incident which made a most fearful impression upon myself, deepening my tendencies to thoughtfulness and abstraction beyond what would seem credible for my years. If there was one thing in this world from which, more than from any other, nature had forced me to revolt, it was brutality and violence. Now, a whisper arose in the family that a female servant,

[1] It is true that in those days *paregoric elixir* was occasionally given to children in colds; and in this medicine there is a small proportion of laudanum. But no medicine was ever administered to any member of our nursery except under medical sanction; and this, assuredly, would not have been obtained to the exhibition of laudanum in a case such as mine. For I was not more than twenty-one months old; at which age the action of opium is capricious, and therefore perilous.

who by accident was drawn off from her proper duties to attend my sister Jane for a day or two, had on one occasion treated her harshly, if not brutally; and as this ill-treatment happened within three or four days of her death, so that the occasion of it must have been some fretfulness in the poor child caused by her sufferings, naturally there was a sense of awe and indignation diffused through the family. I believe the story never reached my mother, and possibly it was exaggerated; but upon me the effect was terrific. I did not often see the person charged with this cruelty; but, when I did, my eyes sought the ground; nor could I have borne to look her in the face; not, however, in any spirit that could be called anger. The feeling which fell upon me was a shuddering horror, as upon a first glimpse of the truth that I was in a world of evil and strife. Though born in a large town (the town of Manchester, even then among the largest of the island), I had passed the whole of my childhood, except for the few earliest weeks, in a rural seclusion. With three innocent little sisters for playmates, sleeping always amongst them, and shut up for ever in a silent garden from all knowledge of poverty, or oppression, or outrage, I had not suspected until this moment the true complexion of the world in which myself and my sisters were living. Henceforward the character of my thoughts changed greatly; for so *representative* are some acts, that one single case of the class is sufficient to throw open before you the whole theatre of possibilities in that direction. I never heard that the woman accused of this cruelty took it at all to heart, even after the event which so immediately succeeded had reflected upon it a more painful emphasis. But for myself, that incident had a lasting revolutionary power in colouring my estimate of life.

So passed away from earth one of those three sisters that made up my nursery playmates; and so did my acquaintance (if such it could be called) commence with mortality. Yet, in fact, I knew little more of mortality than that Jane had disappeared. She had gone away; but, perhaps, she would come back. Happy interval of heaven-born ignorance! Gracious immunity of infancy from sorrow disproportioned to its strength! I was sad for Jane's absence. But still in my heart I trusted that she would come again. Summer and winter came again— crocuses and roses; why not little Jane?

Thus easily was healed, then, the first wound in my infant heart. Not so the second. For thou, dear, noble Elizabeth, around whose ample brow, as often as thy sweet countenance rises upon the darkness, I fancy a *tiara* of light or a gleaming *aureola*[1] in token of thy premature intellectual grandeur—thou whose

---

[1] '*Aureola*': The *aureola* is the name given in the 'Legends of the Christian Saints' to that golden diadem or circlet of supernatural light (that *glory*, as it is commonly called in English) which, amongst the great masters of painting in Italy, surrounded the heads of Christ and of distinguished saints.

head, for its superb developments, was the astonishment of science[1]—thou next, but after an interval of happy years, thou also wert summoned away from our nursery; and the night which for me gathered upon that event ran after my steps far into life; and perhaps at this day I resemble little for good or for ill that which else I should have been. Pillar of fire that didst go before me to guide and to quicken—pillar of darkness, when thy countenance was turned away to God, that didst too truly reveal to my dawning fears the secret shadow of death, by what mysterious gravitation was it that *my* heart had been drawn to thine? Could a child, six years old, place any special value upon intellectual forwardness? Serene and capacious as my sister's mind appeared to me upon after review, was *that* a charm for stealing away the heart of an infant? Oh no! I think of it *now* with interest, because it lends, in a stranger's ear, some justification to the excess of my fondness. But then it was lost upon me; or, if not lost, was perceived only through its effects. Hadst thou been an idiot, my sister, not the less I must have loved thee, having that capacious heart—overflowing, even as mine overflowed, with tenderness, strung, even as mine was strung, by the necessity of loving and being loved. This it was which crowned thee with beauty and power:

> *'Love, the holy sense,*
> *Best gift of God, in thee was most intense.'*

That lamp of Paradise was, for myself, kindled by reflection from the living light which burned so steadfastly in thee; and never but to thee, never again since *thy* departure, had I power or temptation, courage or desire, to utter the feelings which possessed me. For I was the shyest of children; and, at all stages of life, a natural sense of personal dignity held me back from exposing the least ray of feelings which I was not encouraged *wholly* to reveal.

It is needless to pursue, circumstantially, the course of that sickness which carried off my leader and companion. She (according to my recollection at this moment) was just as near to nine years as I to six.[2] And perhaps this natural precedency in authority of years and judgment, united to the tender humility with which she declined to assert it, had been amongst the fascinations of her

---

[1] My sister died of hydrocephalus; and it has been often supposed that the premature expansion of the intellect in cases of that class is altogether morbid—forced on, in fact, by the mere stimulation of the disease. I would, however, suggest, as a possibility, the very opposite order of relation between the disease and the intellectual manifestations. Not the disease may always have caused the preternatural growth of the intellect; but, inversely, this growth of the intellect coming on spontaneously, and outrunning the capacities of the physical structure, may have caused the disease.

[2] For *six* De Quincey should here have written *seven*.—M.

presence. It was upon a Sunday evening, if such conjectures can be trusted, that the spark of fatal fire fell upon that train of predispositions to a brain complaint which had hitherto slumbered within her. She had been permitted to drink tea at the house of a labouring man, the father of a favourite female servant. The sun had set when she returned, in the company of this servant, through meadows reeking with exhalations after a fervent day. From that day she sickened. In such circumstances, a child, as young as myself, feels no anxieties. Looking upon medical men as people privileged, and naturally commissioned, to make war upon pain and sickness, I never had a misgiving about the result. I grieved, indeed, that my sister should lie in bed; I grieved still more to hear her moan. But all this appeared to me no more than as a night of trouble, on which the dawn would soon arise. O! moment of darkness and delirium, when the elder nurse awakened me from that delusion, and launched God's thunderbolt at my heart in the assurance that my sister MUST die. Rightly it is said of utter, utter misery, that it 'cannot be *remembered*.'[1] Itself, as a remembrable thing, is swallowed up in its own chaos. Blank anarchy and confusion of mind fell upon me. Deaf and blind I was, as I reeled under the revelation. I wish not to recall the circumstances of that time, when *my* agony was at his height, and hers, in another sense, was approaching. Enough it is to say, that all was soon over; and the morning of that day had at last arrived which looked down upon her innocent face, sleeping the sleep from which there is no awakening, and upon me sorrowing the sorrow for which there is no consolation.

On the day after my sister's death, whilst the sweet temple of her brain was yet unviolated by human scrutiny, I formed my own scheme for seeing her once more. Not for the world would I have made this known, nor have suffered a witness to accompany me. I had never heard of feelings that take the name of 'sentimental,' nor dreamed of such a possibility. But grief, even in a child, hates the light, and shrinks from human eyes. The house was large enough to have two staircases; and by one of these I knew that about mid-day, when all would be quiet (for the servants dined at one o'clock), I could steal up into her chamber. I imagine that it was about an hour after high noon when I reached the chamber-door; it was locked but the key was not taken away. Entering, I closed the door so softly, that, although it opened upon a hall which ascended through all the storeys, no echo ran along the silent walls. Then, turning round, I sought my sister's face. But the bed had been moved, and the back was now turned towards myself. Nothing met my eyes but one large window, wide open, through which the sun of midsummer at mid-day was showering down torrents of

[1] 'I stood in unimaginable trance
And agony which cannot be remember'd.'
        Speech of Alhadra, In Coleridge's Remorse.

splendour. The weather was dry, the sky was cloudless, the blue depths seemed to express types of infinity; and it was not possible for eye to behold, or for heart to conceive, any symbols more pathetic of life and the glory of life.

Let me pause for one instant in approaching a remembrance so affecting for my own mind, to mention that, in the 'Opium Confessions,' I endeavoured to explain the reason why death, other conditions remaining the same, is more profoundly affecting in summer than in other parts of the year—so far, at least, as it is liable to any modification at all from accidents of scenery or season. The reason, as I there suggested, lies in the antagonism between the tropical redundancy of life in summer, and the frozen sterilities of the grave. The summer we see, the grave we haunt with our thoughts; the glory is around us, the darkness is within us; and, the two coming into collision, each exalts the other into stronger relief. But, in my case, there was even a subtler reason why the summer had this intense power of vivifying the spectacle or the thoughts of death. And, recollecting it, I am struck with the truth, that far more of our deepest thoughts and feelings pass to us through perplexed combinations of *concrete* objects, pass to us as *involutes* (if I may coin that word) in compound experiences incapable of being disentangled, than ever reach us *directly*, and in their own abstract shapes. It had happened, that among our vast nursery collection of books was the Bible illustrated with many pictures. And in long dark evenings, as my three sisters with myself sat by the firelight round the *guard*[1] of our nursery, no book was so much in request amongst us. It ruled us and swayed us as mysteriously as music. Our younger nurse, whom we all loved, would sometimes, according to her simple powers, endeavour to explain what we found obscure. We, the children, were all constitutionally touched with pensiveness; the fitful gloom and sudden lambencies of the room by firelight suited our evening state of feelings; and they suited, also, the divine revelations of power and mysterious beauty which awed us. Above all, the story of a just man—man and yet *not* man, real above all things, and yet shadowy above all things—who had suffered the passion of death in Palestine, slept upon our minds like early dawn upon the waters. The nurse knew and explained to us the chief differences in oriental climates; and all these differences (as it happens) express themselves, more or less, in varying relations to the great accidents and powers of summer. The cloudless sunlights of Syria—those seemed to argue everlasting summer; the disciples plucking the ears of corn—that *must* be summer; but, above all, the very name of Palm Sunday, (a festival in the English Church) troubled me like

[1] '*The guard*': I know not whether the word is a local one in this sense. What I mean is a sort of fender, four or five feet high, which locks up the fire from too near an approach on the part of children.

an anthem. 'Sunday!' what was *that*? That was the day of peace which masked another peace deeper than the heart of man can comprehend. 'Palms!' what were they? *That* was an equivocal word; palms, in the sense of trophies, expressed the pomps of life; palms, as a product of nature, expressed the pomps of summer. Yet still even this explanation does not suffice; it was not merely by the peace and by the summer, by the deep sound of rest below all rest and of ascending glory, that I had been haunted. It was also because Jerusalem stood near to those deep images both in time and in place. The great event of Jerusalem was at hand when Palm Sunday came; and the scene of that Sunday was near in place to Jerusalem. What then was Jerusalem? Did I fancy it to be the *omphalos* (navel) or physical centre of the earth? Why should *that* affect me? Such a pretension had once been made for Jerusalem, and once for a Grecian city; and both pretensions had become ridiculous, as the figure of the planet became known. Yes; but if not of the earth, yet of mortality, for earth's tenant, Jerusalem, had now become the *omphalos* and absolute centre. Yet how? There, on the contrary, it was, as we infants understood, that mortality had been trampled under foot. True; but, for that very reason, there it was that mortality had opened its very gloomiest crater. There it was, indeed, that the human had risen on wings from the grave; but, for that reason, there also it was that the divine had been swallowed up by the abyss; the lesser star could not rise, before the greater should submit to eclipse. Summer, therefore, had connected itself with death, not merely as a mode of antagonism, but also as a phenomenon brought into intricate relations with death by scriptural scenery and events.

Out of this digression, for the purpose of showing how inextricably my feelings and images of death were entangled with those of summer, as connected with Palestine and Jerusalem, let me come back to the bedchamber of my sister. From the gorgeous sunlight I turned round to the corpse. There lay the sweet childish figure; there the angel face; and, as people usually fancy, it was said in the house that no features had suffered any change. Had they not? The forehead, indeed—the serene and noble forehead—*that* might be the same; but the frozen eyelids, the darkness that seemed to steal from beneath them, the marble lips, the stiffening hands, laid palm to palm, as if repeating the supplications of closing anguish—could these be mistaken for life? Had it been so, wherefore did I not spring to those heavenly lips with tears and never-ending kisses? But so it was *not*. I stood checked for a moment; awe, not fear, fell upon me; and, whilst I stood, a solemn wind began to blow—the saddest that ear ever heard. It was a wind that might have swept the fields of mortality for a thousand centuries. Many times since, upon summer days, when the sun is about the hottest, I have remarked the same wind arising and uttering the same hollow, solemn,

Memnonian,[1] but saintly swell: it is in this world the one great audible symbol of eternity. And three times in my life have I happened to hear the same sound in the same circumstances—viz., when standing between an open window and a dead body on a summer day.

Instantly, when my ear caught this vast Æolian intonation, when my eye filled with the golden fullness of life, the pomps of the heavens above, or the glory of the flowers below, and turning when it settled upon the frost which overspread my sister's face, instantly a trance fell upon me. A vault seemed to open in the zenith of the far blue sky, a shaft which ran up for ever. I, in spirit, rose as if on billows that also ran up the shaft for ever; and the billows seemed to pursue the throne of God; but *that* also ran before us and fled away continually. The flight and the pursuit seemed to go on for ever and ever. Frost gathering

[1] '*Memnonian*': For the sake of many readers, whose hearts may go along earnestly with a record of infant sorrow, but whose course of life has not allowed them much leisure for study, I pause to explain—that the head of Memnon, in the British Museum, that sublime head which wears upon its lips a smile co-extensive with all time and all space, an Æonian smile of gracious love and Panlike mystery, the most diffusive and pathetically divine that the hand of man has created, is represented on the authority of ancient traditions to have uttered at sunrise, or soon after, as the sun's rays had accumulated heat enough to rarify the air within certain cavities in the bust, a solemn and dirge-like series of intonations; the simple explanation being, in its general outline, this—that sonorous currents of air were produced by causing chambers of cold and heavy air to press upon other collections of air, warmed, and therefore rarified, and therefore yielding readily to the pressure of heavier air. Currents being thus established, by artificial arrangements of tubes, a certain succession of notes could be concerted and sustained. Near the Red Sea lie a chain of sand hills, which, by a natural system of grooves inosculating with each other, become vocal under changing circumstances in the position of the sun, etc. I knew a boy who, upon observing steadily, and reflecting upon a phenomenon that met him in his daily experience—viz, that tubes, through which a stream of water was passing, gave out a very different sound according to the varying slenderness or fulness of the current—devised an instrument that yielded a rude hydraulic gamut of sounds; and, indeed, upon this simple phenomenon is founded the use and power of the stethoscope. For exactly as a thin thread of water, trickling through a leaden tube, yields a stridulous and plaintive sound compared with the full volume of sound corresponding to the full volume of water—on parity of principles, nobody will doubt that the current of blood pouring through the tubes of the human frame will utter to the learned ear, when armed with the stethoscope, an elaborate gamut or compass of music, recording the ravages of disease, or the glorious plenitudes of health, as faithfully as the cavities within this ancient Memnonian bust reported this mighty event of sunrise to the rejoicing world of light and life—or, again, under the sad passion of the dying day, uttered the sweet requiem that belonged to its departure.

frost, some Sarsar wind of death, seemed to repel me; some mighty relation between God and death dimly struggled to evolve itself from the dreadful antagonism between them; shadowy meanings even yet continue to exercise and torment, in dreams, the deciphering oracle within me. I slept—for how long I cannot say; slowly I recovered my self-possession; and, when I woke, found myself standing, as before, close to my sister's bed.

I have reason to believe that a *very* long interval had elapsed during this wandering or suspension of my perfect mind. When I returned to myself, there was a foot (or I fancied so) on the stairs. I was alarmed; for, if anybody had detected me, means would have been taken to prevent my coming again. Hastily, therefore, I kissed the lips that I should kiss no more, and slunk, like a guilty thing, with stealthy steps from the room. Thus perished the vision, loveliest amongst all the shows which earth has revealed to me; thus mutilated was the parting which should have lasted for ever; tainted thus with fear was that farewell sacred to love and grief, to perfect love and to grief that could not be healed.

'Autobiography': *Tait's Magazine*, Feb. 1834; Masson I.

The Feud

Such, according to the rapid sketch which at this moment my memory furnishes, was the brother who now first laid open to me the gates of war. The occasion was this. He had resented, with a shower of stones, an affront offered to us by an individual boy, belonging to a cotton factory; for more than two years afterwards this became the *teterrima causa* of a skirmish or a battle as often as we passed the factory; and, unfortunately, *that* was twice a-day on every day, except Sunday. Our situation in respect to the enemy was as follows:—Greenhay, a country-house, newly built by my father, at that time was a clear mile from the outskirts of Manchester; but in after years, Manchester, throwing out the *tentacula* of its vast expansions, absolutely enveloped Greenhay; and, for anything I know, the grounds and gardens which then insulated the house may have long disappeared. Being a modest mansion, which (including hot walls, offices, and gardener's house) had cost only six thousand pounds, I do not know how it should have risen to the distinction of giving name to a region of that great town; however, it *has* done so; and at this time, therefore, after changes so great, it will be difficult for the *habitué* of that region to understand how my brother and myself could have a solitary road to traverse between Greenhay and Princess Street, then the termination, on that side, of Manchester. But so it was.

Oxford *Street*, like its namesake in London, was then called the Oxford *Road*; and during the currency of our acquaintance with it, arose the first three houses in its neighbourhood; of which the third was built for the Rev. S. H., one of our guardians, for whom his friends had also built the church of St. Peter's—not a bowshot from the house. At present, however, he resided in Salford, nearly two miles from Greenhay; and to him we went over daily, for the benefit of his classical instructions. One sole cotton factory had then risen along the line of Oxford Street; and this was close to a bridge, which also was a new creation; for previously all passengers to Manchester went round by Garrat. This factory became to us the *officina gentium*, from which swarmed forth those Goths and Vandals that continually threatened our steps; and this bridge became the eternal arena of combat, we taking good care to be on the right side of the bridge for retreat—*i.e.*, on the town side, or the country side, accordingly as we were going out in the morning, or returning in the afternoon. Stones were the implements of warfare; and by continual practice both parties became expert in throwing them.

The origin of the feud it is scarcely requisite to rehearse, since the particular accident which began it was not the true efficient cause of our long warfare, but simply the casual occasion. The cause lay in our aristocratic dress. As children of an opulent family, where all provisions were liberal, and all appointments elegant, we were uniformly well-dressed; and, in particular, we wore trousers (at that time unheard of, except among sailors), and we also wore Hessian boots —a crime that could not be forgiven in the Lancashire of that day, because it expressed the double offence of being aristocratic and being outlandish. We were aristocrats, and it was vain to deny it; could we deny our boots? whilst our antagonists, if not absolutely *sansculottes*, were slovenly and forlorn in their dress, often unwashed, with hair totally neglected, and always covered with flakes of cotton. Jacobins they were not, as regarded any sympathy with the Jacobinism that then desolated France; for, on the contrary, they detested every-thing French, and answered with brotherly signals to the cry of 'Church and King,' or 'King and Constitution.' But, for all that, as they were perfectly inde-pendent, getting very high wages, and these wages in a mode of industry that was then taking vast strides ahead, they contrived to reconcile this patriotic anti-Jacobinism with a personal Jacobinism of that sort which is native to the heart of man, who is by natural impulse (and not without a root of nobility, though also of base envy) impatient of inequality, and submits to it only through a sense of its necessity, or under a long experience of its benefits.

It was on an early day of our new *tyrocinium*, or perhaps on the very first, that, as we passed the bridge, a boy happening to issue from the factory sang out to us, derisively, 'Holloa, Bucks!' In this the reader may fail to perceive any atrocious insult commensurate to the long war which followed. But the reader is wrong. The word '*dandies*,' which was what the villain meant, had not then been born, so that he could not have called us by that name, unless through the spirit of prophecy. *Buck* was the nearest word at hand in his Manchester vocabulary; he gave all he could, and let us dream the rest. But in the next moment he discovered our boots, and he consummated his crime by saluting us as 'Boots! boots!' My brother made a dead stop, surveyed him with intense disdain, and bade him draw near, that he might 'give his flesh to the fowls of the air.' The boy declined to accept this liberal invitation, and conveyed his answer by a most contemptuous and plebeian gesture,[1] upon which my brother drove him in with a shower of stones.

During this inaugural flourish of hostilities, I, for my part, remained inactive, and therefore apparently neutral. But this was the last time that I did so; for the moment, indeed, I was taken by surprise. To be called a *buck* by one that had it in his choice to have called me a coward, a thief, or a murderer, struck me as a most pardonable offence; and as to *boots*, that rested upon a flagrant fact that could not be denied; so that at first I was green enough to regard the boy as very considerate and indulgent. But my brother soon rectified my views; or, if any doubts remained, he impressed me, at least, with a sense of my paramount duty to himself, which was threefold. First, it seems that I owed military allegiance to *him*, as my commander-in-chief, whenever we 'took the field'; secondly, by the law of nations, I, being a cadet of my house, owed suit and service to him who was its head; and he assured me, that twice in a year, on *my* birth-day and on *his*, he had a right, strictly speaking, to make me lie down, and to set his foot upon my neck; lastly, by a law not so rigorous, but valid amongst gentlemen—viz., 'by the *comity* of nations'—it seems I owed eternal deference to one so much older than myself, so much wiser, stronger, braver, more beautiful, and more swift of foot. Something like all this in tendency I had already believed, though I had not so minutely investigated the modes and grounds of my duty. By temperament, and through natural dedication to despondency, I felt resting upon me always too deep and gloomy a sense of obscure duties attached to life, that I never *should* be able to fulfil; a burden which I could not carry, and which yet I did not know how to throw off. Glad, therefore, I was to find the whole tremendous weight of obligations—the law and the prophets—all crowded into this one pocket command, 'Thou shalt obey thy brother as God's vicar upon earth.' For now, if by any future stone levelled at him who had called me a

[1] Precisely, however, the same gesture, plebeian as it was, by which the English commandant at Heligoland replied to the Danes when civilly inviting him to surrender. Southey it was, on the authority of Lieutenant Southey, his brother, who communicated to me this anecdote.

'buck,' I should chance to draw blood—perhaps I might not have committed so serious a trespass on any rights which he could plead: but if I *had* (for on this subject my convictions were still cloudy), at any rate the duty I might have violated in regard to this general brother, in right of Adam, was cancelled when it came into collision with my paramount duty to this liege brother of my own individual house.

From this day, therefore, I obeyed all my brother's military commands with the utmost docility; and happy it made me that every sort of doubt, or question, or opening for demur, was swallowed up in the unity of this one papal principle, discovered by my brother—viz., that all rights and duties of casuistry were transferred from me to himself. *His* was the judgment—*his* was the responsibility; and to me belonged only the sublime obligation of unconditional faith in *him*. That faith I realized. It is true that he taxed me at times, in his reports of particular fights, with 'horrible cowardice,' and even with a 'cowardice that seemed inexplicable, except on the supposition of treachery.' But this was only a *façon de parler* with him: the idea of secret perfidy, that was constantly moving under-ground, gave an interest to the progress of the war, which else tended to the monotonous. It was a dramatic artifice for sustaining the interest, where the incidents might happen to be too slightly diversified. But that he did not believe his own charges was clear, because he never repeated them in his 'General History of the Campaigns,' which was a *resumé*, or recapitulating digest, of his daily reports.

We fought every day; and, generally speaking, *twice* every day; and the result was pretty uniform—viz., that my brother and I terminated the battle by insisting upon our undoubted right to run away. *Magna Charta*, I should fancy, secures that great right to every man; else, surely, it is sadly defective. But out of this catastrophe to most of our skirmishes, and to all our pitched battles except one, grew a standing schism between my brother and myself. My unlimited obedience had respect to action, but not to opinion. Loyalty to my brother did not rest upon hypocrisy; because I was faithful, it did not follow that I must be false in relation to his capricious opinions. And these opinions sometimes took the shape of acts. Twice, at the least, in every week, but sometimes every night, my brother insisted on singing 'Te Deum' for supposed victories he had won; and he insisted also on my bearing a part in these 'Te Deums.' Now, as I knew of no such victories, but resolutely asserted the truth—viz., that we ran away—a slight jar was thus given to the else triumphal effect of these musical ovations. Once having uttered my protest, however, willingly I gave my aid to the chanting; for I loved unspeakably the grand and varied system of chanting in the Romish and English Churches. And, looking back at this day to the ineffable benefits which I derived from the church of my childhood, I account

21

among the very greatest those which reached me through the various chants connected with the 'O, Jubilate,' the 'Magnificat,' the 'Te Deum,' and 'Benedicite,' etc. Through these chants it was that the sorrow which laid waste my infancy, and the devotion which nature had made a necessity of my being, were profoundly interfused: the sorrow gave reality and depth to the devotion; the devotion gave grandeur and idealization to the sorrow. Neither was my love for chanting altogether without knowledge. A son of my reverend guardian, much older than myself, who possessed a singular faculty of producing a sort of organ accompaniment with one-half of his mouth, whilst he sang with the other half, had given me some instructions in the art of chanting: and, as to my brother, he, the hundred-handed Briareus, could do all things; of course, therefore, he could chant.

Once having begun, it followed naturally that the war should deepen in bitterness. Wounds that wrote memorials in the flesh, insults that rankled in the heart—these were not features of the case likely to be forgotten by our enemies, and far less by my fiery brother. I, for my part, entered not into any of the passions that war may be supposed to kindle, except only the chronic passion of anxiety. *Fear* it was not; for experience had taught me that, under the random firing of our undisciplined enemies, the chances were not many of being wounded. But the uncertainties of the war; the doubts in every separate action whether I could keep up the requisite connection with my brother; and, in case I could not, the utter darkness that surrounded my fate; whether, as a trophy won from Israel, I should be dedicated to the service of some Manchester Dagon, or pass through fire to Moloch; all these contingencies, for me that had no friend to consult, ran too violently into the master-current of my constitutional despondency, ever to give way under any casual elation of success. Success, however, we really had at times; in slight skirmishes pretty often; and once, at least, as the reader will find to his mortification, if he is wicked enough to take the side of the Philistines, a most smashing victory in a pitched battle. But even then, and whilst the hurrahs were yet ascending from our jubilating lips, the freezing remembrance came back to my heart of that deadly depression which, duly at the coming round of the morning and evening watches, travelled with me, like my shadow on our approach to the memorable bridge. A bridge of sighs[1] too surely it was for me; and even for my brother it formed an

---

[1] *'Bridge of Sighs'*: Two men of memorable genius, Hood last, and Lord Byron by many years previously, have so appropriated this phrase, and re-issued it as English currency, that many readers suppose it to be theirs. But the genealogies of fine expressions should be more carefully preserved. The expression belongs originally to Venice. This *jus postliminii* becomes of real importance in many cases, but especially in the case of Shakspere. Could one have believed it possible

object of fierce yet anxious jealousy, that he could not always disguise, as we first came in sight of it: for, if it happened to be occupied in strength, there was an end of all hope that we could attempt the passage; and *that* was a fortunate solution of the difficulty, as it imposed no evil beyond a circuit; which, at least, was safe, if the world should choose to call it inglorious. Even this shade of ignominy, however, my brother contrived to colour favourably, by calling us —that is, me and himself—'a corps of observation'; and he condescendingly explained to me, that, although making 'a lateral movement', he had his eye upon the enemy, and 'might yet come round upon his left flank in a way that wouldn't, perhaps, prove very agreeable.' This, from the nature of the ground, never happened. We crossed the river at Garrat, out of sight from the enemy's position; and, on our return in the evening, when we reached that point of our route from which the retreat was secure to Greenhay, we took such revenge for the morning insult as might belong to extra liberality in our stone donations. On this line of policy there was, therefore, no cause for anxiety; but the common case was, that the numbers might not be such as to justify this caution, and yet quite enough for mischief. To my brother, however, stung and carried head-long into hostility by the martial instincts of his nature, the uneasiness of doubt or insecurity was swallowed up by his joy in the anticipation of victory, or even of contest; whilst to myself, whose exultation was purely official and ceremonial, as due by loyalty from a cadet to the head of his house, no such compensation existed. The enemy was no enemy in *my* eyes; his affronts were

beforehand? And yet it is a fact that he is made to seem a robber of the lowest order, by mere dint of suffering robbery. Purely through their own jewelly splendour have many hundreds of his phrases forced themselves into usage so general, under the vulgar infirmity of seeking to strengthen weak prose by shreds of poetic quotation, that at length the majority of careless readers come to look upon these phrases as belonging to the language, and traceable to no distinct proprietor any more than proverbs: and thus, on afterwards observing them in Shakspere, they regard him in the light of one accepting alms (like so many meaner persons) from the common treasury of the universal mind, on which treasury, meantime, he had himself conferred these phrases as original donations of his own. Many expressions in the 'Paradise Lost,' in 'Il Penseroso,' and in 'L'Allegro,' are in the same predicament. And thus the almost incredible case is realized which I have described—viz., that simply by having suffered a robbery through two centuries (for the first attempt at plundering Milton was made upon his juvenile poems), have Shakspere and Milton come to be taxed as robbers. N.B.—In speaking of Hood as having appropriated the phrase *Bridge of Sighs*, I would not be understood to represent him as by possibility aiming at any conceal-ment. He was far above such a meanness by his nobility of heart, as he was raised above all need for it by the overflowing opulence of his genius.

but retaliations; and his insults were so inapplicable to my unworthy self, being of a calibre exclusively meant for the use of my brother, that from me they recoiled, one and all, as cannon-shot from cotton bags.

The ordinary course of our day's warfare was this: between nine and ten in the morning, occurred our first transit, and consequently our earliest opportunity for doing business. But at this time the great sublunary interest of breakfast, which swallowed up all nobler considerations of glory and ambition, occupied the work-people of the factory (or what in the pedantic diction of this day are termed the 'operatives'), so that very seldom any serious business was transacted. Without any formal armistice, the paramount convenience of such an arrangement silently secured its own recognition. Notice there needed none of truce, when the one side yearned for breakfast, and the other for a respite; the groups, therefore, on or about the bridge, if any at all, were loose in their array, and careless. We passed through them rapidly, and, on my part, uneasily; exchanging a few snarls, perhaps, but seldom or ever snapping at each other. The tameness was almost shocking of those who, in the afternoon, would inevitably resume their natural characters of tiger-cats and wolves. Sometimes, however, my brother felt it to be a duty that we should fight in the morning; particularly when any expression of public joy for a victory—bells ringing in the distance— or when a royal birth-day, or some traditional commemoration of ancient feuds (such as the 5th of November), irritated his martial propensities. Some of these, being religious festivals, seemed to require of us an *extra* homage, for which we knew not how to find any natural or significant expression, except through sharp discharges of stones, that being a language older than Hebrew or Sanscrit, and universally intelligible. But, excepting these high days of religious solemnity, when a man is called upon to show that he is not a Pagan or a miscreant in the eldest of senses, by thumping, or trying to thump, somebody who is accused or accusable of being heterodox, the great ceremony of breakfast was allowed to sanctify the hour. Some natural growls we uttered, but hushed them soon, regardless

'*Of the sweeping whirlpool's sway,*
That, hush'd in grim repose, look'd for his evening prey.'

That came but too surely. Yes, evening never forgot to come; this odious necessity of fighting never missed its road back, or fell asleep, or loitered by the way, more than a bill of exchange, or a tertian fever. Five times a-week (Saturday sometimes, and Sunday always, were days of rest) the same scene rehearsed itself in pretty nearly the same succession of circumstances. Betweeen four and five o'clock we had crossed the bridge to the safe, or Greenhay, side; then we paused, and waited for the enemy. Sooner or later a bell rang, and from the smoky hive issued the hornets that night and day stung incurably my peace of

24

mind. The order and procession of the incidents after this were odiously monotonous. My brother occupied the main high-road, precisely at the point where a
very gentle rise of the ground attained its summit; for the bridge lay in a slight
valley; and the main military position was fifty or eighty yards above the
bridge; then—but having first examined my pockets, in order to be sure that
my stock of ammunition—stones, fragments of slate, with a reasonable proportion of brickbats—was all correct and ready for action—he detached me about
forty yards to the right, my orders being invariable, and liable to no doubts or
'quibbling.' Detestable in *my* ears was that word '*quibbling*,' by which, for a
thousand years, if the war had happened to last so long, he would have fastened
upon me the imputation of meaning, or wishing, at least, to do what he called
'pettifogulising'—that is, to plead some distinction, or verbal demur, in bar of
my orders, under some colourable pretence that, according to their literal
construction, they really did not admit of being fulfilled, or perhaps that they
admitted it too much as being capable of fulfilment in two senses, either of
them a practical sense. True it was that my eye was preternaturally keen for
flaws of language, not from pedantic exaction of superfluous accuracy, but, on
the contrary, from too conscientious a wish to escape the mistakes which
language not rigorous is apt to occasion. So far from seeking to 'pettifogulise'—
i.e., to find evasions for any purpose in a trickster's minute tortuosities of construction—exactly in the opposite direction, from mere excess of sincerity, most
unwillingly I found, in almost everybody's words, an unintentional opening left
for double interpretations. Undesigned equivocation prevails everywhere; and
it is not the cavilling hair-splitter, but, on the contrary, the single-eyed servant
of truth, that is most likely to insist upon the limitation of expressions too wide or
too vague, and upon the decisive election between meanings potentially double.
Not in order to resist or evade my brother's directions, but for the very opposite
purpose—viz., that I might fulfil them to the letter—thus and no otherwise it
happened that I showed so much scrupulosity about the exact value and position
of his words, as finally to draw upon myself the vexatious reproach of being
habitually a 'pettifoguliser.'

Meantime, our campaigning continued to rage. Overtures of pacification
were never mentioned on either side. And I, for *my* part, with the passions only
of peace at my heart, did the works of war faithfully, and with distinction. I
presume so, at least, from the results. It is true I was continually falling into
treason, without exactly knowing how I got into it, or how I got out of it. My
brother also, it is true, sometimes assured me that he could, according to the
rigour of martial justice, have me hanged on the first tree we passed; to which
my prosaic answer had been, that of trees there *were* none in Oxford Street—
(which, in imitation of Von Troil's famous chapter on the snakes of Lapland,

the reader may accept, if he pleases, as a complete course of lectures on the 'dendrology' of Oxford Street)—but, notwithstanding such little stumblings in my career, I continued to ascend in the service; and I am sure it will gratify my friendly readers to hear, that, before my eighth birth-day, I was promoted to the rank of major-general. Over this sunshine, however, soon swept a train of clouds. Three times I was taken prisoner; and with different results. The first time I was carried to the rear, and not molested in any way. Finding myself thus ignominiously neglected, I watched my opportunity; and, by making a wide circuit, easily effected my escape. In the next case, a brief council was held over me; but I was not allowed to hear the deliberations; the result only being communicated to me—which result consisted in a message not very complimentary to my brother, and a small present of kicks to myself. This present was paid down without any discount, by means of a general subscription among the party surrounding me—that party, luckily, not being very numerous; besides which, I must, in honesty, acknowledge myself, generally speaking, indebted to their forbearance. They were not disposed to be too hard upon me. But, at the same time, they clearly did not think it right that I should escape altogether from tasting the calamities of war. And this translated the estimate of my guilt from the public jurisdiction to that of the individual, sometimes capricious and harsh, and carrying out the public award by means of legs that ranged through all gradations of weight and agility. One kick differed exceedingly from another kick in dynamic value; and, in some cases, this difference was so distressingly conspicuous, as to imply special malice, unworthy, I conceive, of all generous soldiership.

On returning to our own frontiers, I had an opportunity of displaying my exemplary greenness. That message to my brother, with all its *virus* of insolence, I repeated as faithfully for the spirit, and as literally for the expressions, as my memory allowed me to do: and in that troublesome effort, simpleton that I was, fancied myself exhibiting a soldier's loyalty to his commanding officer. My brother thought otherwise: he was more angry with me than with the enemy. I ought, he said, to have refused all participation in such *sansculottes'* insolence; to carry it, was to acknowledge it as fit to be carried. One grows wiser every day; and on this particular day I made a resolution that, if again made prisoner, I would bring no more 'jaw' (so my brother called it) from the Philistines. If these people *would* send 'jaw', I settled that, henceforwards, it must go through the post-office.

'Autobiography': *Hogg's Instructor*, 1851; Masson I.

Bath

In my twelfth year it was that first of all I entered upon the arena of a great public school—viz., the Grammar School of Bath, over which at that time presided a most accomplished Etonian—Mr. (or was he as yet Doctor?) Morgan. If he was not, I am sure he ought to have been; and, with the reader's concurrence, will therefore create him a doctor on the spot. Every man has reason to rejoice who enjoys the advantage of a public training. I condemned, and *do* condemn, the practice of sending out into such stormy exposures those who are as yet too young, too dependent on female gentleness, and endowed with sensibilities originally too exquisite for such a warfare. But at nine or ten the masculine energies of the character are beginning to develop themselves; or, if not, no discipline will better aid in their development than the bracing intercourse of a great English classical school. Even the selfish are *there* forced into accommodating themselves to a public standard of generosity; and the effeminate into conforming to a rule of manliness. I was myself at two public schools, and I think with gratitude of the benefits which I reaped from both; as also I think with gratitude of that guardian in whose quiet household I learned Latin so effectually. But the small private schools, of which I had opportunities for gathering some brief experience—schools containing thirty to forty boys—were models of ignoble manners as regarded part of the juniors, and of favouritism as regarded the masters. Nowhere is the sublimity of public justice so broadly exemplified as in an English public school on the old Edward the Sixth or Elizabeth foundation. There is not in the universe such an Areopagus for fair play, and abhorrence of all crooked ways, as an English mob, or one of the time-honoured English 'foundation' schools. But my own first introduction to such an establishment was under peculiar and contradictory circumstances. When my 'rating,' or graduation in the school was to be settled, naturally my altitude (to speak astronomically) was taken by my proficiency in Greek. But here I had no advantage over others of my age. My guardian was a feeble Grecian, and had not excited my ambition; so that I could barely construe books as easy as the Greek Testament and the Iliad. This was considered quite well enough for my age; but still it caused me to be placed under the care of Mr. Wilkins, the second master out of four, and not under Dr. Morgan himself. Within one month, however, my talent for Latin verses, which had by this time gathered strength and expansion, became known. Suddenly I was honoured as never was man or boy since Mordecai the Jew. Without any colourable relation to the doctor's jurisdiction, I was now weekly paraded for distinction at the supreme tribunal of the school; out of which, at first, grew nothing but a sunshine of approbation delightful to my heart. Within six weeks all this had

27

changed. The approbation, indeed, continued, and the public expression of it. Neither would there, in the ordinary course, have been any painful reaction from jealousy or fretful resistance to the soundness of my pretensions; since it was sufficiently known to such of my schoolfellows as stood on my own level in the school, that I, who had no male relatives but military men, and those in India, could not have benefited by any clandestine aid. But, unhappily, Dr. Morgan was at that time dissatisfied with some points in the progress of his head class; and, as it soon appeared, was continually throwing in their teeth the brilliancy of my verses at eleven or twelve, by comparison with theirs at seventeen, eighteen, and even nineteen. I had observed him sometimes pointing to myself, and was perplexed at seeing this gesture followed by gloomy looks, and what French reporters call 'sensation', in these young men, whom naturally I viewed with awe as my leaders—boys that were called young men, men that were reading Sophocles (a name that carried with it the sound of something seraphic to my ears), and who never had vouchsafed to waste a word on such a child as myself. The day was come, however, when all that would be changed. One of these leaders strode up to me in the public playground; and, delivering a blow on my shoulder, which was not intended to hurt me, but as a mere formula of introduction, asked me, 'What the devil I meant by bolting out of the course, and annoying other people in that manner? Were "other people" to have no rest for me and my verses, which, after all, were horribly bad?' There might have been some difficulty in returning an answer to this address, but none was required. I was briefly admonished to see that I wrote worse for the future, or else—— At this *aposiopesis* I looked inquiringly at the speaker, and he filled up the chasm by saying, that he would 'annihilate' me. Could any person fail to be aghast at such a demand? I was to write worse than my own standard, which, by his account of my verses, must be difficult; and I was to write worse than himself, which might be impossible. My feelings revolted against so arrogant a demand, unless it had been far otherwise expressed; if death on the spot had awaited me, I could not have controlled myself; and, on the next occasion for sending up verses to the headmaster, so far from attending to the orders issued, I double-shotted my guns; double applause descended on myself; but I remarked, with some awe, though not repenting of what I had done, that double confusion seemed to agitate the ranks of my enemies. Amongst them, loomed out in the distance my 'annihilating' friend, who shook his huge fist at me, but with something like a grim smile about his eyes. He took an early opportunity of paying his respects to me again, saying, 'You little devil, do you call this writing your worst?'—'No,' I replied; 'I call it writing my best.' The annihilator, as it turned out, was really a good-natured young man; but he was on the wing for Cambridge; and with the rest, or some of them, I continued to wage war for more than a year. And yet, for a word spoken with kindness, how readily I would have resigned (had it been altogether at my own choice to do so) the peacock's feather in my cap as the merest of baubles. Undoubtedly, praise sounded sweet in *my* ears also; but that was nothing by comparison with what stood on the other side. I detested distinctions that were connected with mortification to others; and, even if I could have got over *that*, the eternal feud fretted and tormented my nature. Love, that once in childhood had been so mere a necessity to me, *that* had long been a reflected ray from a departed sunset. But peace, and freedom from strife, if love were no longer possible (as so rarely it is in this world), was the clamorous necessity of my nature. To contend with somebody was still my fate; how to escape the contention I could not see; and yet, for itself, and for the deadly passions into which it forced me, I hated and loathed it more than death. It added to the distraction and internal feud of my mind, that I could not *altogether* condemn the upper boys. I was made a handle of humiliation to them. And, in the meantime, if I had an undeniable advantage in one solitary accomplishment, which is still a matter of accident, or sometimes of peculiar direction given to the taste, they, on the other hand, had a great advantage over me in the more elaborate difficulties of Greek, and of choral Greek poetry. I could not altogether wonder at their hatred of myself. Yet still, as they had chosen to adopt this mode of conflict with me, I did not feel that I had any choice but to resist. The contest was terminated for me by my removal from the school, in consequence of a very threatening illness affecting my head; but it lasted more than a year, and it did not close before several among my public enemies had become my private friends. They were much older, but they invited me to the houses of their friends, and showed me a respect which affected me—this respect having more reference, apparently, to the firmness I had exhibited, than to any splendour in my verses. And, indeed, these had rather drooped, from a natural accident: several persons of my own class had formed the practice of asking me to write verses for *them*. I could not refuse. But, as the subjects given out were the same for the entire class, it was not possible to take so many crops off the ground, without starving the quality of all.

'Autobiography': *Tait's Magazine*, Feb. 1834; Masson I.

Manchester Grammar School

On a day, therefore, it was in the closing autumn (or rather in the opening winter) of 1800 that my first introduction took place to the Manchester Grammar School. The school-room showed already in its ample proportions some hint of its pretensions as an endowed school, or school of that class which I believe peculiar to England. To this limited extent had the architectural sense of power been timidly and parsimoniously invoked. Beyond that, nothing had been attempted; and the dreary expanse of whitewashed walls, that at so small a cost might have been embellished by plaster-of-Paris friezes and large medallions, illustrating to the eye of the youthful student the most memorable glorifications of literature—these were bare as the walls of a poor-house or a lazaretto; buildings whose functions, as thoroughly sad and gloomy, the mind recoils from drawing into relief by sculpture or painting. But this building was dedicated to purposes that were noble. The naked walls clamoured for decoration; and how easily might tablets have been moulded—exhibiting (as a first homage to literature) Athens, with the wisdom of Athens, in the person of Pisistratus, concentrating the general energies upon the revisal and the re-casting of the 'Iliad.' Or (second) the Athenian captives in Sicily, within the fifth century B.C., as winning noble mercy for themselves by some

> 'Repeated air
> Of sad Electra's poet.'

Such, and so sudden, had been the oblivion of earthly passions wrought by the contemporary poet of Athens that in a moment the wrath of Sicily, with all its billows, ran down into a heavenly calm; and he that could plead for his redemption no closer relation to Euripides than the accident of recalling some scatterings from his divine verses suddenly found his chains dropping to the ground, and himself, that in the morning had risen a despairing slave in a stone-quarry, translated at once as a favoured brother into a palace of Syracuse. Or, again, how easy to represent (third) 'the great Emathian conqueror,' that in the very opening of his career, whilst visiting Thebes with vengeance, nevertheless relented at the thought of literature, and

> 'Bade spare
> The house of Pindarus, when temple and tower
> Went to the ground.'

Alexander might have been represented amongst the colonnades of some Persian capital—Ecbatana or Babylon, Susa or Persepolis—in the act of receiving from Greece, as a *nuzzur* more awful than anything within the gift of the 'barbaric East,' a jewelled casket containing the 'Iliad' and the 'Odyssey'; creations that already have lived almost as long as the Pyramids.

Puritanically bald and odious, therefore, in my eyes, was the hall up which my guardian and myself paced solemnly—though not Miltonically 'riding up to the Soldan's chair,' yet, in fact, within a more limited kingdom, advancing to the chair of a more absolute despot. This potentate was the head-master, or *archididascalus*, of the Manchester Grammar School; and that school was variously distinguished. It was (1) ancient, having in fact been founded by a bishop of Exeter in an early part of the sixteenth century, so as to be now, in 1856, more than 330 years old; (2) it was rich, and was annually growing richer; and (3) it was dignified by a beneficial relation to the magnificent University of Oxford. ...

Mr. Lawson[1] was in some degree interesting by his position and his recluse habits. Life was over with him, for its hopes and for its trials. Or at most one trial yet awaited him; which was—to fight with a painful malady, and fighting to die. He still had his dying to do: he was in arrear as to *that*: else all was finished. It struck me (but, with such limited means for judging, I might easily be wrong) that his understanding was of a narrow order. But that did not disturb the interest which surrounded him now in his old age (probably seventy-five, or more), nor make any drawback from the desire I had to spell backwards and re-compose the text of his life. What had been his fortunes in this world? Had they travelled upwards or downwards? What triumphs had he enjoyed in the sweet and solemn cloisters of Oxford? What mortifications in the harsh world outside? Two only had survived in the malicious traditions of 'his friends.' He was a Jacobite (as were so many amongst my dear Lancastrian compatriots); had drunk the Pretender's health, and had drunk it in company with that Dr. Byrom who had graced the *symposium* by the famous equivocating *impromptu*[2] to the health of that prince. Mr. Lawson had therefore been obliged to witness the final prostration of his political party. That was his earliest mortification. His second, about seven years later, was that he had been jilted, and with

---

[1] The head-master.—B.D.

[2] '*Equivocating impromptu*': The party had gathered in a tumultuary way; so that some Capulets had mingled with the Montagues, one of whom called upon Dr. Byrom to drink *The King, God bless him! and Confusion to the Pretender!* Upon which the doctor sang out—

> 'God bless the king, of church and state defender;
> God bless (no harm in *blessing*) the Pretender!
> But who Pretender is, and who the King—
> God bless us all! that's quite another thing.'

Dr. Byrom [John Byrom, 1691-1763] was otherwise famous than as a Jacobite— viz., as the author of a very elaborate shorthand, which (according to some who have examined it) rises even to a philosophic dignity. David Hartley in particular said of it that, 'if ever a philosophic language (as projected by Bishop Wilkins, by Leibnitz, &c.) should be brought to bear, in that case Dr. Byrom's work would furnish the proper character for its notation.'

circumstances (at least so I heard) of cruel scorn. Was it that *he* had interpreted in a sense too flattering for himself ambiguous expressions of favour in the lady? or that she in cruel caprice had disowned the hopes which she had authorized? However this might be, half-a-century of soothing and reconciling years had cicatrised the wounds of Mr. Lawson's heart. The Lady of 1752, if living in 1800, must be furiously wrinkled. And a strange metaphysical question arises: Whether, when the object of an impassioned love has herself faded into a shadow, the fiery passion itself can still survive as an abstraction, still mourn over its wrongs, still clamour for redress. I have heard of such cases. In Words-worth's poem of 'Ruth' (which was founded, as I happen to know, upon facts) it is recorded as an affecting incident that, some months after the first frenzy of her disturbed mind had given way to medical treatment, and had lapsed into a gentler form of lunacy, she was dismissed from confinement; and, upon finding herself uncontrolled among the pastoral scenes where she played away her childhood, she gradually fell back to the original habits of her life whilst yet un-disturbed by sorrow. Something similar had happened to Mr. Lawson; and some time after his first shock, amongst other means for effacing that deep-grooved impression, he had laboured to replace himself, as much as was possible, in the situation of a college student. In this effort he was assisted considerably by the singular arrangement of the house attached to his official station. For an English house it was altogether an oddity, being, in fact, built upon a Roman plan. All the rooms on both storeys had their windows looking down upon a little central court. This court was quadrangular, but so limited in its dimensions that by a Roman it would have been regarded as the *impluvium*: for Mr. Law-son, however, with a little exertion of fancy, it transmuted itself into a college quadrangle. Here, therefore, were held the daily 'callings-over', at which every student was obliged to answer upon being named. And thus the unhappy man, renewing continually the fancy that he was still standing in an Oxford quad-rangle, perhaps cheated himself into the belief that all had been a dream which concerned the caprices of the lady, and the lady herself a phantom. ...

... It was honourable both to the masters and the upper boys, through whom only such a result was possible, that in that school, during my knowledge of it (viz. during the closing year of the eighteenth century and the two opening years of the nineteenth), all punishments that appealed to the sense of bodily pain had fallen into disuse; and this at a period long before any public agitation had begun to stir in that direction. How then was discipline maintained? It was maintained through the self-discipline of the senior boys, and through the efficacy of their example, combined with their system of rules. Noble are the impulses of opening manhood where they are not utterly ignoble: at that period,

I mean, when the poetic sense begins to blossom, and when boys are first made sensible of the paradise that lurks in female smiles. Had the school been entirely a day-school, too probable it is that the vulgar brawling tendencies of boys left to themselves would have prevailed. But it happened that the elder section of the school—those on the brink of manhood, and by incalculable degrees the more scholar-like section, all who read, meditated, or began to kindle into the love of literature—were boarders in Mr. Lawson's house. The students, therefore, of the house carried an overwhelming influence into the school. They were bound together by links of brotherhood; whereas the day-scholars were disconnected. Over and above this, it happened luckily that there was no playground, not the smallest, attached to the school; that is, none was attached to the *upper* or *grammar* school. But there was also, and resting on the same liberal endowment, a *lower* school, where the whole machinery of teaching was applied to the lowest mechanical accomplishments of reading and writing. The hall in which this servile business was conducted ran under the upper school; it was, therefore, I presume, a subterraneous duplicate of the upper hall. And, since the upper rose only by two or three feet above the level of the neighbouring streets, the lower school should naturally have been at a great depth *below* these streets. In that case it would be a dark crypt, such as we see under some cathedrals; and it would have argued a singular want of thoughtfulness in the founder to have laid one part of his establishment under an original curse of darkness. As the access to this plebeian school lay downwards through long flights of steps, I never found surplus energy enough for investigating the problem. But, as the ground broke away precipitously at that point into lower levels, I presume, upon consideration, that the subterranean crypt will be found open on one side to visitations from sun and moon. So that, for this base mechanic school there may, after all, have been a playground. But for ours in the upper air, I repeat, there was none; not so much as would have bleached a lady's pocket-handkerchief; and this one defect carried along with it unforeseen advantages. ...

Two or three days after this examination[1]—viz., on the Sunday following—I transferred myself to head-quarters at Mr. Lawson's house. About nine-o'clock in the evening, I was conducted by a servant up a short flight of stairs, through a series of gloomy and unfurnished little rooms, having small windows but no doors, to the common room (as in Oxford it would technically be called) of the senior boys. Everything had combined to depress me. To leave the society of accomplished women—*that* was already a signal privation. The season besides was rainy, which in itself is a sure source of depression; and the forlorn aspect of the rooms completed my dejection. But the scene changed as the door was

[1] The inaugural examination which put him in the highest group.—B.D.

thrown open: faces kindling with animation became visible; and from a company of boys, numbering sixteen or eighteen, scattered about the room, two or three, whose age entitled them to the rank of leaders, came forward to receive me with a courtesy which I had not looked for. The grave kindness and the absolute sincerity of their manner impressed me most favourably. I had lived familiarly with boys gathered from all quarters of the island at the Bath Grammar School: and for some time (when visiting Lord Altamont at Eton) with boys of the highest aristocratic pretensions. At Bath and at Eton, though not equally, there prevailed a tone of higher polish; and in the air, speech, deportment of the majority could be traced at once a premature knowledge of the world. They had indeed the advantage over my new friends in graceful self-possession; but, on the other hand, the best of them suffered by comparison with these Manchester boys in the qualities of visible self-restraint and of self-respect. At Eton high rank was distributed pretty liberally; but in the Manchester school the parents of many boys were artisans, or of that rank; some even had sisters that were menial servants; and those who stood higher by pretensions of birth and gentle blood were, at the most, the sons of rural gentry or of clergymen. And I believe that, with the exception of three or four brothers, belonging to a clergyman's family at York, all were, like myself, natives of Lancashire. At that time my experience was too limited to warrant me in expressing any opinion, one way or the other, upon the relative pretensions—moral and intellectual—of the several provinces in our island. But since then I have seen reason to agree with the late Dr. Cooke Taylor in awarding the pre-eminence, as regards energy, power to face suffering, and other high qualities, to the natives of Lancashire. Even a century back, they were distinguished for the culture of refined tastes. In musical skill and sensibility, no part of Europe, with the exception of a few places in Germany, could pretend to rival them: and, accordingly, even in Handel's days, but for the chorus-singers from Lancashire, his oratorios must have remained a treasure, if not absolutely sealed, at any rate most imperfectly revealed.

One of the young men, noticing my state of dejection, brought out some brandy—a form of alcohol which I, for my part, tasted now for the first time, having previously taken only wine, and never once in quantities to affect my spirits. So much the greater was my astonishment at the rapid change worked in my state of feeling—a change which at once reinstalled me in my natural advantages for conversation. Towards this nothing was wanting but a question of sufficient interest. And a question arose naturally out of a remark addressed by one of the boys to myself, implying that perhaps I had intentionally timed my arrival so as to escape the Sunday evening exercise. No, I replied; not at all; what *was* that exercise? Simply an off-hand translation from the little work of

Grotius[1] on the Evidences of Christianity. Did I know the book? No, I did not; all the direct knowledge which I had of Grotius was built upon his metrical translations into Latin of various fragments surviving from the Greek scenical poets, and these translations had struck me as exceedingly beautiful. On the other hand, his work of highest pretension, 'De Jure Belli et Pacis,' so signally praised by Lord Bacon, I had not read at all; but I had heard such an account of it from a very thoughtful person as made it probable that Grotius was stronger, and felt himself stronger, on literary than on philosophic ground. Then, with regard to his little work on the Mosaic and Christian revelations, I had heard very disparaging opinions about it; two especially. One amounted to no more than this—that the question was argued with a logic far inferior, in point of cogency, to that of Lardner and Paley. Here several boys interposed their loud assent, as regarded Paley in particular. Paley's 'Evidences,' at that time just seven years old,[2] had already become a subject of study amongst them. But the other objection impeached not so much the dialectic acuteness as the learning of Grotius—at least, the appropriate learning. According to the anecdote current upon this subject, Dr. Edward Pococke, the great oriental scholar of England in the seventeenth century, when called upon to translate the little work of Grotius into Arabic or Turkish had replied by pointing to the idle legend of Mahomet's pigeon or dove, as a reciprocal messenger between the prophet and heaven—which legend had been accredited and adopted by Grotius in the blindest spirit of credulity. Such a baseless fable, Pococke alleged, would work a double mischief: not only it would ruin the authority of that particular book in the East, but would damage Christianity for generations, by making known to the followers of the Prophet that their master was undervalued amongst the Franks on the authority of nursery tales, and that these tales were accredited by the leading Frankish scholars. ...

My very first conversation with the boys had arisen naturally upon a casual topic, and had shown them to be tolerably familiar with the outline of the Christian polemics in the warfare with Jew, Mahometan, Infidel, and Sceptic. But this was an exceptional case; and naturally it happened that most of us sought for the ordinary subjects of our conversational discussions in literature— viz., in our own native literature. Here it was that I learned to feel a deep respect for my new school-fellows: deep it was, then; and a larger experience has made it deeper. I have since known many literary men; men whose profession was literature; who were understood to have dedicated themselves to literature; and who sometimes had with some one special section or little nook of literature

[1] Entitled 'De Veritate Christianae Religionis.'
[2] First published in 1794.—M.

an acquaintance critically minute. But amongst such men I have found but three or four who had a knowledge which came as near to what I should consider a comprehensive knowledge as really existed amongst those boys collectively. What one boy had not, another had; and thus, by continual intercourse, the fragmentary contributions of one being integrated by the fragmentary contributions of others, gradually the attainments of each separate individual became, in some degree, the collective attainments of the whole senior common room. It is true, undoubtedly, that some parts of literature were inaccessible, simply because the books were inaccessible to boys at school, —for instance, Froissart in the old translation by Lord Berners, now more than three centuries old; and some parts were, to the young, essentially repulsive. But, measuring the general qualifications by that standard which I have since found to prevail amongst professional *litterateurs*, I felt more respectfully towards the majority of my senior school-fellows than ever I had fancied it possible that I should find occasion to feel towards any boys whatever. My intercourse with those amongst them who had any conversational talents greatly stimulated my intellect. ...

Here then stood arrayed the whole machinery of mischief in good working order; and through six months or more, allowing for one short respite of four weeks, this machinery had been operating with effect. Mr. Lawson, to begin, had (without meaning it, or so much as perceiving it) barred up all avenues from morning to night through which any bodily exercise could be obtained. Two or three chance intervals of five minutes each, and even these not consecutively arranged, composed the whole available fund of leisure out of which any stroll into the country could have been attempted. But in a great city like Manchester the very suburbs had hardly been reached before that little fraction of time was exhausted. Very soon after Mr. Lawson's increasing infirmities had begun to tell severely in the contraction of our spare time, the change showed itself powerfully in my drooping health. Gradually the liver became affected: and connected with that affection arose, what often accompanies such ailments, profound melancholy. In such circumstances, indeed under any the slightest disturbance of my health, I had authority from my guardians to call for medical advice: but I was not left to my own discretion in selecting the adviser. This person was not a physician, who would of course have expected the ordinary fee of a guinea for every visit; nor a surgeon; but simply an apothecary. In any case of serious illness a physician would have been called in. But a less costly style of advice was reasonably held to be sufficient in any illness which left the patient strength sufficient to walk about. Certainly it ought to have been sufficient here: for no case could possibly be simpler. Three doses of calomel or blue pill, which unhappily I did not then know, would no doubt have re-established me in a week. But far better, as acting always upon me with a magical celerity and a magical certainty, would have been the authoritative prescription (privately notified to Mr. Lawson) of seventy miles' walking in each week. Unhappily my professional adviser was a comatose old gentleman, rich beyond all his needs, careless of his own practice, and standing under that painful necessity (according to the custom then regulating medical practice, which prohibited fees to apothecaries) of seeking his remuneration in excessive deluges of medicine. Me, however, out of pure idleness, he forbore to plague with any *variety* of medicines. With sublime simplicity he confined himself to one horrid mixture, that must have suggested itself to him when prescribing for a tiger. In ordinary circumstances, and with plenty of exercise, no creature could be healthier than myself. But my organisation was perilously frail. And to fight simultaneously with such a malady and such a medicine seemed really too much. The proverb tells us that three 'flittings' are as bad as a fire. Very possibly. And I should think that, in the same spirit of reasonable equation, three such tiger-drenches must be equal to one apoplectic fit, or even to the tiger himself. Having taken two of them, which struck me as quite enough for one life, I declined to comply with the injunction of the label pasted upon each several phial—viz., *Repetatur haustus*[1]; and, instead of doing any such dangerous thing, called upon Mr. —— (the apothecary), begging to know if his art had not amongst its reputed infinity of resources any less abominable, and less shattering to a delicate system than this. 'None whatever,' he replied. Exceedingly kind he was; insisted on my drinking tea with his really amiable daughters; but continued at intervals to repeat, 'None whatever—none whatever'; then, as if rousing himself to an effort, he sang out loudly 'None whatever,' which in this final utterance he toned down syllabically into 'what*ever—ever—ver—er*.' The whole wit of man, it seems, had exhausted itself upon the preparation of that one infernal mixture. ...

But now, at last, came over me, from the mere excess of bodily suffering and mental disappointments, a frantic and rapturous re-agency. In the United States the case is well known, and many times has been described by travellers, of that furious instinct which, under a secret call for saline variations of diet, drives all the tribes of buffaloes for thousands of miles to the common centre of the 'Salt-licks.' Under such a compulsion does the locust, under such a compulsion does the leeming, traverse its mysterious path. They are deaf to danger, deaf to the cry of battle, deaf to the trumpets of death. Let the sea cross their path, let armies with artillery bar the road, even these terrific powers can arrest only by

[1] 'Let the draught be repeated.'

destroying; and the most frightful abysses, up to the very last menace of engulfment, up to the very instant of absorption, have no power to alter or retard the line of their inexorable advance.

Such an instinct it was, such a rapturous command—even so potent, and alas! even so blind—that, under the whirl of tumultuous indignation and of new-born hope, suddenly transfigured my whole being. In the twinkling of an eye, I came to an adamantine resolution—not as if issuing from any act or any choice of my own, but as if passively received from some dark oracular legislation external to myself. That I would elope from Manchester—this was the resolution. *Abscond* would have been the word, if I had meditated anything criminal. But whence came the indignation, and the hope? The indignation arose naturally against my three tormentors (guardian, Archididascalus, and the professor of tigrology); for those who *do* substantially co-operate to one result, however little designing it, unavoidably the mind unifies as a hostile confederacy. But the hope—how shall I explain *that*? Was it the first-born of the resolution, or was the resolution the first-born of the hope? Indivisibly they went together, like thunder and lightning; or each interchangeably ran before and after the other. Under that transcendent rapture which the prospect of sudden liberation let loose, all that natural anxiety which should otherwise have interlinked itself with my anticipations was actually drowned in the blaze of joy, as the light of the planet Mercury is lost and confounded on sinking too far within the blaze of the solar beams. Practically I felt no care at all stretching beyond two or three weeks. Not as being heedless and improvident; my tendencies lay generally in the other direction. No; the cause lurked in what Wordsworth, when describing the festal state of France during the happy morning-tide of her First Revolution (1788–1790), calls '*the senselessness of joy*': this it was, joy—headlong—frantic—irreflective—and (as Wordsworth truly calls it), for that very reason, *sublime*[1]—which swallowed up all capacities of rankling care or heart-corroding doubt. I was, I had been long, a captive: I was in a house of bondage: one fulminating word—*Let there be freedom*—spoken from some hidden recess in my own will, had as by an earthquake rent asunder my prison gates. At any minute I could walk out. Already I trod by anticipation the sweet pastoral hills, already I breathed gales of the everlasting mountains, that to my feelings blew from the garden of Paradise; and in that vestibule of an earthly heaven it was no more possible for me to see vividly or in any lingering detail the thorny care which might hereafter multiply around me than amongst the roses of June, and

---

[1] 'The senselessness of joy was then sublime.'—Wordsworth at Calais in 1802 (see his sonnets), looking back through thirteen years to the great era of social resurrection, in 1788–89, from a sleep of ten centuries.

on the loveliest of June mornings, I could gather depression from the glooms of the last December.

To go was settled. But *when* and *whither*? *When* could have but one answer; for on more reasons than one I needed summer weather, and as much of it as possible. Besides that, when August came, it would bring along with it my own birth-day: now, one codicil in my general vow of freedom had been that my seventeenth birth-day should not find me at school. Still I needed some trifle of preparation. Especially I needed a little money. I wrote, therefore, to the only confidential friend that I had—viz., Lady Carbery. Originally, as early friends of my mother's, both she and Lord Carbery had distinguished me at Bath and elsewhere, for some years, by flattering attentions; and, for the last three years in particular, Lady Carbery, a young woman some ten years older than myself, and who was as remarkable for her intellectual pretensions as she was for her beauty and her benevolence, had maintained a correspondence with me upon questions of literature. She thought too highly of my powers and attainments, and everywhere spoke of me with an enthusiasm that, if I had been five or six years older, and had possessed any personal advantages, might have raised smiles at her expense. To her I now wrote, requesting the loan of five guineas. A whole week passed without any answer. This perplexed and made me uneasy: for her ladyship was rich by a vast fortune removed entirely from her husband's control; and, as I felt assured, would have cheerfully sent me twenty times the sum asked, unless her sagacity had suggested some suspicion (which seemed impossible) of the real purposes which I contemplated in the employment of the five guineas. Could I incautiously have said anything in my own letter tending that way? Certainly not; why then—— But at that moment my speculations were cut short by a letter bearing a coroneted seal. It was from Lady Carbery, of course, and enclosed ten guineas instead of five. Slow in those days were the mails; besides which, Lady Carbery happened to be down at the seaside, whither my letter had been sent after her. Now, then, including my own pocket-money, I possessed a dozen guineas; which seemed sufficient for my immediate purpose; and all ulterior emergencies, as the reader understands, I trampled under foot. This sum, however, spent at inns on the most economic footing, could not have held out for much above a calendar month; and, as to the plan of selecting secondary inns, these are not always cheaper; but the main objection is that in the solitary stations amongst the mountains (Cambrian no less than Cumbrian) there is often no choice to be found: the high-priced inn is the only one. Even this dozen of guineas it became necessary to diminish by three. The age of 'vails' and perquisites to three or four servants at any gentleman's house where you dined—this age, it is true, had passed away by thirty years perhaps. But that flagrant abuse had no connexion at all with the English custom of distributing money amongst that part of the domestics whose daily labours may have been increased by a visitor's residence in the family for some considerable space of time. This custom (almost peculiar, I believe, to the English gentry) is honourable and just. I personally had been trained by my mother, who detested sordid habits, to look upon it as ignominious in a gentleman to leave a household without acknowledging the obliging services of those who cannot openly remind him of their claims. On this occasion, mere necessity compelled me to overlook the housekeeper: for to her I could not have offered less than two or three guineas; and, as she was a fixture, I reflected that I might send it at some future period. To three inferior servants I found that I ought not to give less than one guinea each; so much, therefore, I left in the hands of G——, the most honourable and upright of boys; since to have given it myself would have been prematurely to publish my purpose. These three guineas deducted, I still had nine, or thereabouts. And now all things were settled, except one: the *when* was settled, and the *how*; but not the *whither*. That was still *sub judice*. ...

At length all was ready. Midsummer, like an army with banners, was moving through the heavens; already the longest day had passed; those arrangements, few and imperfect, through which I attempted some partial evasion of disagreeable contingencies likely to arise, had been finished: what more remained for me to do of things that I was able to do? None; and yet, though now at last free to move off, I lingered; lingered as under some sense of dim perplexity, or even of relenting love for the very captivity itself which I was making so violent an effort to abjure, but more intelligibly for all the external objects, living or inanimate, by which that captivity had been surrounded and gladdened. What I was hastening to desert, nevertheless I grieved to desert; and, but for the foreign letter, I might have long continued to loiter and procrastinate. That, however, through various and urgent motives which it suggested, quickened my movements; and the same hour which brought this letter into my hands witnessed my resolution (uttered *audibly* to myself in my study) that early on the next day I would take my departure. A day, therefore, had at length arrived, had somewhat suddenly arrived, which would be the last, the very last, on which I should make my appearance in the school. ...

Prayers had finished. The school had dissolved itself. Six o'clock came, seven, eight. By three hours nearer stood the dying day to its departure. By three hours nearer, therefore, stood we to that darkness which our English liturgy calls into such symbolic grandeur, as hiding beneath its shadowy mantle all perils that beseige our human infirmity. But in summer, in the immediate suburbs of midsummer, the vast scale of the heavenly movements is read in their slowness.

Time becomes the expounder of Space. And now, though eight o'clock had struck, the sun was still lingering above the horizon: the light, broad and gaudy, having still two hours of travel to face before it would assume that tender fading hue prelusive to the twilight. Now came the last official ceremony of the day: the students were all mustered; and the names of all were challenged according to the order of precedency. My name, as usual, came first. Stepping forward, I passed Mr. Lawson, and bowed to him, looking earnestly in his face, and saying to myself, 'He is old and infirm, and in this world I shall not see him again.' I was right; I never *did* see him again, nor ever shall. He looked at me complacently; smiled placidly; returned my salutation (not knowing it to be my valediction); and we parted for ever. Intellectually, I might not have seen cause to reverence him in any emphatic sense. But very sincerely I respected him as a conscientious man, faithful to his duties, and as, even in his latter ineffectual struggle with these duties, inflicting more suffering upon himself than upon others; finally, I respected him as a sound and accurate (though not brilliant) scholar. Personally I owed him much gratitude; for he had been uniformly kind to me, and had allowed me such indulgences as lay in his power; and I grieved at the thought of the mortification I should inflict upon him.

The morning came which was to launch me into the world; that morning from which, and from its consequences, my whole succeeding life has, in many important points, taken its colouring. At half after three I rose, and gazed with deep emotion at the ancient collegiate church, 'dressed in earliest light,' and beginning to crimson with the deep lustre of a cloudless July morning. I was firm and immoveable in my purpose, but yet agitated by anticipation of uncertain danger and troubles. To this agitation the deep peace of the morning presented an affecting contrast, and in some degree a medicine. The silence was more profound than that of midnight: and to me the silence of a summer morning is more touching than all other silence, because, the light being broad and strong as that of noonday at other seasons of the year, it seems to differ from perfect day chiefly because man is not yet abroad, and thus the peace of nature, and of the innocent creatures of God, seems to be secure and deep only so long as the presence of man, and his unquiet spirit, are not there to trouble its sanctity. I dressed myself, took my hat and gloves, and lingered a little in the room. For nearly a year and a-half this room had been my 'pensive citadel': here I had read and studied through all the hours of night; and, though true it was that, for the latter part of this time, I had lost my gaiety and peace of mind during the strife and fever of contention with my guardian, yet, on the other hand, as a boy passionately fond of books, and dedicated to intellectual pursuits, I could not fail to have enjoyed many happy hours in the midst of general dejection. ...

A sudden step upon the stairs broke up my dream, and recalled me to myself. Dangerous hours were now drawing near, and I prepared for a hasty farewell.

I shed tears as I looked round on the chair, hearth, writing-table, and other familiar objects, knowing too certainly that I looked upon them for the last time. Whilst I write this, it is nineteen years ago; and yet, at this moment, I see, as if it were but yesterday, the lineaments and expressions of the object on which I fixed my parting gaze. It was the picture of a lovely lady, which hung over the mantelpiece; the eyes and mouth of which were so beautiful, and the whole countenance so radiant with divine tranquillity, that I had a thousand times laid down my pen, or my book, to gather consolation from it, as a devotee from his patron saint. Whilst I was yet gazing upon it, the deep tones of the old church clock proclaimed that it was six o'clock. I went up to the picture, kissed it, then gently walked out, and closed the door for ever.

Revised *Confessions*, 1853; Masson III.

Solitude

There was one reason why I sought solitude at that early age, and sought it in a morbid excess, which must naturally have conferred upon my character some degree of that interest which belongs to all extremes. My eye had been couched into a secondary power of vision, by misery, by solitude, by sympathy with life in all its modes, by experience too early won, and by the sense of danger critically escaped. Suppose the case of a man suspended by some colossal arm over an unfathomed abyss,—suspended, but finally and slowly withdrawn,—it is probable that he would not smile for years. That was my case: for I have not mentioned in the 'Opium Confessions' a thousandth part of the sufferings I underwent in London and in Wales; partly because the misery was too monotonous, and, in that respect, unfitted for description; but still more because there is a mysterious sensibility connected with real suffering, which recoils from circumstantial rehearsal or delineation, as from violation offered to something sacred, and which is, or should be, dedicated to privacy. Grief does not parade its pangs, nor the anguish of despairing hunger willingly count again its groans or its humiliations.

'Autobiography': *Tait's Magazine*, Aug. 1835; Masson II.

Oxford

Thus, then, it was. Past experience of a very peculiar kind, the agitations of many lives crowded into the compass of a year or two, in combination with a peculiar structure of mind, offered one explanation of the very remarkable and unsocial habits which I adopted at college; but there was another not less powerful, and not less unusual. In stating this, I shall seem, to some persons, covertly designing an affront to Oxford. But that is far from my intention. It is noways peculiar to Oxford, but will, doubtless, be found in every University throughout the world, that the younger part of the members—the undergraduates, I mean, generally, whose chief business must have lain amongst the great writers of Greece and Rome—cannot have found leisure to cultivate extensively their own domestic literature. Not so much that time will have been wanting; but that the whole energy of the mind, and the main course of the subsidiary studies and researches, will naturally have been directed to those difficult languages amongst which lie their daily tasks. I make it no subject of complaint or scorn, therefore, but simply state it as a fact, that few or none of the Oxford undergraduates, with whom parity of standing threw me into collision at my first outset, knew anything at all of English Literature. The *Spectator* seemed to me the only English book of a classical rank which they had read; and even this less for its inimitable delicacy, humour, and refined pleasantry in dealing with manners and characters, than for its insipid and meagre essays, ethical or critical. This was no fault of theirs: they had been sent to the book chiefly as a subject for Latin translations, or of other exercises; and, in such a view, the vague generalities of superficial morality were more useful and more manageable than sketches of manner or character, steeped in national peculiarities. To translate the terms of Whig politics into classical Latin would be as difficult as it might be for a Whig himself to give a consistent account of those politics from the year 1688. Natural, however, and excusable, as this ignorance might be, to myself it was intolerable and incomprehensible. Already, at fifteen, I had made myself familiar with the great English poets. About sixteen, or not long after, my interest in the story of Chatterton had carried me over the whole ground of the Rowley controversy; and that controversy, by a necessary consequence, had so familiarised me with the 'Black Letter' that I had begun to find an unaffected pleasure in the ancient English metrical romances; and in Chaucer, though acquainted as yet only with part of his works, I had perceived and had felt profoundly those divine qualities which, even at this day, are so languidly acknowledged by his unjust countrymen. With this knowledge, and this enthusiastic knowledge of the elder poets—of those most remote from easy access—I could not well be a stranger in other walks of our literature, more on a level

43

with the general taste, and nearer to modern diction, and, therefore, more extensively multiplied by the press. Yet, after all—as one proof how much more commanding is that part of a literature which speaks to the elementary affections of men than that which is founded on the mutable aspects of manners—it is a fact that, even in our elaborate system of society, where an undue value is unavoidably given to the whole science of social intercourse, and a continual irritation applied to the sensibilities which point in that direction, still, under all these advantages, Pope himself is less read, less quoted, less thought of, than the elder and graver section of our literature. It is a great calamity for an author such as Pope, that, generally speaking, it requires so much experience of life to enjoy his peculiar felicities as must argue an age likely to have impaired the general capacity for enjoyment. For my part, I had myself a very slender acquaintance with this chapter of our literature; and what little I had was generally, at that period of my life, as with most men it continues to be to the end of life, a reflex knowledge, acquired through those pleasant miscellanies, half gossip, half criticism—such as Warton's *Essay on Pope*, Boswell's *Johnson*, Mathias's *Pursuits of Literature*, and many scores besides of the same indeterminate class: a class, however, which do a real service to literature by diffusing an indirect knowledge of fine writers in their most effective passages, where else, in a direct shape, it would often never extend.

In some parts, then, having even a profound knowledge of our literature, in all parts having some, I felt it to be impossible that I should familiarly associate with those who had none at all; not so much as a mere historical knowledge of the literature in its capital names and their chronological succession. Do I mention this in disparagement of Oxford? By no means. Among the undergraduates of higher standing, and occasionally, perhaps, of my own, I have since learned that many might have been found eminently accomplished in this particular. But seniors do not seek after juniors; they must be sought; and, with my previous bias to solitude, a bias equally composed of impulses and motives, I had no disposition to take trouble in seeking any man for any purpose.

But, on this subject, a fact still remains to be told, of which I am justly proud; and it will serve, beyond anything else that I can say, to measure the degree of my intellectual development. On coming to Oxford, I had taken up one position in advance of my age by full thirty years; that appreciation of Wordsworth, which it has taken full thirty years to establish amongst the public, I had already made, and had made operative to my own intellectual culture, in the same year when I clandestinely quitted school. Already, in 1802, I had addressed a letter of fervent admiration to Mr. Wordsworth. I did not send it until the spring of 1803; and, from misdirection, it did not come into his hands for some months. But I had an answer from Mr. Wordsworth before I was eighteen; and that my letter was thought to express the homage of an enlightened admirer may be inferred from the fact that his answer was long and full. On this anecdote I do not mean to dwell; but I cannot allow the reader to overlook the circumstances of the case. At this day [1835] it is true, no journal can be taken up which does not habitually speak of Mr. Wordsworth as of *a* great, if not *the* great, poet of the age. Mr. Bulwer, living in the intensest pressure of the world, and though recoiling continually from the judgements of the world, yet never in any violent degree ascribes to Mr. Wordsworth (in his *England and the English*, p. 308) 'an influence of a more noble and purely intellectual character than *any* writer of our age or nation has exercised.' Such is the opinion held of this great poet in 1835; but what were those of 1805-15,—nay, of 1825? For twenty years after the date of that letter to Mr. Wordsworth above referred to, language was exhausted, ingenuity was put on the rack, in the search after images and expressions vile enough, insolent enough, to convey the unutterable contempt avowed for all that he had written by the fashionable critics. One critic—who still, I believe, edits a rather popular journal, and who belongs to that class, feeble, fluttering, ingenious, who make it their highest ambition not to lead, but, with a slave's adulation, to obey and to follow all the caprices of the public mind— described Mr. Wordsworth as resembling, in the quality of his mind, an old nurse babbling in her paralytic dotage to sucking babies. If this insult was peculiarly felt by Mr. Wordsworth, it was on a consideration of the unusual imbecility of him who offered it, and not because in itself it was baser or more insolent than the language held by the majority of journalists who then echoed the public voice. *Blackwood's Magazine* (1817) first accustomed the public ear to the language of admiration coupled with the name of Wordsworth. This began with Professor Wilson; and well I remember—nay, the proofs are still easy to hunt up—that, for eight or ten years, this singularity of opinion, having no countenance from other journals, was treated as a whim, a paradox, a bold extravagance, of the *Blackwood* critics. Mr. Wordsworth's neighbours in Westmoreland, who had (generally speaking) a profound contempt for him, used to rebut the testimony of *Blackwood* by one constant reply—'Ay, *Blackwood* praises Wordsworth, but who else praises him?' In short, up to 1820, the name of Wordsworth was trampled under foot; from 1820 to 1830, it was militant; from 1830 to 1835, it has been triumphant. In 1803, when I entered at Oxford, that name was absolutely unknown; and the finger of scorn, pointed at it in 1802 by the first or second number of the *Edinburgh Review*, failed to reach its mark from absolute defect or knowledge in the public mind. Some fifty besides myself knew who was meant by 'that poet who had cautioned his friend against growing double,' etc.; to all others it was a profound secret.

Ibid.

Approach to William Wordsworth

May 31, 1803

Sir,

I suppose that most men would think what I am going to say—strange at least or rude: but I am bold enough to imagine that, as you are not yourself 'in the roll of common men,' you may be willing to excuse anything uncommon in the liberty I am now taking.

My object in troubling you, Sir, is that hereafter I may have the satisfaction of recollecting that I made one effort at least for obtaining your [friendship *scratched out*] notice—and that I did not, through any want of exertion on my own part, miss that without which what good can my life do me? I have no other motive for soliciting your friendship than what (I should think) every man who has read and felt the 'Lyrical Ballads,' must have in common with me. There is no need that I should express my admiration and love for those delightful poems; nor is it possible that I should do so. Besides, I am persuaded that the dignity of your moral character sets you as far above the littleness of any vanity which could be soothed by applause feeble and insignificant as mine—as the transcendency of your genius makes all applause fall beneath it. But I may say in general, without the smallest exaggeration, that the whole aggregate of pleasure I have received from some eight or nine other poets that I have been able to find since the world began—falls infinitely short of what those two enchanting volumes have singly afforded me:—that your name is with me for ever linked to the lovely scenes of nature:—and that not yourself only but that each place and object you have mentioned—and all the souls in that delightful community of your's—to me

> '*Are dearer than the sun!*'

With such opinions, it is not surprising that I should so earnestly and humbly sue for your friendship;—it is not surprising that the hope of that friendship should have sustained me through two years of a life passed partially in the world—and therefore not passed in happiness;—that I should have breathed forth my morning and my evening orisons for the accomplishment of that hope;—that I should now consider it as the only object worthy of my nature or capable of rewarding my pains. Sometimes indeed, in the dreary vacuity of worldly intercourse, this hope will touch those chords that have power to rouse me from the lethargy of despair; and sometimes, from many painful circumstances—many many bitter recollections, it is my only refuge.

But my reasons for seeking your regard—it would be endless to recount and (I am afraid) useless; for I do not forget that the motives of any intimacy must be mutual: and, alas! to me, unknown and unhonored as I am, why should anyone—the meanest of God's creatures—extend his friendship? What claim then can I urge to a fellowship with a society such as yours—beaming (as it does) with genius so wild and so magnificent? I dare not say that I too have some spark of that heavenly fire which blazes there; for, if I have, it has not yet kindled and shone out in any exertion which only could entitle me to your notice. But, though I can shew no positive pretensions to a gift so high, I may yet advance some few negative reasons why you may suffer me, if but at a distance, to buoy myself up with the idea that I am not wholly disregarded in your sight—when I say that my life has been passed chiefly in the contemplation and altogether in the worship of nature—that I am but a boy and have therefore formed no connection which could draw you one step farther from the sweet retreats of poetry to the detested haunts of men—that no one should ever dare, in confidence of any acquaintance he might have with me, to intrude on your hallowed solitude—and lastly that you would at any rate have an opportunity of offering to God the pleasant and greatful incense of a good deed—by blessing the existence of a fellow-creature. As to all external points, I believe that there is nothing in them which would disgrace you.

I cannot say anything more that that, though you may find many minds more congenial with your own—and therefore proportionately more worthy of your regard, you will never find any one more zealously attached to you— more full of admiration for your mental excellence and of reverential love for your moral character—more ready (I speak from my heart!) to sacrifice even his life—whenever it could have a chance of promoting your interest and happiness—than he who bends the knee before you. And I will add that, to no man on earth except yourself and *one* other (a friend of your's)[1], would I thus lowly and suppliantly prostrate myself.

Dear Sir!
Your's for ever,
Thomas de Quincey.

John E. Jordan, *De Quincey to Wordsworth*, University of California Press/ Cambridge University Press, 1962, Letter 2, p. 30.

Original Preface to Confessions

I here present you, courteous reader, with the record of a remarkable period of my life: according to my application of it, I trust that it will prove not merely an interesting record, but, in a considerable degree, useful and instructive. In *that*

[1] Presumably Coleridge.—B.D.

hope it is that I have drawn it up; and *that* must be my apology for breaking through that delicate and honourable reserve which, for the most part, restrains us from the public exposure of our own errors and infirmities. Nothing, indeed, is more revolting to English feelings than the spectacle of a human being obtruding on our notice with his moral ulcers, or scars, and tearing away that 'decent drapery' which time, or indulgence to human frailty, may have drawn over them; accordingly, the greater part of *our* confessions (that is, spontaneous and extra-judicial confessions) proceed from demireps, adventurers, or swindlers; and, for any such acts of gratuitous self-humiliation from those who can be supposed in sympathy with the decent and self-respecting part of society, we must look to French literature, or to that part of the German which is tainted with the spurious and defective sensibility of the French. All this I feel so forcibly, and so nervously am I alive to reproach of this tendency, that I have for many months hesitated about the propriety of allowing this, or any part of my narrative, to come before the public eye until after my death (when, for many reasons, the whole will be published): and it is not without an anxious review of the reasons for and against this step that I have, at last, concluded on taking it.

Guilt and misery shrink, by a natural instinct, from public notice: they court privacy and solitude; and, even in their choice of a grave, will sometimes sequester themselves from the general population of the churchyard, as if declining to claim fellowship with the great family of man, and wishing (in the affecting language of Mr. Wordsworth)

> '*humbly to express*
> *A penitential loneliness.*'

It is well, upon the whole, and for the interest of us all, that it should be so; nor would I willingly, in my own person, manifest a disregard of such salutary feelings; nor in act or word do anything to weaken them. But, on the one hand, as my self-accusation does not amount to a confession of guilt, so, on the other, it is possible that, if it *did*, the benefit resulting to others, from the record of an experience purchased at so heavy a price, might compensate, by a vast overbalance, for any violence done to the feelings I have noticed, and justify a breach of the general rule. Infirmity and misery do not, of necessity, imply guilt. They approach, or recede from, the shades of that dark alliance, in proportion to the probable motives and prospects of the offender, and the palliations, known or secret, of the offence; in proportion as the temptations to it were potent from the first, and the resistance to it, in act or in effort, was earnest to the last. For my own part, without breach of truth or modesty, I may affirm that my life has been, on the whole, the life of a philosopher: from my birth I was made an intellectual creature; and intellectual in the highest sense my pursuits and pleasures have been, even from my school-boy days. If opium-eating be a sensual pleasure, and if I am bound to confess that I have indulged in it to an excess, not yet *recorded*[1] of any other man, it is no less true that I have struggled against this fascinating enthralment with a religious zeal, and have at length accomplished what I never yet heard attributed to any other man—have untwisted, almost to its final links, the accursed chain which fettered me. Such a self-conquest may reasonably be set off in counterbalance to any kind of degree of self-indulgence. Not to insist that, in my case, the self-conquest was unquestionable, the self-indulgence open to doubts of casuistry, according as that name shall be extended to acts aiming at the bare relief of pain, or shall be restricted to such as aim at the excitement of positive pleasure.

Guilt, therefore, I do not acknowledge; and, if I did, it is possible that I might still resolve on the present act of confession, in consideration of the service which I may thereby render to the whole class of opium-eaters. But who are they? Reader, I am sorry to say, a very numerous class indeed. Of this I became convinced, some years ago, by computing, at that time, the number of those in one small class of English society (the class of men distinguished for talents, or of eminent station) who were known to me, directly or indirectly, as opium-eaters: such, for instance, as the eloquent and benevolent ———; the late Dean of ———; Lord ———; Mr. ———, the philosopher; a late under-secretary of state (who described to me the sensation which first drove him to the use of opium in the very same words as the Dean of ———, viz. 'that he felt as though rats were gnawing and abrading the coats of his stomach'); Mr. ———; and many others, hardly less known, whom it would be tedious to mention.[2] Now, if one class, comparatively so limited, could furnish so many scores of cases (and *that* within the knowledge of one single inquirer), it was a natural inference that the entire population of England would furnish a proportionable number. The

---

[1] 'Not yet *recorded*,' I say; for there is one celebrated man of the present day who, if all be true which is reported of him, has greatly exceeded me in quantity.

[2] All the blanks in this sentence were filled up by De Quincey himself in his reprint of this 'Original Preface' of 1822 in the form in which he prefixed it to his Revised and Enlarged Edition of the 'Confessions' in 1856. The 'eloquent and benevolent———,' we there learn, was William Wilberforce; the 'late Dean of ———' was Dr. Isaac Milner, Dean of Carlisle; 'Lord———' was the first Lord Erskine; the 'late under-secretary of state' was Mr. Addington, brother to the first Lord Sidmouth; and 'Mr. ———' was no other than Coleridge. One might have supposed the previous 'Mr. ———, the philosopher,' to be Coleridge; but De Quincey professes to have forgotten in 1856 who this 'Mr. ———, the philosopher,' of 1822 was. See, at the end of this preface, his long double note on Dean Milner and Philosopher Dash, inserted at this point of his reprint of it in 1856.—M.

49

soundness of this inference, however, I doubted, until some facts became known to me, which satisfied me that it was not incorrect. I will mention two. 1. Three respectable London druggists, in widely remote quarters of London, from whom I happened lately to be purchasing small quantities of opium, assured me that the number of *amateur* opium-eaters (as I may term them) was, at this time, immense; and that the difficulty of distinguishing these persons, to whom habit had rendered opium necessary, from such as were purchasing it with a view to suicide, occasioned them daily trouble and disputes. This evidence respected London only. But, 2 (which will possibly surprise the reader more), some years ago, on passing through Manchester, I was informed by several cotton manufacturers that their work-people were rapidly getting into the practice of opium-eating; so much so, that on a Saturday afternoon the counters of the druggists were strewed with pills of one, two, or three grains, in preparation for the known demand of the evening. The immediate occasion of this practice was the lowness of wages, which, at that time, would not allow them to indulge in ale or spirits; and, wages rising, it may be thought that this practice would cease: but, as I do not readily believe that any man, having once tasted the divine luxuries of opium, will afterwards descend to the gross and mortal enjoyments of alcohol, I take it for granted

> *'That those eat now who never ate before,*
> *And those who always ate now eat the more.'*

Indeed, the fascinating powers of opium are admitted even by medical writers, who are its greatest enemies: thus, for instance, Awsiter, apothecary to Greenwich Hospital, in his 'Essay on the Effects of Opium' (published in the year 1763), when attempting to explain why Mead had not been sufficiently explicit on the properties, counter-agents, &c., of this drug, expresses himself in the following mysterious terms (φωνᾶντα συνετοῖσι): 'Perhaps he thought the subject of too delicate a nature to be made common; and, as many people might then indiscriminately use it, it would take from that necessary fear and caution which should prevent their experiencing the extensive power of this drug; *for there are many properties in it, if universally known, that would habituate the use, and make it more in request with us than the Turks themselves*; the result of which knowledge,' he adds, 'must prove a general misfortune.' In the necessity of this conclusion I do not altogether concur; but upon that point I shall have occasion to speak at the close of my Confessions, where I shall present the reader with the *moral* of my narrative.

Confessions of an English Opium-Eater, 1822; Masson III.

How the Opium-Eating Began

It is very long since I first took opium; so long that, if it had been a trifling incident in my life I might have forgotten its date: but cardinal events are not to be forgotten; and, from circumstances connected with it, I remember that this inauguration into the use of opium must be referred to the spring or to the autumn of 1804; during which seasons I was in London, having come thither for the first time since my entrance at Oxford. And this event arose in the following way:—From an early age I had been accustomed to wash my head in cold water at least once a-day. Being suddenly seized with toothache, I attributed it to some relaxation caused by a casual intermission of that practice, jumped out of bed, plunged my head into a basin of cold water, and with hair thus wetted went to sleep. The next morning, as I need hardly say, I awoke with excruciating rheumatic pains of the head and face, from which I had hardly any respite for about twenty days. On the twenty-first day I think it was, and on a Sunday, that I went out into the streets; rather to run away, if possible, from my torments, than with any distinct purpose of relief. By accident, I met a college acquaintance, who recommended opium. Opium! dread agent of unimaginable pleasure and pain! I had heard of it as I had heard of manna or of ambrosia, but no further. How unmeaning a sound was opium at that time! what solemn chords does it now strike upon my heart! what heartquaking vibrations of sad and happy remembrances! Reverting for a moment to these, I feel a mystic importance attached to the minutest circumstances connected with the place, and the time, and the man (if man he was), that first laid open to me the paradise of opium-eaters. It was a Sunday afternoon, wet and cheerless; and a duller spectacle this earth of ours has not to show than a rainy Sunday in London. My road homewards lay through Oxford Street; and near 'the *stately* Pantheon' (as Mr. Wordsworth has obligingly called it) I saw a druggist's shop. The druggist (unconscious minister of celestial pleasures!), as if in sympathy with the rainy Sunday, looked dull and stupid, just as any mortal druggist might be expected to look on a rainy London Sunday; and, when I asked for the tincture of opium, he gave it to me as any other man might do; and, furthermore, out of my shilling returned to me what seemed to be real copper halfpence, taken out of a real wooden drawer. Nevertheless, and notwithstanding all such indications of humanity, he has ever since figured in my mind as a beatific vision of an immortal druggist, sent down to earth on a special mission to myself. And it confirms me in this way of considering him that, when I next came up to London, I sought him near the stately Pantheon, and found him not; and thus to me, who knew not his name (if, indeed, he had one), he seemed rather to have vanished from Oxford Street than to have flitted into any other locality, or (which some abominable man suggested) to have absconded from the rent. The reader may choose to think of him as, possibly, no more than a sublunary druggist; it may be so, but my faith is better. I believe him to have evanesced.[1] So unwillingly would I connect any mortal remembrances with that hour, and place, and creature that first brought me acquainted with the celestial drug.

Arrived at my lodgings, it may be supposed that I lost not a moment in taking the quantity prescribed. I was necessarily ignorant of the whole art and mystery of opium-taking; and what I took I took under every disadvantage. But I took it; and in an hour, O heavens! what a revulsion! what a resurrection, from its lowest depths, of the inner spirit! what an apocalypse of the world within me! That my pains had vanished was now a trifle in my eyes; this negative effect was swallowed up in the immensity of those positive effects which had opened before me, in the abyss of divine enjoyment thus suddenly revealed. Here was a panacea, a φάρμακον νηπενθές for all human woes; here was the secret of happiness, about which philosophers had disputed for so many ages, at once discovered; happiness might now be bought for a penny, and carried in the waistcoat-pocket; portable ecstasies might be had corked up in a pint-bottle; and peace of mind could be sent down by the mail.

Confessions, 1853; Masson III.

General Existence

I have often been asked how it was, and through what series of steps, that I became an opium-eater. Was it gradually, tentatively, mistrustingly, as one goes down a shelving beach into a deepening sea, and with a knowledge from the first of the dangers lying on that path; half-courting those dangers, in fact, whilst seeming to defy them? Or was it, secondly, in pure ignorance of such dangers, under the misleadings of mercenary fraud? since oftentimes lozenges for the relief of pulmonary affections found their efficacy upon the opium which

---

[1] '*Evanesced*': This way of going off from the stage of life appears to have been well known in the seventeenth century, but at that time to have been considered a peculiar privilege of royalty, and by no means open to the use of druggists. For, about the year 1686, a poet of rather ominous name (and who, apparently, did justice to his name)—viz. Mr. FLATMAN—in speaking of the death of Charles II, expresses his surprise that any prince should commit so vulgar an act as dying; because, says he:

'Kings should disdain to die, and only *disappear*.'

they contain,—upon this, and this only, though clamorously disavowing so suspicious an alliance,—and under such treacherous disguises multitudes are seduced into a dependency which they had not foreseen upon a drug which they had not known; not known even by name or by sight: and thus the case is not rare that the chain of abject slavery is first detected when it has inextricably wound itself about the constitutional system. Thirdly, and lastly, was it (*Yes*, by passionate anticipation, I answer, before the question is finished)—was it on a sudden, overmastering impulse derived from bodily anguish? Loudly I repeat, *Yes*; loudly and indignantly—as in answer to a wilful calumny. Simply as an anodyne it was, under the mere coercion of pain the severest, that I first resorted to opium; and precisely that same torment it is, or some variety of that torment, which drives most people to make acquaintance with that same insidious remedy. Such was the fact; such by accident. ...

Coleridge, therefore, was doubly in error when he allowed himself to aim most unfriendly blows at my supposed voluptuousness in the use of opium; in error as to a principle, and in error as to a fact. A letter of his, which I will hope that he did not design to have published, but which, however, *has* been published, points the attention of his correspondent to a broad distinction separating my case as an opium-eater from his own.[1] He, it seems, had fallen excusably (because unavoidably) into this habit of eating opium—as the one sole therapeutic resource available against his particular malady; but I, wretch that I am, being so notoriously charmed by fairies against pain, must have resorted to opium in the abominable character of an adventurous voluptuary, angling in all streams for variety of pleasures. Coleridge is wrong to the whole extent of what was possible; wrong in his fact, wrong in his doctrine; in his little fact, and his

---

[1] The letter was printed in Gillman's *Life of Coleridge*, published in 1838; and the passage in it principally referred to was this—'Nor had I at any time taken the flattering poison as a stimulus, or for any craving after pleasurable sensations. I needed none; and oh! with what unutterable sorrow did I read the *Confessions of an Opium-Eater*, in which the writer, with morbid vanity, makes a boast of what was my misfortune; for he had been faithfully, and with an agony of zeal, warned of the gulf, and yet willingly struck into the current. ... Oh! may He, the God to whom I look for mercy through Christ, show mercy on the author of the *Confessions of an Opium-Eater*, if, as I have strong reason to believe, his book has been the occasion of seducing others into the withering vice through wantonness. From this aggravation I have, I humbly trust, been free. ... Even to the author of that work I pleaded with flowing tears, and with an agony of forewarning. He utterly denied it; but I fear that I had then even to *deter* perhaps, not to forewarn.' The strength of these words may partly account for the strength of De Quincey's language in the comment on them which follows.—M.

big doctrine. I did not do the thing which he charges upon me; and, if I *had* done it, this would not convict me as a citizen of Sybaris or Daphne. There never was a distinction more groundless and visionary than that which it has pleased him to draw between my motives and his own; nor could Coleridge have possibly owed this mis-statement to any false information; since no man surely, on a question of my own private experience, could have pretended to be better informed than myself. Or, if there really is such a person, perhaps he will not think it too much trouble to re-write these Confessions from first to last, correcting their innumerable faults; and, as it happens that some parts of the unpublished sections for the present are missing, would he kindly restore them —brightening the colours that may have faded, rekindling the inspiration that may have drooped; filling up all those chasms which else are likely to remain as permanent disfigurations of my little work? Meantime the reader who takes any interest in such a question will find that I myself (upon such a theme not simply the best, but surely the sole authority) have, without a shadow of variation, always given a different account of the matter. Most truly I have told the reader that not any search after pleasure, but mere extremity of pain from rheumatic toothache—this and nothing else it was that first drove me into the use of opium. Coleridge's bodily affliction was simple rheumatism. Mine, which intermittingly raged for ten years, was rheumatism in the face combined with toothache. This I had inherited from my father; or inherited (I should rather say) from my own desperate ignorance; since a trifling dose of colocynth, or of any similar medicine, taken three times a-week, would more certainly than opium have delivered me from that terrific curse. In this ignorance, however, which misled me into making war upon toothache when ripened and manifesting itself in effects of pain, rather than upon its germs and gathering causes, I did but follow the rest of the world. To intercept the evil whilst yet in elementary stages of formation was the true policy; whereas I in my blindness sought only for some mitigation to the evil when already formed, and past all reach of interception. In this stage of the suffering, formed and perfect, I was thrown passively upon chance advice, and therefore, by a natural consequence, upon opium—that being the one sole anodyne that is almost notoriously such, and which in that great function is universally appreciated.

Coleridge, therefore, and myself, as regards our baptismal initiation into the use of that mighty drug, occupy the very same position. We are embarked in the self-same boat; nor is it within the compass even of angelic hair-splitting to show that the dark shadow thrown by our several trespasses in this field, mine and his, had by so much as a pin's point any assignable difference. Trespass against trespass (if any trespass there were)—shadow against shadow (if any shadow were really thrown by this trespass over the snowy disk of pure ascetic morality)—in any case, that act in either of us would read into the same meaning, would count up as a debt into the same value, would measure as a delinquency into the same burden of responsibility. And vainly, indeed, does Coleridge attempt to differentiate two cases which ran into absolute identity, differing only as rheumatism differs from toothache. Amongst the admirers of Coleridge, I at all times stood in the foremost rank; and the more was my astonishment at being summoned so often to witness his carelessness in the management of controversial questions, and his demoniac inaccuracy in the statement of facts. The more also was my sense of Coleridge's wanton injustice in relation to myself individually. Coleridge's gross misstatement of facts, in regard to our several opium experiences, had its origin, sometimes in flighty reading, sometimes in partial and incoherent reading, sometimes in subsequent forgetfulness; and any one of these lax habits (it will occur to the reader) is a venial infirmity. Certainly it is; but surely *not* venial when it is allowed to operate disadvantageously upon the character for self-control of a brother, who had never spoken of *him* but in the spirit of enthusiastic admiration; of that admiration which his exquisite works so amply challenge. Imagine the case that I really *had* done something wrong, still it would have been ungenerous—me it would have saddened, I confess, to see Coleridge rushing forward with a public denunciation of my fault:—'Know all men by these presents that I, S. T. C., *a noticeable man with large grey eyes,*[1] am a licensed opium-eater, whereas this other man is a buccaneer, a pirate, a flibustier,[2] and can have none but a forged licence in his disreputable pocket. In the name of Virtue, arrest him!' But the truth is, that inaccuracy as to facts and citations from books was in Coleridge a mere necessity of nature. Not three days ago, in reading a short comment of the late Archdeacon Hare ('Guesses at Truth') upon a bold speculation of Coleridge's (utterley baseless) with respect to the machinery of Etonian Latin verses, I found my old feelings upon this subject refreshed by an instance that is irresistibly comic, since everything that Coleridge had relied upon as a citation from a book in support of his own hypothesis turns out to be a pure fabrication of his own dreams; though, doubtless (which indeed it is that constitutes the characteristic interest of the case), without a suspicion on his part of his own furious romanc-

[1] See Wordsworth's exquisite picture of S. T. C. and himself as occasional denizens in the 'Castle of Indolence.'

[2] This word—in common use, and so spelled as I spell it, amongst the grand old French and English buccaneers contemporary with our own admirable Dampier, at the close of the seventeenth century—has recently been revived in the journals of the United States, with a view to the special case of Cuba, but (for what reason I know not) is now written always as *filli*busters. Meantime, written in whatsoever way, it is understood to be a Franco–Spanish corruption of the English word *freebooter.*

ing. The archdeacon's good-natured smile upon that Etonian case naturally reminded me of the case now before us, with regard to the history of our separate careers as opium-eaters. Upon which case I need say no more, as by this time the reader is aware that Coleridge's entire statement upon that subject is perfect moonshine, and, like the sculptured imagery of the pendulous lamp in 'Christabel,'

> *'All carvèd from the carver's brain.'*

This case, therefore, might now be counted on as disposed of; and what sport it could yield might reasonably be thought exhausted. ...

Am I the man to reproach Coleridge with this vassalage to opium? Heaven forbid! Having groaned myself under that yoke, I pity, and blame him not. But, undeniably, such a vassalage must have been created wilfully and consciously by his own craving after genial stimulation; a thing which I do not blame, but Coleridge *did*. For my own part, duly as the torment relaxed in relief of which I had resorted to opium, I laid aside the opium, not under any meritorious effort of self-conquest; nothing of that sort do I pretend to; but simply on a prudential instinct warning me not to trifle with an engine so awful of consolation and support, nor to waste upon a momentary uneasiness what might eventually prove, in the midst of all-shattering hurricanes, the great elixir of resurrection. What was it that did in reality make me an opium-eater? That affection which finally drove me into the *habitual* use of opium, what was it? Pain was it? No, but misery. Casual overcasting of sunshine was it? No, but blank desolation. Gloom was it that might have departed? No, but settled and abiding darkness—

> *'Total eclipse,*
> *Without all hope of day!'*[1]

Yet whence derived? Caused by what? Caused, as I might truly plead, by youthful distresses in London, were it not that these distresses were due, in their ultimate origin, to my own unpardonable folly; and to that folly I trace many ruins. Oh, spirit of merciful interpretation, angel of forgiveness to youth and its aberrations, that hearkenest for ever as if to some sweet choir of far-off female intercessions! will ye, choir that intercede—wilt thou, angel that forgivest—join together, and charm away that mighty phantom, born amidst the gathering mists of remorse, which strides after me in pursuit from forgotten days— towering for ever into proportions more and more colossal, overhanging and over-shadowing my head as if close behind, yet dating its nativity from hours that are fled by more than half-a-century? Oh heavens! that it should be possible for a child not seventeen years old, by a momentary blindness, by listening to a

[1] 'Samson Agonistes.'

false, false whisper from his own bewildered heart, by one erring step, by a motion this way or that, to change the currents of his destiny, to poison the fountains of his peace, and in the twinkling of an eye to lay the foundations of a life-long repentance! Yet, alas! I must abide by the realities of the case. And one thing is clear,—that, amidst such bitter self-reproaches as are now extorted from me by the anguish of my recollections, it cannot be with any purpose of weaving plausible excuses, or of evading blame, that I trace the origin of my confirmed opium-eating to a necessity growing out of my early sufferings in the streets of London. Because, though true it is that the re-agency of these London sufferings did in after years *enforce* the use of opium, equally it is true that the sufferings themselves grew out of my own folly. What really calls for excuse is not the recourse to opium, when opium had become the one sole remedy available for the malady, but those follies which had themselves produced that malady.

I, for my part, after I had become a regular opium-eater, and from mismanagement had fallen into miserable excesses in the use of opium, did nevertheless, four several times, contend successfully against the dominion of this drug; did four several times renounce it; renounced it for long intervals; and finally resumed it upon the warrant of my enlightened and deliberate judgment, as being of two evils by very much the least. In this I acknowledge nothing that calls for excuse. I repeat again and again that not the application of opium, with its deep tranquillising powers to the mitigation of evils, bequeathed by my London hardships, is what reasonably calls for sorrow, but that extravagance of childish folly which precipitated me into scenes naturally producing such hardships.

These scenes I am now called upon to retrace. Possibly they are sufficiently interesting to merit, even on their own account, some short record; but at present, and at this point, they have become indispensable as a key to the proper understanding of all which follows. For in these incidents of my early life is found the entire substratum, together with the secret and underlying motive, of those pompous dreams and dream-sceneries which were in reality the true objects—first and last—contemplated in these Confessions.

Ibid.

General Existence and Ann

This house I have described as roomy and respectable. It stands in a conspicuous situation, and in a well-known part of London. Many of my readers will have passed it, I doubt not, within a few hours of reading this. For myself, I never fail to visit it when accident draws me to London. About ten o'clock this very night (August 15, 1821, being my birthday), I turn aside from my evening walk along Oxford Street, in order to take a glance at it. It is now in the occupation of some family, apparently respectable. The windows are no longer coated by a paste composed of ancient soot and superannuated rain; and the whole exterior no longer wears an aspect of gloom. By the lights in the front drawing-room, I observed a domestic party, assembled, perhaps, at tea, and apparently cheerful and gay—marvellous contrast, in my eyes, to the darkness, cold, silence, and desolation, of that same house nineteen years ago, when its nightly occupants were one famishing scholar and a poor, neglected child. Her, by the bye, in after years, I vainly endeavoured to trace. Apart from her situation, she was not what would be called an interesting child. She was neither pretty, nor quick in understanding, nor remarkably pleasing in manners. But, thank God! even in those years I needed not the embellishments of elegant accessories to conciliate my affections. Plain human nature, in its humblest and most homely apparel, was enough for me; and I loved the child because she was my partner in wretchedness. If she is now living, she is probably a mother, with children of her own; but, as I have said, I could never trace her.

This I regret; but another person there was, at that time, whom I have since sought to trace with far deeper earnestness, and with far deeper sorrow at my failure. This person was a young woman, and one of that unhappy class who belong to the outcasts and pariahs of our female population. I feel no shame, nor have any reason to feel it, in avowing that I was then on familiar and friendly terms with many women in that unfortunate condition. Smile not, reader too carelessly facile! Frown not, reader too unseasonably austere! Little call was there here either for smiles or frowns. A penniless schoolboy could not be supposed to stand within the range of such temptations; besides that, according to the ancient Latin proverb, '*sine Cerere et Baccho*,' &c. These unhappy women, to me, were simply sisters in calamity; and sisters amongst whom, in as large measure as amongst any other equal number of persons commanding more of the world's respect, were to be found humanity, disinterested generosity, courage that would not falter in defence of the helpless, and fidelity that would have scorned to take bribes for betraying. But the truth is that at no time of my life have I been a person to hold myself polluted by the touch or approach of any creature that wore a human shape. I cannot suppose, I will not believe, that any creatures wearing the form of man or woman are so absolutely rejected and reprobate outcasts that merely to talk with them inflicts pollution. On the contrary, from my very earliest youth, it has been my pride to converse familiarly, *more Socratico*, with all human beings—man, woman, and child— that chance might fling in my way; for a philosopher should not see with the eyes of the poor limitary creature calling himself a man of the world, filled with narrow and self-regarding prejudices of birth and education, but should look upon himself as a catholic creature, and as standing in an equal relation to high and low, to educated and uneducated, to the guilty and the innocent. Being myself, at that time, of necessity a peripatetic, or a walker of the streets, I naturally fell in more frequently with those female peripatetics who are technically called street-walkers. Some of these women had occasionally taken my part against watchmen who wished to drive me off the steps of houses where I was sitting; others had protected me against more serious aggressions. But one amongst them—the one on whose account I have at all introduced this subject— yet no! let me not class thee, O noble-minded Ann——, with that order of women; let me find, if it be possible, some gentler name to designate the condition of her to whose bounty and compassion—ministering to my necessities when all the world stood aloof from me—I owe it that I am at this time alive. For many weeks I had walked, at nights, with this poor friendless girl up and down Oxford Street, or had rested with her on steps and under the shelter of porticos.

She could not be so old as myself: she told me, indeed, that she had not completed her sixteenth year. By such questions as my interest about her prompted, I had gradually drawn forth her simple history. Hers was a case of ordinary occurrence (as I have since had reason to think), and one in which, if London beneficence had better adapted its arrangements to meet it, the power of the law might oftener be interposed to protect and to avenge. But the stream of London charity flows in a channel which, though deep and mighty, is yet noiseless and underground;—not obvious or readily accessible to poor, houseless wanderers; and it cannot be denied that the outside air and framework of society in London, as in all vast capitals, is unavoidably harsh, cruel, and repulsive. In any case, however, I saw that part of her injuries might have been redressed; and I urged her often and earnestly to lay her complaint before a magistrate. Friendless as she was, I assured her that she would meet with immediate attention; and that English justice, which was no respecter of persons, would speedily and amply avenge her on the brutal ruffian who had plundered her little property. She promised me often that she would; but she delayed taking the steps I pointed out, from time to time; for she was timid and dejected to a degree which showed how deeply sorrow had taken hold of her young heart; and perhaps she thought justly that the most upright judge and the most righteous tribunals could do nothing to repair her heaviest wrongs. Something, however, would perhaps have been done; for it had been settled between us at length (but, unhappily, on the very last time but one that I was ever to see her) that in a day or two I, accompanied by her, should state her case to a magistrate. This little service it was destined, however, that I should never realize. Meantime, that which she rendered to me, and which was greater than I could ever have repaid her, was this:—One night, when we were pacing slowly along Oxford Street, and after a day when I had felt unusually ill and faint, I requested her to turn off with me into Soho Square. Thither we went; and we sat down on the steps of a house, which to this hour I never pass without a pang of grief, and an inner act of homage to the spirit of that unhappy girl, in memory of the noble act which she there performed. Suddenly, as we sat, I grew much worse. I had been leaning my head against her bosom, and all at once I sank from her arms, and fell backwards on the steps. From the sensations I then had, I felt an inner conviction of the liveliest kind that, without some powerful and reviving stimulus, I should either have died on the spot, or should, at least, have sunk to a point of exhaustion from which all re-ascent, under my friendless circumstances, would soon have become hopeless. Then it was, at this crisis of my fate, that my poor orphan companion, who had herself met with little but injuries in this world, stretched out a saving hand to me. Uttering a cry of terror, but without a moment's delay, she ran off into Oxford Street, and, in less time than could be imagined, returned to me with a glass of port-wine and spices, that acted upon my empty stomach (which at that time would have rejected all solid food) with an instantaneous power of restoration; and for this glass the generous girl, without a murmur, paid out of her own humble purse, at a time, be it remembered, when she had scarcely wherewithal to purchase the bare necessaries of life, and when she could have no reason to expect that I should ever be able to reimburse her. O youthful benefactress! how often in succeeding years, standing in solitary places, and thinking of thee with grief of heart and perfect love—how often have I wished that, as in ancient times the curse of a father was believed to have a supernatural power, and to pursue its object with a fatal necessity of self-fulfilment, even so the benediction of a heart oppressed with gratitude might have a like prerogative; might have power given it from above to chase, to haunt, to waylay, to pursue thee into the central darkness of a London brothel, or (if it were possible) even into the darkness of the grave, there to awaken thee with an authentic message of peace and forgiveness, and of final reconciliation!

Some feelings, though not deeper or more passionate, are more tender than others; and often when I walk, at this time, in Oxford Street by dreamy lamp-light, and hear those airs played on a common street-organ which years ago solaced me and my dear youthful companion, I shed tears, and muse with myself at the mysterious dispensation which so suddenly and so critically separated us for ever. How it happened, the reader will understand from what remains of this introductory narration.

Ibid.

Ann

Meantime, what had become of Ann? Where was she? Whither had she gone? According to our agreement, I sought her daily, and waited for her every night, so long as I staid in London, at the corner of Tichfield Street; and during the last days of my stay in London I put into activity every means of tracing her that my knowledge of London suggested, and the limited extent of my power made possible. The street where she had lodged I knew, but not the house; and I remembered at last, some account which she had given of ill-treatment from her landlord, which made it probable that she had quitted those lodgings before we parted. She had few acquaintance; most people, besides, thought that the earnestness of my inquiries arose from motives which moved their laughter or their slight regard; and others, thinking that I was in chase of a girl who had robbed me of some trifles, were naturally and excusably indisposed to give me any clue to her, if indeed they had any to give. Finally, as my despairing resource, on the day I left London I put into the hands of the only person who (I was sure) must know Ann by sight, from having been in company with us once or twice, an address to the Priory. All was in vain. To this hour I have never heard a syllable about her. This, amongst such troubles as most men meet with in this life, has been my heaviest affliction. If she lived, doubtless we must have been sometimes in search of each other, at the very same moment, through the mighty labyrinths of London; perhaps even within a few feet of each other—a barrier no wider, in a London street, often amounting in the end to a separation for eternity! During some years I hoped that she *did* live; and I suppose that, in the literal and unrhetorical use of the word *myriad*, I must, on my different visits to London, have looked into many myriads of female faces, in the hope of meeting Ann. I should know her again amongst a thousand, and if seen but for a moment. Handsome she was not; but she had a sweet expression of countenance, and a peculiarly graceful carriage of the head. I sought her, I have said, in hope. So it was for years; but now I should fear to see her; and her cough, which grieved me when I parted with her, is now my consolation. Now I wish to see her no longer, but think of her, more gladly, as one long since laid in the grave —in the grave, I would hope, of a Magdalen; taken away before injuries and cruelty had blotted out and transfigured her ingenuous nature, or the brutalities of ruffians had completed the ruin they had begun.

So then, Oxford Street, stony-hearted stepmother, thou that listenest to the sighs of orphans, and drinkest the tears of children, at length I was dismissed from thee! The time was come that I no more should pace in anguish thy never-ending terraces, no more should wake and dream in captivity to the pangs of hunger. Successors too many to myself and Ann have, doubtless, since then trodden in our footsteps, inheritors of our calamities. Other orphans than Ann have sighed; tears have been shed by other children; and thou, Oxford Street, hast since those days echoed to the groans of innumerable hearts. For myself, however, the storm which I had outlived seemed to have been the pledge of a long fair weather; the premature sufferings which I had paid down to have been accepted as a ransom for many years to come, as a price of long immunity from sorrow; and, if again I walked in London, a solitary and contemplative man (as oftentimes I did), I walked for the most part in serenity and peace of mind. And, although it is true that the calamities of my novitiate in London had struck root so deeply in my bodily constitution that afterwards they shot up and flourished afresh, and grew into a noxious umbrage that has overshadowed and darkened my latter years, yet these second assaults of suffering were met with a fortitude more confirmed, with the resources of a mature intellect, and with alleviations, how deep! from sympathizing affection.

Ibid.

Dreams

Ann Dream

Many years ago, when I was looking over Piranesi's 'Antiquities of Rome,' Coleridge, then standing by, described to me a set of plates from that artist, called his 'Dreams,' and which record the scenery of his own visions during the delirium of a fever. Some of these (I describe only from memory of Coleridge's account) represented vast Gothic halls; on the floor of which stood mighty engines and machinery, wheels, cables, catapults, &c., expressive of enormous power put forth, or resistance overcome. Creeping along the sides of the walls, you perceived a staircase; and upon this, groping his way upwards, was Piranesi himself. Follow the stairs a little farther, and you perceive them reaching an abrupt termination, without any balustrade, and allowing no step onwards to him who should reach the extremity, except into the depths below. Whatever is to become of poor Piranesi, at least you suppose that his labours must now in some way terminate. But raise your eyes, and behold a second flight of stairs still higher, on which again Piranesi is perceived, by this time standing on the very brink of the abyss. Once again elevate your eye, and a still more aerial flight of stairs is descried; and there, again, is the delirious Piranesi, busy on his aspiring labours: and so on, until the unfinished stairs and the hopeless Piranesi both are lost in the upper gloom of the hall. With the same power of endless growth and self-reproduction did my architecture proceed in dreams. In the early stage of the malady, the splendours of my dreams were indeed chiefly architectural; and I beheld such pomp of cities and palaces as never yet was beheld by the waking eye, unless in the clouds. From a great modern poet[1] I cite the part of a passage which describes, as an appearance actually beheld in the clouds, what in many of its circumstances I saw frequently in sleep:

> '*The appearance, instantaneously disclosed,*
> *Was of a mighty city—boldly say*
> *A wilderness of building, sinking far*
> *And self-withdrawn into a wondrous depth,*
> *Far sinking into splendour without end!*
> *Fabric it seemed of diamond and of gold,*
> *With alabaster domes and silver spires,*
> *And blazing terrace upon terrace, high*
> *Uplifted; here, serene pavilions bright,*
> *In avenues disposed; there, towers begirt*
> *With battlements that on their restless fronts*
> *Bore stars—illumination of all gems!*
> *By earthly nature had the effect been wrought*
> *Upon the dark materials of the storm*
> *Now pacified; on them, and on the coves,*
> *And mountain-steeps and summits, whereunto*
> *The vapours had receded, taking there*
> *Their station under a cerulean sky.*'

[1] '*From a great modern poet*' What poet? It was Wordsworth; and why did I not formally name him? This throws a light backwards upon the strange history of Wordsworth's reputation. The year in which I wrote and published these Confessions was 1821; and at that time the name of Wordsworth, though beginning to emerge from the dark cloud of scorn and contumely which had hitherto overshadowed it, was yet most imperfectly established. Not until ten years later was his greatness cheerfully and generally acknowledged. I, therefore, as the very earliest (without one exception) of all who came forward, in the beginning of his career, to honour and welcome him, shrank with disgust from making any sentence of mine the occasion for an explosion of vulgar malice against him. But the grandeur of the passage here cited inevitably spoke for itself; and he that would have been most scornful on hearing the name of the poet coupled with this epithet of 'great' could not but find his malice intercepted, and himself cheated into cordial admiration, by the splendour of the verses. [The passage is from *The Excursion*, Book II.—M.]

The sublime circumstances—'that on their *restless* fronts bore stars'—might have been copied from my own architectural dreams, so often did it occur. We hear it reported of Dryden, and in later times of Fuseli, that they ate raw meat for the sake of obtaining splendid dreams: how much better, for such a purpose, to have eaten opium, which yet I do not remember that any poet is recorded to have done, except the dramatist Shadwell; and in ancient days, Homer is, I think rightly reputed to have known the virtues of opium as a φάρμακον νηπενθές —*i.e.* as an anodyne.

To my architecture succeeded dreams of lakes and silvery expanses of water: these haunted me so much that I feared lest some dropsical state or tendency of the brain might thus be making itself (to use a metaphysical word) *objective*, and that the sentient organ might be projecting itself as its own object. For two months I suffered greatly in my head—a part of my bodily structure which had hitherto been so clear from all touch or taint of weakness (physically, I mean) that I used to say of it, as the last Lord Orford said of his stomach, that it seemed likely to survive the rest of my person. Till now I had never felt a headache even, or any the slightest pain, except rheumatic pains caused by my own folly.

The waters gradually changed their character—from translucent lakes, shining like mirrors, they became seas and oceans. And now came a tremendous change, which, unfolding itself slowly like a scroll, through many months, promised an abiding torment; and, in fact, it never left me, though recurring more or less intermittingly. Hitherto the human face had often mixed in my dreams, but not despotically, nor with any special power of tormenting. But now that affection which I have called the tyranny of the human face began to unfold itself. Perhaps some part of my London life (the searching for Ann amongst fluctuating crowds) might be answerable for this. Be that as it may, now it was that upon the rocking waters of the ocean the human face began to reveal itself; the sea appeared paved with innumerable faces, upturned to the heavens; faces, imploring, wrathful, despairing; faces that surged upwards by thousands, by myriads, by generations: infinite was my agitation; my mind tossed, as it seemed, upon the billowy ocean, and weltered upon the weltering waves.

Ibid.

Ann Dream

I thought that it was a Sunday morning in May; that it was Easter Sunday, and as yet very early in the morning. I was standing, as it seemed to me, at the door of my own cottage. Right before me lay the very scene which could really be commanded from that situation, but exalted, as was usual, and solemnised by the power of dreams. There were the same mountains, and the same lovely valley at their feet; but the mountains were raised to more than Alpine height, and there was interspace far larger between them of savannahs and forest lawns; the hedges were rich with white roses; and no living creature was to be seen, excepting that in the green churchyard there were cattle tranquilly reposing upon the verdant graves, and particularly round about the grave of a child whom I had once tenderly loved, just as I had really beheld them, a little before sunrise, in the same summer when that child died.[1] I gazed upon the well-known scene, and I said to myself, 'It yet wants much of sunrise; and it is Easter Sunday; and that is the day on which they celebrate the first-fruits of Resurrection. I will walk abroad; old griefs shall be forgotten to-day: for the air is cool and still, and the hills are high, and stretch away to heaven; and the churchyard is as verdant as the forest lawns, and the forest lawns are as quiet as the churchyard; and with the dew I can wash the fever from my forehead; and then I shall be unhappy no longer.' I turned, as if to open my garden gate, and immediately I saw upon the left a scene far different; but which yet the power of dreams had reconciled into harmony. The scene was an oriental one; and there also it was Easter Sunday, and very early in the morning. And at a vast distance were visible, as a stain upon the horizon, the domes and cupolas of a great city—an image or faint abstraction, caught perhaps in childhood from some picture of Jerusalem. And not a bow-shot from me, upon a stone, shaded by Judean palms, there sat a woman; and I looked, and it was—Ann! She fixed her eyes upon me earnestly; and I said to her at length, 'So, then, I have found you at last.' I waited; but she answered me not a word. Her face was the same as when I saw it last; the same, and yet, again, how different! Seventeen years ago, when the lamp-light of mighty London fell upon her face, as for the last time I kissed her lips (lips, Ann, that to me were not polluted!), her eyes were streaming with tears. The tears were now no longer seen. Sometimes she seemed altered; yet again sometimes *not* altered; and hardly older. Her looks were tranquil, but with unusual solemnity of expression, and I now gazed upon her with some awe. Suddenly her countenance grew dim; and, turning to the mountains, I perceived vapours rolling between us; in a moment all had vanished; thick darkness came on; and in the twinkling of an eye I was far away from mountains, and by lamp-light in London, walking again with Ann—just as we had walked, when both children, eighteen years before, along the endless terraces of Oxford Street.

Then suddenly would come a dream of far different character—a tumultuous dream—commencing with a music such as now I often heard in sleep—music of

[1] Kate Wordsworth.

preparation and of awakening suspense. The undulations of fast-gathering tumults were like the opening of the Coronation Anthem; and, like *that*, gave the feeling of a multitudinous movement, of infinite cavalcades filing off, and the tread of innumerable armies. The morning was come of a mighty day—a day of crisis and of ultimate hope for human nature, then suffering mysterious eclipse, and labouring in some dread extremity. Somewhere, but I knew not where—somehow, but I knew not how—by some beings, but I knew not by whom—a battle, a strife, an agony, was travelling through all its stages—was evolving itself, like the catastrophe of some mighty drama, with which my sympathy was the more insupportable from deepening confusion as to its local scene, its cause, its nature, and its undecipherable issue. I (as is usual in dreams where, of necessity, we make ourselves central to every movement) had the power, and yet had not the power, to decide it. I had the power, if I could raise myself to will it; and yet again had not the power, for the weight of twenty Atlantics was upon me, or the oppression of inexpiable guilt. 'Deeper than ever plummet sounded,' I lay inactive. Then like a chorus, the passion deepened. Some greater interest was at stake, some mightier cause, than ever yet the sword had pleaded, or trumpet had proclaimed. Then came sudden alarms; hurryings to and fro; trepidations of innumerable fugitives, I knew not whether from the good cause or the bad; darkness and lights; tempest and human faces; and at last, with the sense that all was lost, female forms, and the features that were worth all the world to me; and but a moment allowed—and clasped hands, with heart-breaking partings, and then—everlasting farewells! and, with a sigh such as the caves of hell sighed when the incestuous mother uttered the abhorred name of Death, the sound was reverberated—everlasting farewells! and again, and yet again reverberated—everlasting farewells!

And I awoke in struggles, and cried aloud, 'I will sleep no more!'

Ibid.

On Dreaming

In 1821, as a separate contribution to a periodical work,—in 1822, as a separate volume,—appeared the 'Confessions of an English Opium-Eater.' The object of that work was to reveal something of the grandeur which belongs *potentially* to human dreams. Whatever may be the number of those in whom this faculty of dreaming splendidly can be supposed to lurk, there are not, perhaps, very many in whom it is developed. He whose talk is of oxen will probably dream of oxen; and the condition of human life which yokes so vast a majority to a daily experience incompatible with much elevation of thought oftentimes neutralises the tone of grandeur in the reproductive faculty of dreaming, even for those whose minds are populous with solemn imagery. Habitually to dream magnificently, a man must have a constitutional determination to reverie. This in the first place; and even this, where it exists strongly, is too much liable to disturbance from the gathering agitation of our present English life. Already, what by the procession through fifty years of mighty revolutions amongst the kingdoms of the earth, what by the continual development of vast physical agencies,—steam in all its applications, light getting under harness as a slave for man, powers from heaven descending upon education and accelerations of the press, powers from hell (as it might seem, but these also celestial) coming round upon artillery and the forces of destruction,—the eye of the calmest observer is troubled; the brain is haunted as if by some jealousy of ghostly beings moving amongst us; and it becomes too evident that, unless this colossal pace of advance can be retarded (a thing not to be expected), or, which is happily more probable, can be met by counter-forces of corresponding magnitude,—forces in the direction of religion or profound philosophy that shall radiate centrifugally against this storm of life so perilously centripetal towards the vortex of the merely human,—left to itself, the natural tendency of so chaotic a tumult must be to evil; for some minds to lunacy, for others a reagency of fleshly torpor. How much this fierce condition of eternal hurry upon an arena too exclusively human in its interests is likely to defeat the grandeur which is latent in all men, may be seen in the ordinary effect from living too constantly in varied company. The word *dissipation*, in one of its uses, expresses that effect; the action of thought and feeling is consciously dissipated and squandered. To reconcentrate them into meditative habits, a necessity is felt by all observing persons for sometimes retiring from crowds. No man ever will unfold the capacities of his own intellect who does not at least checker his life with solitude. How much solitude, so much power. Or, if not true in that rigour of expression, to this formula undoubtedly it is that the wise rule of life must approximate.

Among the powers in man which suffer by this too intense life of the *social* instincts, none suffers more than the power of dreaming. Let no man think this a trifle. The machinery for dreaming planted in the human brain was not planted for nothing. That faculty, in alliance with the mystery of darkness, is the one great tube through which man communicates with the shadowy. And the dreaming organ, in connexion with the heart, the eye, and the ear, composes the magnificent apparatus which forces the infinite into the chambers of a human brain, and throws dark reflections from eternities below all life upon the mirrors of that mysterious *camera obscura*—the sleeping mind.

'Suspiria': *Blackwood's Magazine*, 1849; Masson XIII.

Levana

Oftentimes at Oxford I saw Levana in my dreams. I knew her by her Roman symbols. Who is Levana? Reader, that do not pretend to have leisure for very much scholarship, you will not be angry with me for telling you. Levana was the Roman goddess that performed for the newborn infant the earliest office of ennobling kindness,—typical, by its mode, of that grandeur which belongs to man everywhere, and of that benignity in powers invisible which even in Pagan worlds sometimes descends to sustain it. At the very moment of birth, just as the infant tasted for the first time the atmosphere of our troubled planet, it was laid on the ground. *That* might bear different interpretations. But immediately, lest so grand a creature should grovel there for more than one instant, either the paternal hand, as proxy for the goddess Levana, or some near kinsman, as proxy for the father, raised it upright, bade it look erect as the king of all this world, and presented its forehead to the stars, saying perhaps, in his heart, 'Behold what is greater than yourselves!' This symbolic act represented the function of Levana. And that mysterious lady, who never revealed her face (except to me in dreams), but always acted by delegation, had her name from the Latin verb (as still it is the Italian verb) *levare*, to raise aloft.

This is the explanation of Levana. And hence it has arisen that some people have understood by Levana the tutelary power that controls the education of the nursery. She, that would not suffer at his birth even a prefigurative or mimic degradation for her awful ward, far less could be supposed to suffer the real degradation attaching to the non-development of his powers. She therefore watches over human education. Now, the word *edŭco*, with the penultimate short, was derived (by a process often exemplified in the crystallisation of languages) from the word *edūco*, with the penultimate long. Whatsoever *educes*, or develops, *educates*. By the education of Levana, therefore, is meant, —not the poor machinery that move by spelling-books and grammars, but by that mighty system of central forces hidden in the deep bosom of human life, which by passion, by strife, by temptation, by the energies of resistance, works for ever upon children,—resting not day or night, any more than the mighty wheel of day and night themselves, whose moments, like restless spokes, are glimmering[1] for ever as they revolve.

[1] As I have never allowed myself to covet any man's ox nor his ass, nor anything that is his, still less would it become a philosopher to covet other people's images or metaphors. Here, therefore, I restore to Mr. Wordsworth this fine image of the revolving wheel and the glimmering spokes, as applied by him to the flying successions of day and night. I borrowed it for one moment in order to point my own sentence; which being done, the reader is witness that I now pay

If, then, *these* are the ministries by which Levana works, how profoundly must she reverence the agencies of grief! But you, reader, think that children generally are not liable to grief such as mine. There are two senses in the word *generally*,—the sense of Euclid, where it means *universally* (or in the whole extent of the *genus*), and a foolish sense of this world, where it means *usually*. Now, I am far from saying that children universally are capable of grief like mine. But there are more than you ever heard of who die of grief in this island of ours. I will tell you a common case. The rules of Eton require that a boy on the *foundation* should be there twelve years: he is superannuated at eighteen; consequently he must come at six. Children torn away from mothers and sisters at that age not unfrequently die. I speak of what I know. The complaint is not entered by the registrar as grief; but *that* it is. Grief of that sort, and at that age, has killed more than ever have been counted amongst its martyrs.

Therefore it is that Levana often communes with the powers that shake man's heart; therefore it is that she dotes upon grief. 'These ladies,' said I softly to myself, on seeing the ministers with whom Levana was conversing, 'these are the Sorrows; and they are three in number: as the *Graces* are three, who dress man's life with beauty; the *Parcæ* are three, who weave the dark arras of man's life in their mysterious loom always with colours sad in part, sometimes angry with tragic crimson and black; the *Furies* are three, who visit with retributions called from the other side of the grave offences that walk upon this; and once even the *Muses* were but three, who fit the harp, the trumpet, or the lute, to the great burdens of man's impassioned creations. These are the Sorrows; all three of whom I know.' The last words I say *now*; but in Oxford I said, 'one of whom I know, and the others too surely I *shall* know.' For already, in my fervent youth, I saw (dimly relieved upon the dark background of my dreams) the imperfect lineaments of the awful Sisters.

These Sisters—by what name shall we call them? If I say simply 'The Sorrows,' there will be a chance of mistaking the term; it might be understood of individual sorrow,—separate cases of sorrow,—whereas I want a term expressing the mighty abstractions that incarnate themselves in all individual sufferings of man's heart, and I wish to have these abstractions presented as impersonations,—that is, as clothed with human attributes of life, and with functions pointing to flesh. Let us call them, therefore, *Our Ladies of Sorrow*.

I know them thoroughly, and have walked in all their kingdoms. Three

it back instantly by a note made for that sole purpose. On the same principle I often borrow their seals from young ladies, when closing my letters, because there is sure to be some tender sentiment upon them about 'memory,' or 'hope,' or 'roses,' or 'reunion,' and my correspondent must be a sad brute who is not touched by the eloquence of the seal, even if his taste is so bad that he remains deaf to mine.

sisters they are, of one mysterious household; and their paths are wide apart; but of their dominion there is no end. Them I saw often conversing with Levana, and sometimes about myself. Do they talk, then? O no! Mighty phantoms like these disdain the infirmities of language. They may utter voices through the organs of man when they dwell in human hearts, but amongst themselves is no voice nor sound; eternal silence reigns in *their* kingdoms. They spoke not as they talked with Levana; they whispered not; they sang not; though oftentimes methought they *might* have sung: for I upon earth had heard their mysteries oftentimes deciphered by harp and timbrel, by dulcimer and organ. Like God, whose servants they are, they utter their pleasure not by sounds that perish, or by words that go astray, but by signs in heaven, by changes on earth, by pulses in secret rivers, heraldries painted on darkness, and hieroglyphics written on the tablets of the brain. *They* wheeled in mazes: *I* spelled the steps. *They* telegraphed from afar; *I* read the signals. *They* conspired together; and on the mirrors of darkness *my* eye traced the plots. *Theirs* were the symbols; *mine* are the words.

What is it the Sisters are? What is it that they do? Let me describe their form and their presence, if form it were that still fluctuated in its outline, or presence it were that for ever advanced to the front or for ever receded amongst shades.

The eldest of the three is named *Mater Lachrymarum*, Our Lady of Tears. She it is that night and day raves and moans, calling for vanished faces. She stood in Rama, where a voice was heard of lamentation,—Rachel weeping for her children, and refusing to be comforted. She it was that stood in Bethlehem on the night when Herod's sword swept its nurseries of Innocents, and the little feet were stiffened for ever which, heard at times as they trotted along floors overhead, woke pulses of love in household hearts that were not unmarked in heaven. Her eyes are sweet and subtle, wild and sleepy, by turns; oftentimes rising to the clouds, oftentimes challenging the heavens. She wears a diadem round her head. And I knew by childish memories that she could go abroad upon the winds, when she heard the sobbing of litanies, or the thundering of organs, and when she beheld the mustering of summer clouds. This Sister, the elder, it is that carries keys more than papal at her girdle, which open every cottage and every palace. She, to my knowledge, sat all last summer by the bedside of the blind beggar, him that so often and so gladly I talked with, whose pious daughter, eight years old, with the sunny countenance, resisted the temptations of play and village mirth, to travel all day long on dusty roads with her afflicted father. For this did God send her a great reward. In the spring time of the year, and whilst yet her own spring was budding, He recalled her to himself. But her blind father mourns for ever over *her*: still he dreams at midnight that the little guiding hand is locked within his own; and still he wakens to a darkness that is *now* within a second and a deeper darkness. This *Mater Lachrymarum* also has been sitting all this winter of 1844-5 within the bedchamber of the Czar, bringing before his eyes a daughter (not less pious) that vanished to God not less suddenly, and left behind her a darkness not less profound. By the power of the keys it is that Our Lady of Tears glides, a ghostly intruder, into the chambers of sleepless men, sleepless women, sleepless children, from Ganges to the Nile, from Nile to Mississippi. And her, because she is the first-born of her house, and has the widest empire, let us honour with the title of 'Madonna.'

The second Sister is called *Mater Suspiriorum*, Our Lady of Sighs. She never scales the clouds, nor walks abroad upon the winds. She wears no diadem. And her eyes, if they were ever seen, would be neither sweet nor subtle; no man could read their story; they would be found filled with perishing dreams, and with wrecks of forgotten delirium. But she raises not her eyes; her head, on which sits a dilapidated turban, droops for ever, for ever fastens on the dust. She weeps not. She groans not. But she sighs inaudibly at intervals. Her sister, Madonna, is oftentimes stormy and frantic, raging in the highest against heaven, and demanding back her darlings. But Our Lady of Sighs never clamours, never defies, dreams not of rebellious aspirations. She is humble to abjectness. Hers is the meekness that belongs to the hopeless. Murmur she may, but it is in her sleep. Whisper she may, but it is to herself in the twilight. Mutter she does at times, but it is in solitary places that are desolate as she is desolate, in ruined cities, and when the sun has gone down to his rest. This sister is the visitor of the Pariah, of the Jew, of the bondsman to the oar in the Mediterranean galleys; of the English criminal in Norfolk Island, blotted out from the books of remembrance in sweet far-off England; of the baffled penitent reverting his eyes for ever upon a solitary grave, which to him seems the altar overthrown of some past and bloody sacrifice, on which altar no oblations can now be availing, whether towards pardon that he might implore, or towards reparation that he might attempt. Every slave that at noonday looks up to the tropical sun with timid reproach, as he points with one hand to the earth, our general mother, but for *him* a stepmother, as he points with the other hand to the Bible, our general teacher, but against *him* sealed and sequestered[1]; every woman sitting in darkness, without love to shelter her head, or hope to illumine her solitude, because the heaven-born instincts kindling in her nature germs of holy affections, which God implanted in her womanly bosom, having been stifled by

---

[1] This, the reader will be aware, applies chiefly to the cotton and tobacco States of North America; but not to them only; on which account I have not scrupled to figure the sun which looks down upon slavery as *tropical*,—no matter if strictly within the tropics, or simply so near to them as to produce a similar climate.

social necessities, now burn sullenly to waste, like sepulchral lamps amongst the ancients; every nun defrauded of her unreturning May-time by wicked kinsman, whom God will judge; every captive in every dungeon; all that are betrayed, and all that are rejected; outcasts by traditionary law, and children of *hereditary* disgrace: all these walk with Our Lady of Sighs. She also carries a key; but she needs it little. For her kingdom is chiefly amongst the tents of Shem, and the houseless vagrant of every clime. Yet in the very highest ranks of man she finds chapels of her own; and even in glorious England there are some that, to the world, carry their heads as proudly as the reindeer, who yet secretly have received her mark upon their foreheads.

But the third Sister, who is also the youngest——! Hush! whisper whilst we talk of *her*! Her kingdom is not large, or else no flesh should live; but within that kingdom all power is hers. Her head, turreted like that of Cybele, rises almost beyond the reach of sight. She droops not; and her eyes, rising so high, *might* be hidden by distance. But, being what they are, they cannot be hidden: through the treble veil of crape which she wears the fierce light of a blazing misery, that rests not for matins or for vespers, for noon of day or noon of night, for ebbing or for flowing tide, may be read from the very ground. She is the defier of God. She also is the mother of lunacies, and the suggestress of suicides. Deep lie the roots of her power; but narrow is the nation that she rules. For she can approach only those in whom a profound nature has been upheaved by central convulsions; in whom the heart trembles, and the brain rocks under conspiracies of tempest from without and tempest from within. Madonna moves with uncertain steps, fast or slow, but still with tragic grace. Our Lady of Sighs creeps timidly and stealthily. But this youngest Sister moves with incalculable motions, bounding and with tiger's leaps. She carries no key; for, though coming rarely amongst men, she storms all doors at which she is permitted to enter at all. And *her* name is *Mater Tenebrarum*,—our Lady of Darkness.

Ibid.

Dream Fugue

> 'Whence the sound
> Of instruments, that made melodious chime,
> Was heard, of harp and organ; and who moved
> Their stops and chords was seen; his volant touch
> Instinct through all proportions, low and high
> Fled and pursued transverse the resonant fugue.
>
> Par. Lost, Bk. XI.

TUMULTUOSISSIMAMENTE

Passion of sudden death! that once in youth I read and interpreted by the shadows of thy averted signs!—rapture of panic taking the shape (which amongst tombs in churches I have seen) of woman bursting her sepulchral bonds—of woman's Ionic form bending forward from the ruins of her grave with arching foot, with eyes upraised, with clasped adoring hands—waiting, watching, trembling, praying for the trumpet's call to rise from dust for ever! Ah, vision too fearful of shuddering humanity on the brink of almighty abysses!—vision that didst start back, that didst reel away, like a shrivelling scroll from before the wrath of fire racing on the wings of the wind! Epilepsy so brief of horror, wherefore is it that thou canst not die? Passing so suddenly into darkness, wherefore is it that still thou sheddest thy sad funeral blights upon the gorgeous mosaics of dreams? Fragment of music too passionate, heard once, and heard no more, what aileth thee, that thy deep rolling chords come up at intervals through all the worlds of sleep, and after forty years have lost no element of horror?

I

Lo, it is summer—almighty summer! The everlasting gates of life and summer are thrown open wide; and on the ocean, tranquil and verdant as a savannah, the unknown lady from the dreadful vision and I myself are floating—she upon a fairy pinnace, and I upon an English three-decker. Both of us are wooing gales of festal happiness within the domain of our common country, within that ancient watery park, within the pathless chase of ocean, where England takes her pleasure as a huntress through winter and summer, from the rising to the setting sun. Ah, what a wilderness of floral beauty was hidden, or was suddenly revealed, upon the tropic islands through which the pinnace moved! And upon her deck what a bevy of human flowers; young women how lovely, young men how noble, that were dancing together, and slowly drifting towards *us* amidst music and incense, amidst blossoms from forests and gorgeous corymbi[1] from vintages, amidst natural carolling, and the echoes of sweet girlish laughter. Slowly the pinnace nears us, gaily she hails us, and silently she disappears beneath the shadow of our mighty bows. But then, as at some signal from heaven, the music, and the carols, and the sweet echoing of girlish laughter—all are hushed. What evil has smitten the pinnace, meeting or overtaking her? Did ruin to our friends couch within our own dreadful shadow? Was our shadow the shadow of death? I looked over the bow for an answer, and, behold! the pinnace was dismantled; the revel and the revellers were found no more; the

---

[1] *Corymbus*, a cluster of fruit or flowers.—M.

glory of the vintage was dust; and the forests with their beauty were left without a witness upon the seas. 'But where,' and I turned to our crew—'where are the lovely women that danced beneath the awning of flowers and clustering corymbi? Whither have fled the noble young men that danced with *them*?' Answer there was none. But suddenly the man at the mast-head, whose countenance darkened with alarm, cried out, 'Sail on the weather beam! Down she comes upon us: in seventy seconds she also will founder.'

II

I looked to the weather side, and the summer had departed. The sea was rocking, and shaken with gathering wrath. Upon its surface sat mighty mists, which grouped themselves into arches and long cathedral aisles. Down one of these, with the fiery pace of a quarrel from a cross-bow,[1] ran a frigate right athwart our course. 'Are they mad?' some voice exclaimed from our deck. 'Do they woo their ruin?' But in a moment, as she was close upon us, some impulse of a heady current or local vortex gave a wheeling bias to her course, and off she forged without a shock. As she ran past us, high aloft amongst the shrouds stood the lady of the pinnace. The deeps opened ahead in malice to receive her, towering surges of foam ran after her, the billows were fierce to catch her. But far away she was borne into desert spaces of the sea: whilst still by sight I followed her, as she ran before the howling gale, chased by angry sea-birds and by maddening billows; still I saw her, as at the moment when she ran past us, standing amongst the shrouds, with her white draperies streaming before the wind. There she stood, with hair dishevelled, one hand clutched amongst the tackling— rising, sinking, fluttering, trembling, praying; there for leagues I saw her as she stood, raising at intervals one hand to heaven, amidst the fiery crests of the pursuing waves and the raving of the storm; until at last, upon a sound from afar of malicious laughter and mockery, all was hidden for ever in driving showers; and afterwards, but when I know not, nor how.

III

Sweet funeral bells from some incalculable distance, wailing over the dead that die before the dawn, awakened me as I slept in a boat moored to some familiar shore. The morning twilight even then was breaking; and, by the dusky

[1] *Quarrel*, a cross-bow bolt, an arrow with a four-square head; connected with *quadratus*, made square. Richardson's Dictionary gives this example from Robert Brunne—

'A quarrelle lete he flie,
And smote him in the schank.'—M.

revelations which it spread, I saw a girl, adorned with a garland of white roses about her head for some great festival, running along the solitary strand in extremity of haste. Her running was the running of panic; and often she looked back as to some dreadful enemy in the rear. But, when I leaped ashore, and followed on her steps to warn her of a peril in front, alas! from me she fled as from another peril, and vainly I shouted to her of quicksands that lay ahead. Faster and faster she ran; round a promontory of rocks she wheeled out of sight; in an instant I also wheeled round it, but only to see the treacherous sands gathering above her head. Already her person was buried; only the fair young head and the diadem of white roses around it were still visible to the pitying heavens; and, last of all, was visible one white marble arm. I saw by the early twilight this fair young head, as it was sinking down to darkness—saw this marble arm, as it rose above her head and her treacherous grave, tossing, faltering, rising, clutching, as at some false deceiving hand stretched out from the clouds—saw this marble arm uttering her dying hope, and then uttering her dying despair. The head, the diadem, the arm—these all had sunk; at last over these also the cruel quicksand had closed; and no memorial of the fair young girl remained on earth, except my own solitary tears, and the funeral bells from the desert seas, that, rising again more softly, sang a requiem over the grave of the buried child, and over her blighted dawn.

I sat, and wept in secret the tears that men have ever given to the memory of those that died before the dawn, and by the treachery of earth, our mother. But suddenly the tears and funeral bells were hushed by a shout as of many nations, and by a roar as from some great king's artillery, advancing rapidly along the valleys, and heard afar by echoes from the mountains. 'Hush!' I said, as I bent my ear earthwards to listen—'Hush!—this either is the very anarchy of strife, or else'—and then I listened more profoundly, and whispered as I raised my head— 'or else, oh heavens! it is *victory* that is final, victory that swallows up all strife.'

IV

Immediately, in trance, I was carried over land and sea to some distant kingdom, and placed upon a triumphal car, amongst companions crowned with laurel. The darkness of gathering midnight, brooding over all the land, hid from us the mighty crowds that were weaving restlessly about ourselves as a centre: we heard them, but saw them not. Tidings had arrived, within an hour, of a grandeur that measured itself against centuries; too full of pathos they were too full of joy, to utter themselves by other language than by tears, by restless anthems, and *Te Deums* reverberated from the choirs and orchestras of earth. These tidings we that sat upon the laurelled car had it for our privilege to publish amongst all nations. And already, by signs audible through the darkness,

75

by snortings and tramplings, our angry horses, that knew no fear of fleshly weariness, upbraided us with delay. Wherefore *was* it that we delayed? We waited for a secret word, that should bear witness to the hope of nations as now accomplished for ever. At midnight the secret word arrived; which word was—*Waterloo and Recovered Christendom!* The dreadful word shone by its own light; before us it went; high above our leaders' heads it rode, and spread a golden light over the paths which we traversed. Every city, at the presence of the secret word, threw open its gates. The rivers were conscious as we crossed. All the forests, as we ran along their margins, shivered in homage to the secret word. And the darkness comprehended it.

Two hours after midnight we approached a mighty Minster. Its gates, which rose to the clouds, were closed. But, when the dreadful word that rode before us reached them with its golden light, silently they moved back upon their hinges; and at a flying gallop our equipage entered the grand aisle of the cathedral. Headlong was our pace; and at every altar, in the little chapels and oratories to the right hand and left of our course, the lamps, dying or sickening, kindled anew in sympathy with the secret word that was flying past. Forty leagues we might have run in the cathedral, and as yet no strength of morning light had reached us, when before us we saw the aerial galleries of organ and choir. Every pinnacle of the fretwork, every station of advantage amongst the traceries, was crested by white-robed choristers that sang deliverance; that wept no more tears, as once their fathers had wept; but at intervals that sang together to the generations, saying,

> '*Chant the deliverer's praise in every tongue,*'

and receiving answers from afar,

> '*Such as once in heaven and earth were sung.*'

And of their chanting was no end; of our headlong pace was neither pause nor slackening.

Thus as we ran like torrents—thus as we swept with bridal rapture over the Campo Santo[1] of the cathedral graves—suddenly we became aware of a vast

---

[1] '*Campo Santo.*' It is probable that most of my readers will be acquainted with the history of the Campo Santo (or cemetery) at Pisa, composed of earth brought from Jerusalem from a bed of sanctity, as the highest prize which the noble piety of crusaders could ask or imagine. To readers who are unacquainted with England or who (being English) are yet unacquainted with the cathedral cities of England, it may be right to mention that the graves within-side the cathedrals often form a flat pavement over which carriages and horses *might* run; and perhaps a boyish remembrance of one particular cathedral, across which I had seen passengers walk and burdens carried, as about two centuries back they were through the middle of St. Paul's in London, may have assisted my dream.

necropolis rising upon the far-off horizon—a city of sepulchres, built within the saintly cathedral for the warrior dead that rested from their feuds on earth. Of purple granite was the necropolis; yet, in the first minute, it lay like a purple stain upon the horizon, so mighty was the distance. In the second minute it trembled through many changes, growing into terraces and towers of wondrous altitude, so mighty was the pace. In the third minute already, with our dreadful gallop, we were entering its suburbs. Vast sarcophagi rose on every side, having towers and turrets that, upon the limits of the central aisle, strode forward with haughty intrusion, that ran back with mighty shadows into answering recesses. Every sarcophagus showed many bas-reliefs—bas-reliefs of battles and of battle-fields; battles from forgotten ages, battles from yesterday; battle-fields that long since, nature had healed and reconciled to herself with the sweet oblivion of flowers; battle-fields that were yet angry and crimson with carnage. Where the terraces ran, there did *we* run; where the towers curved, there did *we* curve. With the flight of swallows our horses swept round every angle. Like rivers in flood wheeling round headlands, like hurricanes that ride into the secrets of forests, faster than ever light unwove the mazes of darkness, our flying equipage carried earthly passions, kindled warrior instincts, amongst the dust that lay around us—dust oftentimes of our noble fathers that had slept in God from Créci to Trafalgar. And now had we reached the last sarcophagus, now were we abreast of the last bas-relief, already had we recovered the arrow-like flight of the illimitable central aisle, when coming up this aisle to meet us we beheld afar off a female child, that rode in a carriage as frail as flowers. The mists which went before her hid the fawns that drew her, but could not hide the shells and tropic flowers with which she played—but could not hide the lovely smiles by which she uttered her trust in the mighty cathedral, and in the cherubim that looked down upon her from the mighty shafts of its pillars. Face to face she was meeting us,; face to face she rode, as if danger there were none. 'Oh, baby!' I exclaimed, 'shalt thou be the ransom for Waterloo? Must we, that carry tidings of great joy to every people, be messengers of ruin to thee!' In horror I rose at the thought; but then also, in horror at the thought, rose one that was sculptured on a bas-relief—a Dying Trumpeter. Solemnly from the field of battle he rose to his feet; and, unslinging his stony trumpet, carried it, in his dying anguish, to his stony lips—sounding once, and yet once again; proclamation that, in *thy* ears, oh baby! spoke from the battlements of death. Immediately deep shadows fell between us, and aboriginal silence. The choir had ceased to sing. The hoofs of our horses, the dreadful rattle of our harness, the groaning of our wheels, alarmed the graves no more. By horror the bas-relief had been unlocked unto life. By horror we, that were so full of life, we men and our horses, with their fiery fore-legs rising in mid-air to their

77

everlasting gallop, were frozen to a bas-relief. Then a third time the trumpet sounded; the seals were taken off all pulses; life, and the frenzy of life, tore into their channels again; again the choir burst forth in sunny grandeur, as from the muffling of storms and darkness; again the thunderings of our horses carried temptation into the graves. One cry burst from our lips, as the clouds, drawing off from the aisle, showed it empty before us.—'Whither has the infant fled?— is the young child caught up to God?' Lo! afar off, in a vast recess, rose three mighty windows to the clouds; and on a level with their summits, at height insuperable to man, rose an altar of purest alabaster. On its eastern face was trembling a crimson glory. A glory was it from the reddening dawn that now streamed *through* the windows? Was it from the crimson robes of the martyrs painted *on* the windows? Was it from the bloody bas-reliefs of earth? There, suddenly, within that crimson radiance, rose the apparition of a woman's head, and then of a woman's figure. The child it was—grown up to woman's height. Clinging to the horns of the altar, voiceless she stood—sinking, rising, raving, despairing; and behind the volume of incense that, night and day, streamed upwards from the altar, dimly was seen the fiery font, and the shadow of that dreadful being who should have baptized her with the baptism of death. But by her side was kneeling her better angel, that hid his face with wings; that wept and pleaded for *her*; that prayed when *she* could *not*; that fought with Heaven by tears for *her* deliverance; which also, as he raised his immortal countenance from his wings, I saw, by the glory in his eye, that from Heaven he had won at last.

V

Then was completed the passion of the mighty fugue. The golden tubes of the organ, which as yet had but muttered at intervals—gleaming amongst clouds and surges of incense—threw up, as from fountains unfathomable, columns of heart-shattering music. Choir and anti-choir were filling fast with unknown voices. Thou also, Dying Trumpeter, with thy love that was victorious, and thy anguish that was finishing, didst enter the tumult; trumpet and echo—farewell love, and farewell anguish—rang through the dreadful *sanctus*. Oh, darkness of the grave! that from the crimson altar and from the fiery font wert visited and searched by the effulgence in the angel's eye—were these indeed thy children? Pomps of life, that, from the burials of centuries, rose again to the voice of perfect joy, did ye indeed mingle with the festivals of Death? Lo! as I looked back for seventy leagues through the mighty cathedral, I saw the quick and the dead that sang together to God, together that sang to the generations of man. All the hosts of jubilation, like armies that ride in pursuit, moved with one step. Us, that, with laurelled heads, were passing from the cathedral, they overtook, and, as with a garment, they wrapped us round with thunders greater than our own. As brothers we moved together; to the dawn that advanced, to the stars that fled; rendering thanks to God in the highest—that, having hid His face through one generation behind thick clouds of War, once again was ascending, from the Campo Santo of Waterloo was ascending, in the visions of Peace; rendering thanks for thee, young girl! whom having overshadowed with His ineffable passion of death, suddenly did God relent, suffered thy angel to turn aside His arm, and even in thee, sister unknown! shown to me for a moment only to be hidden for ever, found an occasion to glorify His goodness. A thousand times, amongst the phantoms of sleep, have I seen thee entering the gates of the golden dawn, with the secret word riding before thee, with the armies of the grave behind thee,—seen thee sinking, rising, raving, despairing; a thousand times in the worlds of sleep have seen thee followed by God's angel through storms, through desert seas, through the darkness of quicksands, through dreams and the dreadful revelations that are in dreams; only that at the last, with one sling of His victorious arm, He might snatch thee back from ruin, and might emblazon in thy deliverance the endless resurrections of His love!

'The English Mail Coach': *Blackwood's Magazine*, 1849; Masson XIII.

Set Pieces

The Knocking at the Gate in Macbeth

From my boyish days I had always felt a great perplexity on one point in *Macbeth*. It was this: The knocking at the gate which succeeds to the murder of Duncan produced to my feelings an effect for which I never could account. The effect was that it reflected back upon the murderer a peculiar awfulness and a depth of solemnity; yet, however obstinately I endeavoured with my understanding to comprehend this, for many years I never could see *why* it should produce such an effect.

Here I pause for one moment, to exhort the reader never to pay any attention to his understanding when it stands in opposition to any other faculty of his mind. The mere understanding, however useful and indispensable, is the meanest faculty in the human mind, and the most to be distrusted; and yet the great majority of people trust to nothing else,—which may do for ordinary life, but not for philosophical purposes. Of this out of ten thousand instances that I might produce I will cite one. Ask of any person whatsoever who is not previously prepared for the demand by a knowledge of the perspective to draw in the rudest way the commonest appearance which depends upon the laws of that science,—as, for instance, to represent the effect of two walls standing at right angles to each other, or the appearance of the houses on each side of a street as seen by a person looking down the street from one extremity. Now, in all cases, unless the person has happened to observe in pictures how it is that artists produce these effects, he will be utterly unable to make the smallest approximation to it. Yet why? For he has actually seen the effect every day of his life. The reason is that he allows his understanding to overrule his eyes. His understanding, which includes no intuitive knowledge of the laws of vision, can furnish him with no reason why a line which is known and can be proved to be a horizontal line should not *appear* a horizontal line: a line that made any angle with the perpendicular less than a right angle would seem to him to indicate that his houses were all tumbling down together. Accordingly, he makes the line of his houses a horizontal line, and fails, of course, to produce the effect demanded. Here, then, is one instance out of many in which not only the understanding is allowed to overrule the eyes, but where the understanding is positively allowed to obliterate the eyes, as it were; for not only does the man believe the evidence of his understanding in opposition to that of his eyes, but (what is monstrous) the idiot is not aware that his eyes ever gave such evidence. He does not know that he has seen (and therefore *quoad* his consciousness has *not* seen) that which he *has* seen every day of his life.

But to return from this digression. My understanding could furnish no reason why the knocking at the gate in Macbeth should produce any effect, direct or reflected. In fact, my understanding said positively that it could *not* produce any effect. But I knew better; I felt that it did; and I waited and clung to the problem until further knowledge should enable me to solve it. At length, in 1812, Mr. Williams made his *début* on the stage of Ratcliffe Highway, and executed those unparalleled murders which have procured for him such a brilliant and undying reputation. On which murders, by the way, I must observe that in one respect they have had an ill effect, by making the connoisseur in murder very fastidious in his taste, and dissatisfied by anything that has been since done in that line. All other murders look pale by the deep crimson of his; and, as an amateur once said to me in a querulous tone, 'There has been absolutely nothing *doing* since his time, or nothing that's worth speaking of.' But this is wrong; for it is unreasonable to expect all men to be great artists, and born with the genius of Mr. Williams.[1] Now, it will be remembered that in the first of these murders (that of the Marrs) the same incident (of a knocking at the door soon after the work of extermination was complete) did actually occur which the genius of Shakspere has invented; and all good judges, and the most eminent dilettanti, acknowledged the felicity of Shakspere's suggestion as soon as it was actually realized. Here, then was a fresh proof that I was right in relying on my own feeling, in opposition to my understanding; and I again set myself to study the problem. At length I solved it to my own satisfaction; and my solution is this: —Murder, in ordinary cases, where the sympathy is wholly directed to the case of the murdered person, is an incident of coarse and vulgar horror; and for this reason,—that it flings the interest exclusively upon the natural but ignoble instinct by which we cleave to life: an instinct which, as being indispensable to the primal law of self-preservation, is the same in kind (though different in degree) amongst all living creatures. This instinct, therefore, because it annihilates all distinctions, and degrades the greatest of men to the level of 'the poor beetle that we tread on,' exhibits human nature in its most abject and humiliating attitude. Such an attitude would little suit the purposes of the poet. What then must he do? He must throw the interest on the murderer. Our sympathy must be with *him* (of course I mean a sympathy of comprehension, a sympathy by which we enter into his feelings, and are made to understand them,—not a sympathy of pity or approbation).[2] In the murdered person, all

---

[1] A kind of presentiment of De Quincey's subsequent extravaganza called *Murder considered as one of the Fine Arts*.—M.

[2] It seems almost ludicrous to guard and explain my use of a word in a situation where it would naturally explain itself. But it has become necessary to do so, in consequence of the unscholarlike use of the word sympathy, at present so general,

strife of thought, all flux and reflux of passion and of purpose, are crushed by one overwhelming panic; the fear of instant death smites him 'with its petrific mace.' But in the murderer, such a murderer as a poet will condescend to, there must be raging some great storm of passion,—jealousy, ambition, vengeance, hatred,—which will create a hell within him; and into this hell we are to look.

In *Macbeth*, for the sake of gratifying his own enormous and teeming faculty of creation, Shakspere has introduced two murderers: and, as usual in his hands, they are remarkably discriminated: but,—though in Macbeth the strife of mind is greater than in his wife, the tiger spirit not so awake, and his feelings caught chiefly by contagion from her,—yet, as both were finally involved in the guilt of murder, the murderous mind of necessity is finally to be presumed in both. This was to be expressed; and, on its own account, as well as to make it a more proportionable antagonist to the unoffending nature of their victim, 'the gracious Duncan,' and adequately to expound 'the deep damnation of his taking off,' this was to be expressed with peculiar energy. We were to be made to feel that the human nature,—*i.e.* the divine nature of love and mercy, spread through the hearts of all creatures, and seldom utterly withdrawn from man,—was gone, vanished, extinct, and that the fiendish nature had taken its place. And, as this effect is marvellously accomplished in the *dialogues* and *soliloquies* themselves, so it is finally consummated by the expedient under consideration; and it is to this that I now solicit the reader's attention. If the reader has ever witnessed a wife, daughter, or sister in a fainting fit, he may chance to have observed that the most affecting moment in such a spectacle is *that* in which a sigh and a stirring announce the recommencement of suspended life. Or, if the reader has ever been present in a vast metropolis on the day when some great national idol was carried in funeral pomp to his grave, and, chancing to walk near the course through which it passed, has felt powerfully, in the silence and desertion of the streets, and in the stagnation of ordinary business, the deep interest which at that moment was possessing the heart of man,—if all at once he should hear the death-like stillness broken up by the sound of wheels rattling away from the scene, and making known that the transitory vision was dissolved, he will be aware that at no moment was his sense of the complete suspension and pause in ordinary human concerns so full and affecting as at that moment when the suspension ceases, and the goings on of human life are suddenly resumed. All action in any direction is best expounded, measured, and

by which, instead of taking it in its proper sense, as the act of reproducing in our minds the feelings of another, whether for hatred, indignation, love, pity, or approbation, it is made a mere synonym of the word *pity*; and hence, instead of saying 'sympathy *with* another,' many writers adopt the monstrous barbarism of 'sympathy *for* another.'

made apprehensible, by reaction. Now, applying this to the case in *Macbeth*: Here, as I have said, the retiring of the human heart and the entrance of the fiendish heart was to be expressed and made sensible. Another world has stept in; and the murderers are taken out of the region of human things, human purposes, human desires. They are transfigured: Lady Macbeth is 'unsexed'; Macbeth has forgot that he was born of woman; both are conformed to the image of devils; and the world of devils is suddenly revealed. But how shall this be conveyed and made palpable? In order that a new world may step in, this world must for a time disappear. The murderers and the murder must be insulated—cut off by an immeasurable gulf from the ordinary tide and succession of human affairs—locked up and sequestered in some deep recess; we must be made sensible that the world of ordinary life is suddenly arrested, laid asleep, tranced, racked into a dread armistice; time must be annihilated, relation to things without abolished; and all must pass self-withdrawn into a deep syncope and suspension of earthly passion. Hence it is that, when the deed is done, when the work of darkness is perfect, then the world of darkness passes away like a pageantry in the clouds: the knocking at the gate is heard, and it makes known audibly that the reaction has commenced; the human has made its reflux upon the fiendish; the pulses of life are beginning to beat again; and the re-establishment of the goings-on of the world in which we live first makes us profoundly sensible of the awful parenthesis that had suspended them.

O mighty poet! Thy works are not as those of other men, simply and merely great works of art, but are also like the phenomena of nature, like the sun and the sea, the stars and the flowers, like frost and snow, rain and dew, hail-storm and thunder, which are to be studied with entire submission of our own faculties, and in the perfect faith that in them there can be no too much or too little, nothing useless or inert, but that, the farther we press in our discoveries, the more we shall see proofs of design and self-supporting arrangement where the careless eye had seen nothing but accident!

London Magazine, Oct. 1823; Masson X.

Murder Considered as One of the Fine Arts

FIRST PAPER

1. *Advertisement of a Man morbidly Virtuous*[1]

Most of us who read books have probably heard of a Society for the Promotion of Vice, of the Hell-Fire Club founded in the last century by Sir Francis Dashwood, &c.[2] At Brighton I think it was that a Society was formed for the Suppression of Virtue. That society was itself suppressed; but I am sorry to say that another exists in London, of a character still more atrocious. In tendency, it may be denominated a Society for the Encouragement of Murder; but, according to their own delicate εὐφημισμός, it is styled, the Society of Connoisseurs in Murder. They profess to be curious in homicide, amateurs and dilettanti in the various modes of carnage, and, in short, Murder-Fanciers. Every fresh atrocity of that class which the police annals of Europe bring up, they meet and criticise as they would a picture, statue, or other work of art. But I need not trouble myself with any attempt to describe the spirit of their proceedings, as the reader will collect *that* much better from one of the Monthly Lectures read before the society last year. This has fallen into my hands accidentally, in spite of all the vigilance exercised to keep their transactions from the public eye. The publication of it will alarm them; and my purpose is that it should. For I would much rather put them down quietly, by an appeal to public opinion, than by such an exposure of names as would follow an appeal to Bow Street; which last appeal,

[1] This sub-title for the introductory paragraph was invented by De Quincey when he reprinted the paper in 1854. As originally printed in *Blackwood*, the paper opened thus:—'*To the Editor of Blackwood's Magazine.*—Sir, We have all heard of a Society for the Promotion of Vice,' &c.—M.

[2] Convivial fraternities under the outrageous name of *Hell-Fire Clubs*,—because founded on a principle of ostentatious contempt and ridicule of the established religion and of all ordinary morality, and indulging, it was supposed, in blasphemous and profligate orgies,—came into being in the early part of the eighteenth century, and spread like an epidemic through the British Islands during the next fifty or sixty years. The particular club of this kind which De Quincey here mentions was the famous fraternity of the *Monks of St. Francis*, called also *The Medmenham Club*, whose usual place of meeting was the mansion-house of Medmenham in Buckinghamshire, originally a Cistercian monastery. The most notorious members of the club were Sir Francis Dashwood, baronet (known from 1763 onwards as Lord Le Despencer), and John Wilkes; but it included the poet Churchill, the less-known poets Lloyd and Whitehead, Sir John Dashwood King, Bubb Dodington, and others.—M.

however, if this should fail, I must really resort to. For my intense virtue will not put up with such things in a Christian land. Even in a heathen land the toleration of murder—viz., in the dreadful shows of the amphitheatre—was felt by a Christian writer to be the most crying reproach of the public morals. This writer was Lactantius[1]; and with his words, as singularly applicable to the present occasion, I shall conclude: —'Quid tam horribile,' says he, 'tam tetrum 'quam hominis trucidatio? Ideo severissimis legibus vita nostra munitur; ideo 'bella execrabilia sunt. Invenit tamen consuetudo quatenus homicidium sine 'bello ac sine legibus faciat; et hoc sibi voluptas quod scelus vindicavit. Quod, si 'interesse homicidio sceleris conscientia est, et eidem facinori spectator ob-'strictus est cui et admissor, ergo et in his gladiatorum cædibus non minus 'cruore profunditur qui spectat quam ille qui facit: nec potest esse immunis a 'sanguine qui voluit effundi, aut videri non interfecisse qui interfectori et favit et 'præmium postulavit.'—'What is so dreadful,' says Lactantius, 'what so dismal 'and revolting, as the murder of a human creature? Therefore it is that life for 'us is protected by laws the most rigorous; therefore it is that wars are objects 'of execration. And yet the traditional usage of Rome has devised a mode of 'authorising murder apart from war, and in defiance of law; and the demands of 'taste (voluptas) are now become the same as those of abandoned guilt.' Let the Society of Gentlemen Amateurs consider this; and let me call their especial attention to the last sentence, which is so weighty, that I shall attempt to convey it in English: 'Now, if merely to be present at a murder fastens on a man the 'character of an accomplice; if barely to be a spectator involves us in one com-'mon guilt with the perpetrator: it follows, of necessity, that, in these murders 'of the amphitheatre, the hand which inflicts the fatal blow is not more deeply 'imbrued in blood than his who passively looks on; neither can *he* be clear of 'blood who has countenanced its shedding; nor that man seem other than a 'participator in murder who gives his applause to the murderer and calls for 'prizes on his behalf.' The '*præmia postulavit*' I have not yet heard charged upon the Gentlemen Amateurs of London, though undoubtedly their proceedings tend to that; but the '*interfectori favit*' is implied in the very title of this association, and expressed in every line of the lecture which follows.   X. Y. Z.

II. *The Lecture*

Gentlemen: I have had the honour to be appointed by your committee to the trying task of reading the Williams Lecture on Murder Considered as One of the Fine Arts,—a task which might be easy enough three or four centuries ago, when the art was little understood, and few great models had been exhibited; but in this age, when masterpieces of excellence have been executed by

---

[1] Latin Christian writer of the fourth century.—M.

professional men, it must be evident that in the style of criticism applied to them the public will look for something of a corresponding improvement. Practice and theory must advance *pari passu*. People begin to see that something more goes to the composition of a fine murder than two blockheads to kill and be killed, a knife, a purse, and a dark lane. Design, gentlemen, grouping, light and shade, poetry, sentiment, are now deemed indispensable to attempts of this nature. Mr. Williams has exalted the ideal of murder to all of us,[1] and to me, therefore, in particular, has deepened the arduousness of my task. Like Æschylus or Milton in poetry, like Michael Angelo in painting, he has carried his art to a point of colossal sublimity, and as Mr. Wordsworth observes, has in a manner 'created the taste by which he is to be enjoyed.' To sketch the history of the art, and to examine its principles critically, now remains as a duty for the connoisseur, and for judges of quite another stamp from his Majesty's Judges of Assize.

Before I begin, let me say a word or two to certain prigs, who affect to speak of our society as if it were in some degree immoral in its tendency. Immoral! God bless my soul, gentlemen! what is it that people mean? I am for morality, and always shall be, and for virtue, and all that; and I do affirm, and always shall (let what will come of it), that murder is an improper line of conduct, highly improper; and I do not stick to assert that any man who deals in murder must have very incorrect ways of thinking, and truly inaccurate principles; and, so far from aiding and abetting him by pointing out his victim's hiding-place, as a great moralist of Germany declared it to be every good man's duty to do,[2] I would subscribe one shilling and sixpence to have him apprehended,—which is more by eighteenpence than the most eminent moralists have hitherto subscribed for that purpose. But what then? Everything in this world has two handles. Murder, for instance, may be laid hold of by its moral handle (as it generally is in the pulpit and at the Old Bailey), and *that*, I confess, is its weak side; or it may also be treated *æsthetically*, as the Germans call it—that is, in relation to good taste.

To illustrate this, I will urge the authority of three eminent persons: viz. S. T. Coleridge, Aristotle, and Mr. Howship the surgeon.

---

[1] John Williams, the London murderer of 1811. The story of his murders is told in the *Postscript*.—M.

[2] Kant—who carried his demands of unconditional veracity to so extravagant a length as to affirm that, if a man were to see an innocent person escape from a murderer, it would be his duty, on being questioned by the murderer, to tell the truth, and to point out the retreat of the innocent person, under any certainty of causing murder. Lest this doctrine should be supposed to have escaped him in any heat of dispute, on being taxed with it by a celebrated French writer, he solemnly re-affirmed it, with his reasons.

To begin with S. T. C.:—One night, many years ago, I was drinking tea with him in Berners Street (which, by the way, for a short street, has been uncommonly fruitful in men of genius). Others were there besides myself; and, amidst some carnal considerations of tea and toast, we were all imbibing a dissertation on Plotinus from the Attic lips of S. T. C. Suddenly a cry arose of 'Fire—fire!' upon which all of us, master and disciples, Plato and οἱ περὶ τὸν Πλατῶνα, rushed out, eager for the spectacle. The fire was in Oxford Street, at a pianoforte-maker's; and, as it promised to be a conflagration of merit, I was sorry that my engagements forced me away from Mr. Coleridge's party before matters had come to a crisis. Some days after, meeting with my Platonic host, I reminded him of the case, and begged to know how that very promising exhibition had terminated. 'Oh, sir,' said he, 'it turned out so ill that we dammed it unanimously.' Now, does any man suppose that Mr. Coleridge—who, for all he is too fat to be a person of active virtue, is undoubtedly a worthy Christian—that this good S. T. C., I say, was an incendiary, or capable of wishing any ill to the poor man and his pianofortes (many of them, doubtless, with the additional keys)? On the contrary, I know him to be that sort of man that I durst stake my life upon it he would have worked an engine in a case of necessity, although rather of the fattest for such fiery trials of his virtue. But how stood the case? Virtue was in no request. On the arrival of the fire engines, morality had devolved wholly on the insurance office. This being the case, he had a right to gratify his taste. He had left his tea. Was he to have nothing in return?

I contend that the most virtuous man, under the premises stated, was entitled to make a luxury of the fire, and to hiss it, as he would any other performance that raised expectations in the public mind which afterwards it disappointed. Again, to cite another great authority, what says the Stagirite? He (in the Fifth Book, I think it is, of his Metaphysics) describes what he calls κλέπτην τέλειον —i.e. a perfect thief[1]; and, as to Mr. Howship, in a work of his on Indigestion he makes no scruple to talk with admiration of a certain ulcer which he had seen, and which he styles 'a beautiful ulcer.' Now, will any man pretend that, abstractly considered, a thief could appear to Aristotle a perfect character, or that Mr. Howship could be enamoured of an ulcer? Aristotle, it well known, was himself so very moral a character that, not content with writing his Nicomachean Ethics in one volume octavo, he also wrote another system, called Magna Moralia, or Big Ethics. Now, it is impossible that a man who composes

---

[1] It is in the Fourth Book, chap. xvi, and stands thus:—'A perfect or finished physician, and a perfect or finished musician, are such when they are in no wise deficient as far as regards the species of excellence that is proper to their professions: so also, transferring our remarks to the case of evil things, we say a perfect or finished sycophant, and a finished thief.'—M.

any ethics at all, big or little, should admire a thief *per se*; and, as to Mr. How-ship, it is well known that he makes war upon all ulcers, and, without suffering himself to be seduced by their charms, endeavours to banish them from the county of Middlesex. But the truth is that, however objectionable *per se*, yet, relatively to others of their class, both a thief and an ulcer may have infinite degrees of merit. They are both imperfections, it is true; but, to be imperfect being their essence, the very greatness of their imperfection becomes their per-fection. *Spartam nactus es, hanc exorna.* A thief like Autolycus or the once famous George Barrington,[1]—and a grim phagedænic ulcer,[2]—superbly defined, and running regularly through all its natural stages, may no less justly be regarded as ideals after *their* kind than the most faultless moss-rose amongst flowers, in its progress from bud to 'bright consummate flower,' or, amongst human flowers, the most magnificent young female, apparelled in the pomp of womanhood. And thus not only the ideal of an inkstand may be imagined, as Mr. Coleridge illustrated in his celebrated correspondence with Mr. Black-wood,[3]—in which, by the way, there is not so much, because an inkstand is a laudable sort of thing, and a valuable member of society,—but even imperfec-tion itself may have its ideal or perfect state.

Really, gentlemen, I beg pardon for so much philosophy at one time; and now let me apply it. When a murder is in the paulo-post-futurum tense—not done, not even (according to modern purism) *being* done, but only going to be done—and a rumour of it comes to our ears, by all means let us treat it morally. But suppose it over and done, and that you can say of it, Τετέλεσται, It is finished, or (in that adamantine molossus[4] of *Medea*) Εἴργασται, Done it is, it is a *fait accompli*; suppose the poor murdered man to be out of his pain, and the rascal that did it off like a shot nobody knows whither; suppose, lastly, that we have done our best, by putting out our legs, to trip up the fellow in his flight, but all to no purpose—'abiit, evasit, excessit, erupit,' etc.—why, then, I say, what's the use of any more virtue? Enough has been given to morality; now

[1] George Waldron *alias* Barrington, the most famous gentleman-pickpocket of his time, was transported to Botany Bay in 1790, and died there in 1804, in respectable employment and with the reputation of a reformed character.—M.

[2] *Phagedænic*, Greek for 'eating' or 'corrosive': the word, whether in the form of the noun *phagedæna*, or of the adjective *phagedænic* or *phagedænous*, is a surgical definition of a special kind of ulcer.—M.

[3] Refers to certain whimsical letters of Coleridge in *Blackwood* for October 1821, in one of which are enumerated the requisites for a perfect or ideal ink-stand.—M.

[4] *Molossus* is the name in Greek prosody for a word or foot of three consecutive long syllables. The particular molossus which De Quincey goes on to quote,—the word εἴργασται,—occurs in line 293 of the *Medea* of Euripides.—M.

comes the turn of Taste and the Fine Arts. A sad thing it was, no doubt, very sad; but *we* can't mend it. Therefore let us make the best of a bad matter; and, as it is impossible to hammer anything out of it for moral purposes, let us treat it æsthetically, and see if it will turn to account in that way. Such is the logic of a sensible man; and what follows? We dry up our tears, and have the satisfaction perhaps, to discover that a transaction which, morally considered, was shocking and without a leg to stand upon, when tried by principles of Taste, turns out to be a very meritorious performance. Thus all the world is pleased; the old proverb is justified, that it is an ill wind which blows nobody good; the amateur, from looking bilious and sulky by too close an attention to virtue, begins to pick up his crumbs; and general hilarity prevails. Virtue has had her day; and henceforward, *Virtù*, so nearly the same thing as to differ only by a single letter (which surely is not worth haggling or higgling about)—*Virtù*, I repeat, and Connoisseurship, have leave to provide for themselves. Upon this principle, gentlemen, I propose to guide your studies from Cain to Mr. Thurtell. Through this great gallery of murder, therefore, together let us wander hand in hand, in delighted admiration; while I endeavour to point your attention to the objects of profitable criticism.

The first murder is familiar to you all. As the inventor of murder, and the father of the art, Cain must have been a man of first-rate genius. All the Cains were men of genius. Tubal Cain invented tubes, I think, or some such thing. But, whatever might be the originality and genius of the artist, every art was then in its infancy; and the works turned out from each several *studio* must be criticised with a recollection of that fact. Even Tubal's work would probably be little approved at this day in Sheffield; and therefore of Cain (Cain senior, I mean) it is no disparagement to say that his performance was but so-so. Milton, however, is supposed to have thought differently. By his way of relating the case, it should seem to have been rather a pet murder with him, for he retouches it with an apparent anxiety for its picturesque effect:

> '*Whereat he inly raged, and, as they talked,*
> *Smote him into the midriff with a stone*
> *That beat out life: he fell, and, deadly pale,*
> *Groaned out his soul, with gushing blood effused.*'
> *Par. Lost*, Bk. XI.

Upon this Richardson the painter, who had an eye for effect, remarks as follows in his 'Notes on Paradise Lost,' p. 497:—'It has been thought,' says he, 'that Cain beat (as the common saying is) the breath out of his brother's body 'with a great stone: Milton gives in to this, with the addition, however, of a 'large wound.' In this place it was a judicious addition: for the rudeness of the weapon, unless raised and enriched by a warm, sanguinary colouring, has too much of the naked air of the savage school; as if the deed were perpetrated by a Polypheme, without science, premeditation, or anything but a mutton-bone. However, I am chiefly pleased with the improvement, as it implies that Milton was an amateur. As to Shakspere, there never was a better; witness his description of the murdered Duncan, Banquo, &c.; and above all witness his incomparable miniature, in 'Henry VI,' of the murdered Gloucester.

The foundation of the art having been once laid, it is pitiable to see how it slumbered without improvement for ages. In fact, I shall now be obliged to leap over all murders, sacred and profane, as utterly unworthy of notice until long after the Christian era. Greece, even in the age of Pericles, produced no murder, or at least none is recorded, of the slightest merit; and Rome had too little originality of genius in any of the arts to succeed where her model failed her. In fact, the Latin language sinks under the very idea of murder. 'The man was murdered;'—how will this sound in Latin? *Interfectus est, interemptus est*—which simply expresses a homicide; and hence the Christian Latinity of the middle ages was obliged to introduce a new word, such as the feebleness of classic conceptions never ascended to. *Murdratus est*, says the sublime dialect of Gothic ages. Meantime, the Jewish school of murder kept alive whatever was yet known in the art, and gradually transferred it to the Western World. Indeed, the Jewish school was always respectable, even in its mediæval stages, as the case of Hugh of Lincoln shows, which was honoured with the approbation of Chaucer, on occasion of another performance from the same school, which, in his Canterbury Tales, he puts into the mouth of the Lady Abbess.[1]

Recurring, however, for one moment, to classical antiquity, I cannot but think that Catiline, Clodius, and some of that coterie, would have made first-

---

[1] Chaucer's *Prioresses Tale* in his Canterbury Pilgrimage is the story of a little Christian boy in a city in Asia, supposed to have been murdered by the Jews of the city because of the offence he gave them by always singing the Christian hymn O *Alma Redemptoris Mater* through the streets as he went to school. The Prioress concludes the story by referring to a specially English legend of a like character,— that of young 'Hugh of Lincoln,' whom some Jews of that town were said to have put to death for similar reasons by a horrible crucifixion. The historian Matthew Paris, who relates the thing as a fact that happened in his own lifetime, dates it in the year 1255 and adds that a number of Jews were executed for the crime in London in the following year. This explains the wording of the reference to it by the Prioress:—

> 'O yonge Hugh of Lincoln, sleyn also
> With cursed Jewes, as it is notable,
> For it is but a little whyle ago.'—M.

rate artists; and it is on all accounts to be regretted that the priggism of Cicero robbed his country of the only chance she had for distinction in this line. As the *subject* of a murder, no person could have answered better than himself. Oh Lord! how he would have howled with panic, if he had heard Cethegus under his bed. It would have been truly diverting to have listened to him; and satisfied I am, gentlemen, that he would have preferred the *utile* of creeping into a closet, or even into a *cloaca*, to the *honestum* of facing the bold artist.

To come now to the Dark Ages—(by which we that speak with precision mean, *par excellence*, the tenth century as a meridian line, and the two centuries immediately before and after, full midnight being from A.D. 888 to A.D. 1111)—those ages ought naturally to be favourable to the art of murder, as they were to church architecture, to stained glass, &c.; and, accordingly, about the latter end of this period, there arose a great character in our art,—I mean the Old Man of the Mountains. He was a shining light indeed, and I need not tell you that the very word 'assassin' is deduced from him. So keen an amateur was he that on one occasion, when his own life was attempted by a favourite assassin, he was so much pleased with the talent shown that, notwithstanding the failure of the artist, he created him a duke upon the spot, with remainder to the female line, and settled a pension on him for three lives. Assassination is a branch of the art which demands a separate notice; and it is possible that I may devote an entire lecture to it. Meantime, I shall only observe how odd it is that this branch of the art has flourished by intermitting fits. It never rains but it pours. Our own age can boast of some fine specimens, such, for instance, as Bellingham's affair with the prime minister Perceval, the Duc de Berri's case at the Parisian Opera House, the Maréchal Bessières's case at Avignon; and about two and a half centuries ago, there was a most brilliant constellation of murders in this class. I need hardly say that I allude especially to those seven splendid works: the assassinations of William I of Orange; of the three French Henries, viz., of Henri, Duke of Guise, that had a fancy for the throne of France, of Henri III, last prince of the line of Valois, who then occupied that throne, and finally of Henri IV, his brother-in-law, who succeeded to that throne as first prince in the line of Bourbon: not eighteen years later came the 5th on the roll, viz. that of our Duke of Buckingham (which you will find excellently described in the letters published by Sir Henry Ellis, of the British Museum), 6thly of Gustavus Adolphus, and 7thly of Wallenstein. What a glorious Pleiad of Murders! And it increases one's admiration that this bright constellation of artistic displays, comprehending 3 Majesties, 3 Serene Highnesses, and 1 Excellency, all lay within so narrow a field of time as between A.D. 1588 and 1635. The King of Sweden's assassination, by the bye, is doubted by many writers, Harte amongst others; but they are wrong. He *was* murdered; and I consider his murder unique in its excellence;

for he was murdered at noon-day, and on the field of battle—a feature of original conception which occurs in no other work of art that I remember. To conceive the idea of a secret murder on private account as enclosed within a little parenthesis on a vast stage of public battle-carnage is like Hamlet's subtle device of a tragedy within a tragedy. Indeed, all of these assassinations may be studied with profit by the advanced connoisseur. They are all of them *exemplaria*, model murders, pattern murders, of which one may say

'*Nocturna versate manu, versate diurna*'—

especially *nocturna*.

In these assassinations of princes and statesmen there is nothing to excite our wonder. Important changes often depend on their deaths; and, from the eminence on which they stand, they are peculiarly exposed to the aim of every artist who happens to be possessed by the craving for scenical effect. But there is another class of assassinations, which has prevailed from an early period of the seventeenth century, that really *does* surprise me: I mean the assassination of philosophers. For, gentlemen, it is a fact that every philosopher of eminence for the two last centuries has either been murdered, or at the least been very near it,—insomuch that, if a man calls himself a philosopher and never had his life attempted, rest assured there is nothing in him; and against Locke's Philosophy in particular I think it an unanswerable objection (if we needed any) that, although he carried his throat about with him in this world for seventy-two years, no man ever condescended to cut it.[1] As these cases of philosophers are not much known, and are generally good and well composed in their circumstances, I shall here read an excursus on that subject, chiefly by way of showing my own learning.

The first great philosopher of the seventeenth century (if we except Bacon and Galileo) was Des Cartes; and, if ever one could say of a man that he was all *but* murdered—murdered within an inch—one must say it of him. The case was this, as reported by Baillet in his *Vie de M. Des Cartes*, tom. i. pp. 102-3 :—In the year 1621, when Des Cartes might be about twenty-six years old, he was touring about as usual (for he was as restless as a hyena); and, coming to the Elbe, either at Gluckstadt or at Hamburgh, he took shipping for East Friezland. What he could want in East Friezland no man has ever discovered; and perhaps he took this into consideration himself: for, on reaching Embdem, he resolved to sail instantly for *West* Friezland: and, being very impatient of delay, he hired a bark, with a few mariners to navigate it. No sooner had he got out to sea than he made a pleasing discovery, viz. that he had shut himself up in a den of

---

[1] Locke, born 1632, died 1704. This is not the only place in De Quincey's writings in which he shows his dislike of Locke and Locke's philosophy.—M.

murderers. His crew, says M. Baillet, he soon found out to be 'des scélérats'—not *amateurs*, gentlemen, as we are, but professional men, the height of whose ambition at that moment was to cut his individual throat. But the story is too pleasing to be abridged; I shall give it, therefore, accurately from the French of his biographer: 'M. Des Cartes had no company but that of his servant, with 'whom he was conversing in French. The sailors, who took him for a foreign 'merchant, rather than a cavalier, concluded that he must have money about 'him. Accordingly, they came to a resolution by no means advantageous to his 'purse. There is this difference, however, between sea-robbers and the robbers 'in forests, that the latter may without hazard spare the lives of their victims, 'whereas the others cannot put a passenger on shore in such a case without run-'ning the risk of being apprehended. The crew of M. Des Cartes arranged their 'measures with a view to evade any danger of that sort. They observed that he 'was a stranger from a distance, without acquaintance in the country, and that 'nobody would take any trouble to inquire about him, in case he should never 'come to land (*quand il viendroit à manquer*).' Think, gentlemen, of these Friezland dogs discussing a philosopher as if he were a puncheon of rum consigned to some shipbroker. 'His temper, they remarked, was very mild and patient; and, 'judging from the gentleness of his deportment, and the courtesy with which he 'treated themselves, that he could be nothing more than some green young man, 'without station or root in the world, they concluded that they should have all 'the easier task in disposing of his life. They made no scruple to discuss the whole 'matter in his presence, as not supposing that he understood any other language 'than that in which he conversed with his servant; and the amount of their 'deliberation was—to murder him, then to throw him into the sea, and to 'divide his spoils.'

Excuse my laughing, gentlemen; but the fact is I always *do* laugh when I think of this case—two things about it seem so droll. One is the horrid panic or 'funk' (as the men of Eton call it) in which Des Cartes must have found himself upon hearing this regular drama sketched for his own death, funeral, succession and administration to his effects. But another thing which seems to me still more funny about this affair is that, if these Friezland hounds had been 'game,' we should have no Cartesian philosophy; and how we could have done without *that*, considering the world of books it has produced, I leave to any respectable trunk-maker to declare.

However, to go on: spite of his enormous funk, Des Cartes showed fight, and by that means awed these Anti-Cartesian rascals. 'Finding,' says M. Baillet, 'that the matter was no joke, M. Des Cartes leaped upon his feet in a trice, 'assumed a stern countenance that these cravens had never looked for, and, 'addressing them in their own language, threatened to run them through on the 'spot if they dared to give him any insult.' Certainly, gentlemen, this would have been an honour far above the merits of such inconsiderable rascals—to be spitted like larks upon a Cartesian sword; and therefore I am glad M. Des Cartes did not rob the gallows by executing his threat, especially as he could not possibly have brought his vessel to port after he had murdered his crew; so that he must have continued to cruise for ever in the Zuyder Zee, and would probably have been mistaken by sailors for the *Flying Dutchman* homeward bound. 'The 'spirit which M. Des Cartes manifested,' says his biographer, 'had the effect of 'magic on these wretches. The suddenness of their consternation struck their 'minds with a confusion which blinded them to their advantage, and they 'conveyed him to his destination as peaceably as he could desire.'

Possibly, gentlemen, you may fancy that, on the model of Cæsar's address to his poor ferryman—'*Cæsarem vehis et fortunas ejus*'—M. Des Cartes needed only to have said, 'Dogs, you cannot cut my throat, for you carry Des Cartes and his philosophy,' and might safely have defied them to do their worst. A German emperor had the same notion when, being cautioned to keep out of the way of a cannonading, he replied, 'Tut! man. Did you ever hear of a cannon-ball that killed an emperor'?[1] As to an emperor I cannot say, but a less thing has sufficed to smash a philosopher; and the next great philosopher of Europe undoubtedly *was* murdered. This was Spinoza.

I know very well the common opinion about him is that he died in his bed. Perhaps he did, but he was murdered for all that; and this I shall prove by a book published at Brussels in the year 1731, entitled 'La Vie de Spinoza, par M. Jean Colerus,' with many additions from a MS. life by one of his friends. Spinoza died on the 21st February, 1677, being then little more than forty-four years old. This, of itself, looks suspicious; and M. Jean admits that a certain expression in the MS. life of him would warrant the conclusion 'que sa mort n'a pas été tout-à-fait naturelle.' Living in a damp country, and a sailor's country, like Holland, he may be thought to have indulged a good deal in grog, especially in punch, which was then newly discovered. Undoubtedly he might have done so; but the fact is that he did not. M. Jean calls him 'extrêmement sobre en son boire et en son manger.' And, though some wild stories were afloat about his using the juice of mandragora (p. 140) and opium (p. 144), yet neither of these articles is found in his druggist's bill. Living, therefore, with such sobriety, how was it possible that he should die a natural death at forty-four? Hear his biographer's

---

[1] This same argument has been employed at least once too often. Some centuries back a dauphin of France, when admonished of his risk from small-pox, made the same demand as the emperor—'Had any gentleman heard of a dauphin killed by small-pox?' No; not any gentleman *had* heard of such a case. And yet, for all that, this dauphin died of that same small-pox.

account:—'Sunday morning, the 21st of February, before it was church time, 'Spinoza came downstairs, and conversed with the master and mistress of the 'house.' At this time, therefore, perhaps ten o'clock on Sunday morning, you see that Spinoza was alive, and pretty well. But it seems 'he had summoned 'from Amsterdam a certain physician, whom,' says the biographer, 'I shall not 'otherwise point out to notice than by these two letters, L. M.' This L. M. had directed the people of the house to purchase 'an ancient cock,' and to have him boiled forthwith, in order that Spinoza might take some broth about noon; which in fact he did, and ate some of the *old cock* with a good appetite, after the landlord and his wife had returned from church.

'In the afternoon, L. M. staid alone with Spinoza, the people of the house 'having returned to church; on coming out from which, they learned, with 'much surprise, that Spinoza had died about three o'clock, in the presence of 'L. M., who took his departure for Amsterdam that same evening, by the night-'boat, without paying the least attention to the deceased,'—and probably without paying very much attention to the payment of his own little account. 'No 'doubt, he was the readier to dispense with these duties as he had possessed him-'self of a ducatoon, and a small quantity of silver, together with a silver-hafted 'knife, and had absconded with his pillage.' Here you see, gentlemen, the murder is plain, and the manner of it. It was L. M. who murdered Spinoza for his money. Poor Spinoza was an invalid, meagre and weak; as no blood was observed, L. M. no doubt threw him down, and smothered him with pillows —the poor man being already half suffocated by his infernal dinner. After masticating that 'ancient cock,' which I take to mean a cock of the preceding century, in what condition could the poor invalid find himself for a stand-up fight with L. M. ? But who was L. M. ? It surely never could be Lindley Murray, for I saw him at York in 1825; and, besides, I do not think he would do such a thing—at least, not to a brother-grammarian: for you know, gentlemen, that Spinoza wrote a very respectable Hebrew grammar.

Hobbes—but why, or on what principle, I never could understand—was not murdered. This was a capital oversight of the professional men in the seven-teenth century; because in every light he was a fine subject for murder, except, indeed, that he was lean and skinny; for I can prove that he had money, and (what was very funny) he had no right to make the least resistance; since, according to himself, irresistible power creates the very highest species of right, so that it is rebellion of the blackest dye to refuse to be murdered when a competent force appears to murder you. However, gentlemen, though he was not murdered, I am happy to assure you that (by his own account) he was three times very near being murdered,—which is consolatory. The first time was in the spring of 1640, when he pretends to have circulated a little MS. on the

King's behalf against the Parliament. He never could produce this MS., by the bye; but he says that, 'had not His Majesty dissolved the Parliament' (in May), 'it had brought him into danger of his life.' Dissolving the Parliament, however, was of no use; for in November of the same year the Long Parliament assembled, and Hobbes, a second time fearing he should be murdered, ran away to France. This looks like the madness of John Dennis, who thought that Louis XIV would never make peace with Queen Anne unless he (Dennis to wit) were given up to French vengeance, and actually ran away from the sea-coast under that belief. In France, Hobbes managed to take care of his throat pretty well for ten years; but at the end of that time, by way of paying court to Cromwell, he published his 'Leviathan.' The old coward now began to 'funk' horribly for the third time; he fancied the swords of the Cavaliers were constantly at his throat, recollecting how they had served the Parliament ambassadors at the Hague and Madrid. '*Tum*,' says he, in his dog-Latin life of himself,—

'*Tum venit in mentem mihi Dorislaus et Ascham;*
Tanquam proscripto terror ubique aderat.'[1]

And, accordingly, he ran home to England. Now, certainly, it is very true that a man deserved a cudgelling for writing 'Leviathan,' and two or three cudgellings for writing a pentameter ending so villainously as '*terror ubique aderat*'! But no man ever thought him worthy of anything beyond cudgelling. And, in fact, the whole story is a bounce of his own. For, in a most abusive letter which he wrote 'to a learned person' (meaning Wallis the mathematician), he gives quite another account of the matter, and says (p. 8), he ran home 'because he would not trust his safety with the French clergy'; insinuating that he was likely to be murdered for his religion; which would have been a high joke indeed—Tom's being brought to the stake for religion!

Bounce or not bounce, however, certain it is that Hobbes, to the end of his life, feared that somebody would murder him. This is proved by the story I am going to tell you; it is not from a manuscript, but (as Mr. Coleridge says) it is as

---

[1] 'Then there came into my mind Dorislaus and Ascham; fear attended me everywhere as one proscribed.' The quotation is from Hobbes's Life of himself in Latin elegiac verse, first published in December 1679, about three weeks after his death.—Dr. Isaac Dorislaus, a Dutchman naturalised in England, and who had acted as one of the counsel for the prosecution at the trial of Charles I., was sent to the Hague as envoy for the English Commonwealth in the first year of its existence, but had no sooner arrived than he was assassinated in his inn (3d May 1649) by some Royalist exiles. Anthony Ascham, sent to Spain in the following years as envoy for the Commonwealth, had a similar fate, being assassinated in Madrid by English Royalist refugees, 27th May 1650.—M.

good as manuscript; for it comes from a book now entirely forgotten, viz. 'The Creed of Mr. Hobbes Examined: in a Conference between him and a Student in Divinity' (published about ten years before Hobbes's death). The book is anonymous; but it was written by Tenison,—the same who, about thirty years after, succeeded Tillotson as Archbishop of Canterbury. The introductory anecdote is as follows:—'A certain divine' (no doubt Tenison himself) 'took an annual tour of one month to different parts of the island.' In one of these excursions (1670), he visited the Peak in Derbyshire, partly in consequence of Hobbes's description of it.[1] Being in that neighbourhood, he could not but pay a visit to Buxton; and at the very moment of his arrival he was fortunate enough to find a party of gentlemen dismounting at the inn-door, amongst whom was a long thin fellow, who turned out to be no less a person than Mr. Hobbes, who probably had ridden over from Chatsworth.[2] Meeting so great a lion, a tourist in search of the picturesque could do no less than present himself in the character of bore. And, luckily for this scheme, two of Mr. Hobbes's companions were suddenly summoned away by express; so that, for the rest of his stay at Buxton, he had Leviathan entirely to himself, and had the honour of boozing with him in the evening. Hobbes, it seems, at first showed a good deal of stiffness, for he was shy of divines; but this wore off, and he became very sociable and funny, and they agreed to go into the bath together. How Tenison could venture to gambol in the water with Leviathan I cannot explain; but so it was: they frolicked about like two dolphins, though Hobbes must have been as old as the hills; and 'in those intervals wherein they abstained from swimming and 'plunging themselves' (i.e. diving) 'they discoursed of many things relating to 'the baths of the Ancients, and the Origine of Springs. When they had in this 'manner passed away an hour, they stepped out of the bath; and, having dried 'and cloathed themselves, they sate down in expectation of such a supper as the 'place afforded; designing to refresh themselves like the Deipnosophistæ, and 'rather to reason than to drink profoundly. But in this innocent intention they 'were interrupted by the disturbance arising from a little quarrel in which some 'of the ruder people in the house were for a short time engaged. At this Mr. 'Hobbes seemed much concerned, though he was at some distance from the

[1] One of Hobbes's earliest publications was a Latin poem De Mirabilibus Pecci ('On the Wonders of the Peak'). It was first printed in London in 1638, when the author was in his forty-eighth year; and there was a second edition in 1666.—M.

[2] Chatsworth was then, as now, the superb seat of the Cavendishes in their highest branch—in those days Earl, at present Duke, of Devonshire. It is to the honour of this family that, through two generations, they gave an asylum to Hobbes. It is noticeable that Hobbes was born in the year of the Spanish Armada, i.e. in 1588; such, at least, is my belief. And, therefore, at this meeting with Tenison in 1670 he must have been about eighty-two years old.

'persons.' And why was he concerned, gentlemen? No doubt, you fancy, from some benign and disinterested love of peace, worthy of an old man and a philosopher. But listen—'For a while he was not composed, but related it once or twice, as to himself, with a low and careful, *i.e.* anxious, tone, how Sextus 'Roscius was murthered after supper by the Balneæ Palatinæ.[1] Of such general 'extent is that remark of Cicero in relation to Epicurus the Atheist, of whom he 'observed that he of all men dreaded most those things which he contemned— 'Death and the Gods.' Merely because it was supper-time, and in the neighbour-hood of a bath, Mr. Hobbes must have the fate of Sextus Roscius! He must be murthered, because Sextus Roscius was murthered! What logic was there in this, unless to a man who was always dreaming of murder? Here was Leviathan, no longer afraid of the daggers of English cavaliers or French clergy, but 'fright-ened from his propriety' by a row in an alehouse between some honest clod-hoppers of Derbyshire, whom his own gaunt scarecrow of a person, that belonged to quite another century, would have frightened out of their wits.

Malebranche, it will give you pleasure to hear, *was* murdered. The man who murdered him is well known: it was Bishop Berkeley. The story is familiar, though hitherto not put in a proper light. Berkeley, when a young man, went to Paris, and called on Père Malebranche. He found him in his cell cooking. Cooks have ever been a *genus irritabile*; authors still more so: Malebranche was both: a dispute arose; the old father, warm already, became warmer; culinary and metaphysical irritations united to derange his liver: he took to his bed, and died. Such is the common version of the story: 'so the whole ear of Denmark is abused.' The fact is that the matter was hushed up, out of consideration for Berkeley, who (as Pope justly observes) had 'every virtue under heaven': else it was well known that Berkeley, feeling himself nettled by the waspishness of the old Frenchman, squared at him; a *turn-up* was the consequence: Malebranche was floored in the first round; the conceit was wholly taken out of him, and he would perhaps have given in; but Berkeley's blood was now up, and he in-sisted on the old Frenchman's retracting his doctrine of Occasional Causes. The vanity of the man was too great for this; and he fell a sacrifice to the impetuosity of Irish youth, combined with his own absurd obstinacy.[2]

---

[1] Sextus Roscius, a wealthy citizen of Ameria, who often visited Rome, was assassinated there on one of his visits (B.C. 80) near the Palatine Baths, as he was returning from a banquet. The assassins were two of his relatives; who, to shield themselves and secure his property, accused his son, also called Sextus Roscius, of the crime. Cicero's first speech in a criminal case was in defence of this Sextus; and he was acquitted.—M.

[2] Berkeley was certainly in Paris on a visit in 1713, when he was twenty-eight years of age, and a Junior Fellow of Trinity College, Dublin. In a letter of his

Leibnitz being every way superior to Malebranche, one might, *a fortiori*, have counted on *his* being murdered; which, however, was not the case. I believe he was nettled at this neglect, and felt himself insulted by the security in which he passed his days. In no other way can I explain his conduct at the latter end of his life, when he chose to grow very avaricious, and to hoard up large sums of gold, which he kept in his own house. This was at Vienna, where he died; and letters are still in existence describing the immeasurable anxiety which he entertained for his throat. Still, his ambition for being *attempted* at least was so great that he would not forgo the danger. A later English pedagogue of Birmingham manufacture—viz. Dr. Parr[1]—took a more selfish course under the same circumstances. He had amassed a considerable quantity of gold and silver plate, which was for some time deposited in his bedroom at his parsonage-house, Hatton. But, growing every day more afraid of being murdered,—which he knew that he could not stand (and to which, indeed, he never had the slightest pretensions),—he transferred the whole to the Hatton blacksmith; conceiving, no doubt, that the murder of a blacksmith would fall more lightly on the *salus reipublicæ* than that of a pedagogue. But I have heard this greatly disputed; and it seems now generally agreed that one good horseshoe is worth about two and a quarter Spital sermons.[2]

dated 'Paris, November 25, 1713, N.S.' he says 'To-morrow I intend to visit Father Malebranche, and discourse him on certain points.' Whether he made out this visit is unknown; and, if he did, it is not to this visit in 1713 that De Quincey refers, but to a second one in October 1715. On the 13th of that month Malebranche died, in the 77th year of his age; and the story, as told in Stock's Life of Berkeley, published in 1776, is that it was Berkeley's visit that had caused his death. 'He found the ingenious Father in a cell, cooking, in a small pipkin, a 'medicine for a disorder with which he was then troubled,—an inflammation 'on the lungs. The conversation naturally turned on Berkeley's system, of which 'he had received some knowledge from a translation just published. But the issue 'of the debate proved tragical to poor Malebranche. In the heat of the disputation 'he raised his voice too high, and gave way so freely to the natural impetuosity of 'a man of parts and a Frenchman, that he brought on himself a violent increase of 'his disorder, which carried him off in a few days.' This quotation from Stock is from Professor Campbell Fraser's *Life and Letters of Berkeley* (1871); where the authenticity of the story is carefully discussed. 'It is unfortunate,' says Professor Fraser, 'that we have no authentic account of the meeting, especially one by 'Berkeley himself, nor any authority that I can find, except the biographer's, for 'its having occurred at all.'—M.

[1] Dr. Samuel Parr, born 1747, died 1825.

[2] '*Spital Sermons*': Dr. Parr's chief public appearances as an author, after his original appearance in the famous Latin preface to Bellendĕnus (don't say Bellendēnus), occurred in certain sermons at periodic intervals, delivered on

As Leibnitz, though not murdered, may be said to have died partly of the fear that he should be murdered, and partly of vexation that he was not, Kant, on the other hand—who manifested no ambition in that way—had a narrower escape from a murderer than any man we read of except Des Cartes. So absurdly does fortune throw about her favours! The case is told, I think, in an anonymous life of this very great man. For health's sake, Kant imposed upon himself, at one time, a walk of six miles every day along a high-road. This fact becoming known to a man who had his private reasons for committing murder, at the third milestone from Königsberg he waited for his 'intended,' who came up to time as duly as a mail-coach. But for an accident, Kant was a dead man. This accident lay in the scrupulous, or what Mrs. Quickly would have called the *peevish*, morality of the murderer. An old professor, he fancied, might be laden with sins. Not so a young child. On this consideration, he turned away from Kant at the critical moment, and soon after murdered a child of five years old. Such is the German account of the matter; but my opinion is that the murderer was an amateur, who felt how little would be gained to the cause of good taste by murdering an old, arid, and adust metaphysician: there was no room for display, as the man could not possibly look more like a mummy when dead than he had done alive. ...

But it is now time that I should say a few words about the principles of murder, not with a view to regulate your practice, but your judgment. As to old women, and the mob of newspaper readers, they are pleased with anything, provided it is bloody enough. But the mind of sensibility requires something more. *First*, then, let us speak of the kind of person who is adapted to the purpose of the murderer; *secondly*, of the place where; *thirdly*, of the time when, and other little circumstances.

As to the person, I suppose it is evident that he ought to be a good man, because, if he were not, he might himself, by possibility, be contemplating murder at the very time; and such 'diamond-cut-diamond' tussles, though pleasant enough where nothing better is stirring, are really not what a critic can allow himself to call murders. I could mention some people (I name no names) who have been murdered by other people in a dark lane; and so far all seemed correct enough; but, on looking further into the matter, the public have become aware that the murdered party was himself, at the moment, planning to rob his murderer, at the least, and possibly to murder him, if he had been strong enough. Whenever that is the case, or may be thought to be the case, farewell to all the genuine effects of the art. For the final purpose of murder, considered

behalf of some hospital (I really forget what) which retained for its official designation the old word *Spital*; and thus it happened that the sermons themselves were generally known by the title of *Spital* Sermons.

as a fine art, is precisely the same as that of tragedy in Aristotle's account of it; viz. 'to cleanse the heart by means of pity and terror.' Now, terror there may be, but how can there be any pity for one tiger destroyed by another tiger?

It is also evident that the person selected ought not to be a public character. For instance, no judicious artist would have attempted to murder Abraham Newland.[1] For the case was this: everybody read so much about Abraham Newland, and so few people ever saw him, that to the general belief he was a mere abstract idea. And I remember that once, when I happened to mention that I had dined at a coffee-house in company with Abraham Newland, everybody looked scornfully at me, as though I had pretended to have played at billiards with Prester John, or to have had an affair of honour with the Pope. And, by the way, the Pope would be a very improper person to murder; for he has such a virtual ubiquity as the father of Christendom, and, like the cuckoo, is so often heard but never seen, that I suspect most people regard *him* also as an abstract idea. Where, indeed, a public man is in the habit of giving dinners, 'with every delicacy of the season,' the case is very different: every person is satisfied that *he* is no abstract idea; and, therefore, there can be no impropriety in murdering him; only that his murder will fall into the class of assassinations, which I have not yet treated.

Thirdly. The subject chosen ought to be in good health; for it is absolutely barbarous to murder a sick person, who is usually quite unable to bear it. On this principle, no tailor ought to be chosen who is above twenty-five, for after that age he is sure to be dyspeptic. Or, at least, if a man will hunt in that warren, he will of course think it his duty, on the old established equation, to murder some multiple of 9—say 18, 27, or 36. And here, in this benign attention to the comfort of sick people, you will observe the usual effect of a fine art to soften and refine the feelings. The world in general, gentlemen, are very bloody-minded; and all they want in a murder is a copious effusion of blood; gaudy display in this point is enough for *them*. But the enlightened connoisseur is more refined in his taste; and from our art, as from all the other liberal arts when thoroughly mastered, the result is, to humanise the heart; so true is it that

> *'Ingenuas didicisse fideliter artes*
> *Emollit mores, nec sinit esse feros.'*

[1] Abraham Newland [chief cashier of the Bank of England, who died 1807.—M.] is now utterly forgotten. But, when this was written [1827], his name had not ceased to ring in British ears, as the most familiar and most significant that perhaps has ever existed. It was the name which appeared on the face of all Bank of England notes, great or small; and had been, for more than a quarter of a century (especially through the whole career of the French Revolution), a shorthand expression for paper money in its safest form.

A philosophic friend, well known for his philanthropy and general benignity, suggests that the subject chosen ought also to have a family of young children wholly dependent on his exertions, by way of deepening the pathos. And, undoubtedly, this is a judicious caution. Yet I would not insist too keenly on such a condition. Severe good taste unquestionably suggests it; but still, where the man was otherwise unobjectionable in point of morals and health, I would not look with too curious a jealousy to a restriction which might have the effect of narrowing the artist's sphere.

So much for the person. As to the time, the place, and the tools, I have many things to say which at present I have no room for. The good sense of the practitioner has usually directed him to night and privacy. Yet there have not been wanting cases where this rule was departed from with excellent effect. In respect to time, Mrs. Ruscombe's case is a beautiful exception which I have already noticed; and in respect both to time and place there is a fine exception in the annals of Edinburgh (year 1805), familiar to every child in Edinburgh, but which has unaccountably been defrauded of its due portion of fame amongst English amateurs. The case I mean is that of a porter to one of the banks, who was murdered whilst carrying a bag of money, in broad daylight, on turning out of the High Street, one of the most public streets in Europe; and the murderer is to this hour undiscovered.

> *'Sed fugit interea, fugit irreparabile tempus,*
> *Singula dum capti circumvectamur amore.'*

And now, gentlemen, in conclusion, let me again solemnly disclaim all pretensions on my own part to the character of a professional man. I never attempted any murder in my life, except in the year 1801,—upon the body of a tom-cat; and *that* turned out differently from my intention. My purpose, I own, was downright murder. 'Semper ego auditor tantum?' said I 'nunquamne reponam?' And I went downstairs in search of Tom at one o'clock on a dark night, with the 'animus,' and no doubt with the fiendish looks, of a murderer. But, when I found him, he was in the act of plundering the pantry of bread and other things. Now this gave a new turn to the affair; for, the time being one of general scarcity, when even Christians were reduced to the use of potato-bread, rice-bread, and all sorts of things, it was downright treason in a tom-cat to be wasting good wheaten-bread in the way he was doing. It instantly became a patriotic duty to put him to death; and, as I raised aloft and shook the glittering steel, I fancied myself rising, like Brutus, effulgent from a crowd of patriot's, and, as I stabbed him, I

> *'Called aloud on Tully's name,*
> *And bade the father of his country hail!'*

Since then, what wandering thoughts I may have had of attempting the life of an ancient ewe, of a superannuated hen, and such 'small deer,' are locked up in the secrets of my own breast; but for the higher departments of the art I confess myself to be utterly unfit. My ambition does not rise so high. No, gentlemen: in the words of Horace,

'*Fungar vice cotis, acutum*
Reddere quæ ferrum valet, exsors ipsa secandi.'

Blackwood's Magazine, Feb. 1827; Masson XIII.

A Vision of Sudden Death

What is to be taken as the predominant opinion of man, reflective and philosophic, upon SUDDEN DEATH? It is remarkable that, in different conditions of society, sudden death has been variously regarded as the consummation of an earthly career most fervently to be desired, or, again, as that consummation which is with most horror to be deprecated. Cæsar the Dictator, at his last dinner-party (*cæna*), on the very evening before his assassination, when the minutes of his earthly career were numbered, being asked what death, in *his* judgment, might be pronounced the most eligible, replied 'That which should be most sudden.' On the other hand, the divine Litany of our English Church, when breathing forth supplications, as if in some representative character, for the whole human race prostrate before God, places such a death in the very van of horrors: 'From lightning and tempest, from plague, pestilence, and famine; from battle and murder, and from SUDDEN DEATH—*Good Lord, deliver us.*' Sudden death is here made to crown the climax in a grand ascent of calamities; it is ranked among the last of curses; and yet by the noblest of Romans it was ranked as the first of blessings. In that difference most readers will see little more than the essential difference between Christianity and Paganism. But this, on consideration, I doubt. The Christian Church may be right in its estimate of sudden death; and it is a natural feeling, though after all it may also be an infirm one, to wish for a quiet dismissal from life, as that which *seems* most reconcilable with meditation, with penitential retrospects, and with the humilities of farewell prayer. There does not, however, occur to me any direct scriptural warrant for this earnest petition of the English Litany, unless under a special construction of the word 'sudden.' It seems a petition indulged rather and conceded to human infirmity than exacted from human piety. It is not so much a doctrine built upon the eternities of the Christian system as a plausible opinion built upon special varieties of physical temperament. Let that, however, be as it may, two remarks suggest themselves as prudent restraints upon a doctrine which else *may* wander, and *has* wandered, into an uncharitable superstition. The first is this: that many people are likely to exaggerate the horror of a sudden death from the disposition to lay a false stress upon words or acts simply because by an accident they have become *final* words or acts. If a man dies, for instance, by some sudden death when he happens to be intoxicated, such a death is falsely regarded with peculiar horror; as though the intoxication were suddenly exalted into a blasphemy. But *that* is unphilosophic. The man was, or he was not, *habitually* a drunkard. If not, if his intoxication were a solitary accident, there can be no reason for allowing special emphasis to this act simply because through misfortune it became his final act. Nor, on the other hand, if it were no accident, but one of his *habitual* transgressions, will it be the more habitual or the more a transgression because some sudden calamity, surprising him, has caused this habitual transgression to be also a final one. Could the man have had any reason even dimly to foresee his own sudden death, there would have been a new feature in his act of intemperance—a feature of presumption and irreverence, as in one that, having known himself drawing near to the presence of God, should have suited his demeanour to an expectation so awful. But this is no part of the case supposed. And the only new element in the man's act is not any element of special immorality, but simply of special misfortune.

The other remark has reference to the meaning of the word *sudden*. Very possibly Cæsar and the Christian Church do not differ in the way supposed,— that is, do not differ by any difference of doctrine as between Pagan and Christian views of the moral temper appropriate to death; but perhaps they are contemplating different cases. Both contemplate a violent death, a Βιαθάνατος —death that is βιαῖος, or, in other words, death that is brought about, not by internal and spontaneous change, but by active force having its origin from without.[1] In this meaning the two authorities agree. Thus far they are in harmony. But the difference is that the Roman by the word 'sudden' means *unlingering*, whereas the Christian Litany by 'sudden death' means a death *without warning*, consequently without any available summons to religious preparation. The poor mutineer who kneels down to gather into his heart the bullets from twelve firelocks of his pitying comrades dies by a most sudden death in Cæsar's sense; one shock, one mighty spasm, one (possibly *not* one) groan, and all is over. But, in the sense of the Litany, the mutineer's death is far from sudden; his offence originally, his imprisonment, his trial, the interval between his sentence and its execution, having all furnished him with separate

[1] *Biaios*, Greek for 'forcible' or 'violent': hence *Biathanatos*, violent death.—M.

warnings of his fate—having all summoned him to meet it with solemn preparation.

Here at once, in this sharp verbal distinction, we comprehend the faithful earnestness with which a holy Christian Church pleads on behalf of her poor departing children that God would vouchsafe to them the last great privilege and distinction possible on a death-bed, viz. the opportunity of untroubled preparation for facing this mighty trial. Sudden death, as a mere variety in the modes of dying where death in some shape is inevitable, proposes a question of choice which, equally in the Roman and the Christian sense, will be variously answered according to each man's variety of temperament. Meantime, one aspect of sudden death there is, one modification, upon which no doubt can arise, that of all martyrdoms it is the most agitating—viz. where it surprises a man under circumstances which offer (or which seem to offer) some hurrying, flying, inappreciably minute chance of evading it. Sudden as the danger which it affronts must be any effort by which such an evasion can be accomplished. Even *that*, even the sickening necessity for hurrying in extremity where all hurry seems destined to be vain,—even that anguish is liable to a hideous exasperation in one particular case: viz. where the appeal is made not exclusively to the instinct of self-preservation, but to the conscience, on behalf of some other life besides your own, accidentally thrown upon *your* protection. To fail, to collapse in a service merely your own, might seem comparatively venial; though, in fact, it is far from venial. But to fail in a case where Providence has suddenly thrown into your hands the final interests of another,—a fellow-creature shuddering between the gates of life and death: this, to a man of apprehensive conscience, would mingle the misery of an atrocious criminality with the misery of a bloody calamity. You are called upon, by the case supposed, possibly to die, but to die at the very moment when, by any even partial failure or effeminate collapse of your energies, you will be self-denounced as a murderer. You had but the twinkling of an eye for your effort, and that effort might have been unavailing; but to have risen to the level of such an effort would have rescued you, though not from dying, yet from dying as a traitor to your final and farewell duty.

The situation here contemplated exposes a dreadful ulcer, lurking far down in the depths of human nature. It is not that men generally are summoned to face such awful trials. But potentially, and in shadowy outline, such a trial is moving subterraneously in perhaps all men's natures. Upon the secret mirror of our dreams such a trial is darkly projected, perhaps, to every one of us. That dream, so familiar to childhood, of meeting a lion, and, through languishing prostration in hope and the energies of hope, that constant sequel of lying down before the lion, publishes the secret frailty of human nature—reveals its deep-seated falsehood to itself—records its abysmal treachery. Perhaps not one of us escapes that dream; perhaps, as by some sorrowful doom of man, that dream repeats for every one of us, through every generation, the original temptation in Eden. Every one of us, in this dream, has a bait offered to the infirm places of his own individual will; once again a snare is presented for tempting him into captivity to a luxury of ruin; once again, as in aboriginal Paradise, the man falls by his own choice; again, by infinite iteration, the ancient earth groans to Heaven, through her secret caves, over the weakness of her child. 'Nature, from her seat, sighing through all her works,' again 'gives signs of woe that all is lost'; and again the counter-sigh is repeated to the sorrowing heavens for the endless rebellion against God. It is not without probability that in the world of dreams every one of us ratifies for himself the original transgression. In dreams, perhaps under some secret conflict of the midnight sleeper, lighted up to the consciousness at the time, but darkened to the memory as soon as all is finished, each several child of our mysterious race completes for himself the treason of the aboriginal fall.

The incident, so memorable in itself by its features of horror, and so scenical by its grouping for the eye, which furnished the text for this reverie upon *Sudden Death*, occurred to myself in the dead of night, as a solitary spectator, when seated on the box of the Manchester and Glasgow mail, in the second or third summer after Waterloo. I find it necessary to relate the circumstances, because they are such as could not have occurred unless under a singular combination of accidents. In those days, the oblique and lateral communications with many rural post-offices were so arranged, either through necessity or through defect of system, as to make it requisite for the main north-western mail (*i.e.* the *down* mail) on reaching Manchester to halt for a number of hours; how many, I do not remember; six or seven, I think; but the result was that, in the ordinary course, the mail recommenced its journey northwards about midnight. Wearied with the long detention at a gloomy hotel, I walked out about eleven o'clock at night for the sake of fresh air; meaning to fall in with the mail and resume my seat at the post-office. The night, however, being yet dark, as the moon had scarcely risen, and the streets being at that hour empty, so as to offer no opportunities for asking the road, I lost my way, and did not reach the post-office until it was considerably past midnight; but, to my great relief (as it was important for me to be in Westmorland by the morning), I saw in the huge saucer eyes of the mail, blazing through the gloom, an evidence that my chance was not yet lost. Past the time it was; but, by some rare accident, the mail was not even yet ready to start. I ascended to my seat on the box, where my cloak was still lying as it had lain at the Bridgewater Arms. I had left it there in imitation of a nautical discoverer, who leaves a bit of bunting on the shore of his discovery, by way of warning off the ground the whole human race, and notifying to the Christian and the heathen worlds, with his best compliments, that he has hoisted his pocket-handkerchief once and for ever upon that virgin soil: thenceforward claiming the *jus dominii* to the top of the atmosphere above it, and also the right of driving shafts to the centre of the earth below it; so that all people found after this warning either aloft in upper chambers of the atmosphere, or groping in subterraneous shafts, or squatting audaciously on the surface of the soil, will be treated as trespassers— kicked, that is to say, or decapitated, as circumstances may suggest, by their very faithful servant, the owner of the said pocket-handkerchief. In the present case, it is probable that my cloak might not have been respected, and the *jus gentium* might have been cruelly violated in my person—for, in the dark, people commit deeds of darkness, gas being a great ally of morality; but it so happened that on this night there was no other outside passenger; and thus the crime, which else was but too probable, missed fire for want of a criminal.

Having mounted the box, I took a small quantity of laudanum, having already travelled two hundred and fifty miles—viz. from a point seventy miles beyond London. In the taking of laudanum there was nothing extraordinary. But by accident it drew upon me the special attention of my assessor on the box, the coachman. And in *that* also there was nothing extraordinary. But by accident, and with great delight, it drew my own attention to the fact that this coachman was a monster in point of bulk, and that he had but one eye. In fact, he had been foretold by Virgil as

'*Monstrum horrendum, informe, ingens, cui lumen ademptum.*'

He answered to the conditions in every one of the items: 1, a monster he was; 2, dreadful; 3, shapeless; 4, huge; 5, who had lost an eye. But why should *that* delight me? Had be been one of the Calendars in the *Arabian Nights*, and had paid down his eye as the price of his criminal curiosity, what right had *I* to exult in his misfortune? I did *not* exult; I delighted in no man's punishment, though it were even merited. But these personal distinctions (Nos. 1, 2, 3, 4, 5) identified in an instant an old friend of mine whom I had known in the south for some years as the most masterly of mail-coachmen. He was the man in all Europe that could (if *any* could) have driven six-in-hand full gallop over *Al Sirat*—that dreadful bridge of Mahomet, with no side battlements, and of *extra* room not enough for a razor's edge—leading right across the bottomless gulf. Under this eminent man, whom in Greek I cognominated Cyclops *Diphrélates* (Cyclops the Charioteer), I, and others known to me, studied the diphrelatic art. Excuse, reader, a word too elegant to be pedantic.[1] As a pupil, though I paid extra fees, it is to be lamented that I did not stand high in his esteem. It showed his dogged honesty (though, observe, not his discernment) that he could not see my merits. Let us excuse his absurdity in this particular by remembering his want of an eye. Doubtless *that* made him blind to my merits. In the art of conversation, however, he admitted that I had the whip-hand of him. On this present occasion great joy was at our meeting. But what was Cyclops doing here? Had the medical men recommended northern air, or how? I collected, from such explanations as he volunteered, that he had an interest at stake in some suit-at-law now pending at Lancaster; so that probably he had got himself transferred to this station for the purpose of connecting with his professional pursuits an instant readiness for the calls of his lawsuit.

Meantime, what are we stopping for? Surely we have now waited long enough. Oh, this procrastinating mail, and this procrastinating post-office! Can't they take a lesson upon that subject from *me*? Some people have called *me* procrastinating. Yet you are witness, reader, that I was here kept waiting for the post-office. Will the post-office lay its hand on its heart, in its moments of sobriety, and assert that ever it waited for me? What are they about? The guard tells me that there is a large extra accumulation of foreign mails this night, owing to irregularities caused by war, by wind, by weather, in the packet service, which as yet does not benefit at all by steam. For an *extra* hour, it seems, the post-office has been engaged in threshing out the pure wheaten correspondence of Glasgow, and winnowing it from the chaff of all baser intermediate towns. But at last all is finished. Sound your horn, guard! Manchester, good-bye! we've lost an hour by your criminal conduct at the post-office: which, however, though I do not mean to part with a serviceable ground of complaint, and one which really *is* such for the horses, to me secretly is an advantage, since it compels us to look sharply for this lost hour amongst the next eight or nine, and to recover it (if we can) at the rate of one mile extra per hour. Off we are at last, and at eleven miles an hour; and for the moment I detect no changes in the energy or in the skill of Cyclops.

From Manchester to Kendal, which virtually (though not in law) is the

[1] For the last two sentences the original in *Blackwood* had these four:—'I used to call him *Cyclops Mastigophoros*, Cyclops the Whip-bearer, until I observed that his skill made whips useless, except to fetch off an impertinent fly from a leader's head; upon which I changed his Grecian name to Cyclops *Diphrélates* (Cyclops the Charioteer). I, and others known to me, studied under him the diphrelatic art. Excuse, reader, a word too elegant to be pedantic, And also take this remark from me as a *gage d'amitié*—that no word ever was or *can* be pedantic which, by supporting a distinction, supports the accuracy of logic, or which fills up a chasm for the understanding.'—M.

capital of Westmorland, there were at this time seven stages of eleven miles each. The first five of these, counting from Manchester, terminate in Lancaster; which is therefore fifty-five miles north of Manchester, and the same distance exactly from Liverpool. The first three stages terminate in Preston (by way of distinction from other towns of that name, *Proud* Preston); at which place it is that the separate roads from Liverpool and from Manchester to the north become confluent. Within these first three stages lay the foundation, the progress, and termination of our night's adventure. During the first stage, I found out that Cyclops was mortal: he was liable to the shocking affection of sleep—a thing which previously I had never suspected. If a man indulges in the vicious habit of sleeping, all the skill in aurigation of Apollo himself, with the horses of Aurora to execute his notions, avails him nothing. 'Oh, Cyclops!' I exclaimed, 'thou art mortal. My friend, thou snorest.' Through the first eleven miles, however, this infirmity—which I grieve to say that he shared with the whole Pagan Pantheon—betrayed itself only by brief snatches. On waking up, he made an apology for himself which, instead of mending matters, laid open a gloomy vista of coming disasters. The summer assizes, he reminded me, were now going on at Lancaster: in consequence of which for three nights and three days he had not lain down in a bed. During the day he was waiting for his own summons as a witness on the trial in which he was interested, or else, lest he should be missing at the critical moment, was drinking with the other witnesses under the pastoral surveillance of the attorneys. During the night, or that part of it which at sea would form the middle watch, he was driving. This explanation certainly accounted for his drowsiness, but in a way which made it much more alarming; since now, after several days' resistance to this infirmity, at length he was steadily giving way. Throughout the second stage he grew more and more drowsy. In the second mile of the third stage he surrendered himself finally and without a struggle to his perilous temptation. All his past resistance had but deepened the weight of this final oppression. Seven atmospheres of sleep rested upon him; and, to consummate the case, our worthy guard, after singing 'Love amongst the Roses' for perhaps thirty times, without invitation and without applause, had in revenge moodily resigned himself to slumber— not so deep, doubtless, as the coachman's, but deep enough for mischief. And thus at last, about ten miles from Preston, it came about that I found myself left in charge of his Majesty's London and Glasgow mail, then running at the least twelve miles an hour.

What made this negligence less criminal than else it must have been thought was the condition of the roads at night during the assizes. At that time, all the law business of populous Liverpool, and also of populous Manchester, with its vast cincture of populous rural districts, was called up by ancient usage to the tribunal of Lilliputian Lancaster. To break up this old traditional usage required, 1, a conflict with powerful established interests, 2, a large system of new arrangements, and 3, a new parliamentary statute. But as yet this change was merely in contemplation. As things were at present, twice in the year[1] so vast a body of business rolled northwards from the southern quarter of the county that for a fortnight at least it occupied the severe exertions of two judges in its despatch. The consequence of this was that every horse available for such a service, along the whole line of road, was exhausted in carrying down the multitudes of people who were parties to the different suits. By sunset, therefore, it usually happened that, through utter exhaustion amongst men and horses, the road sank into profound silence. Except the exhaustion in the vast adjacent county of York from a contested election, no such silence succeeding to no such fiery uproar was ever witnessed in England.

On this occasion the usual silence and solitude prevailed along the road. Not a hoof nor a wheel was to be heard. And, to strengthen this false luxurious confidence in the noiseless roads, it happened also that the night was one of peculiar solemnity and peace. For my own part, though slightly alive to the possibilities of peril, I had so far yielded to the influence of the mighty calm as to sink into a profound reverie. The month was August, in the middle of which lay my own birthday—a festival to every thoughtful man suggesting solemn and often sigh-born[2] thoughts. The county was my own native county—upon which, in its southern section, more than upon any equal area known to man past or present, had descended the original curse of labour in its heaviest form, not mastering the bodies only of men, as of slaves, or criminals in mines, but working through the fiery will. Upon no equal space of earth was, or ever had been, the same energy of human power put forth daily. At this particular season also of the assizes, that dreadful hurricane of flight and pursuit, as it might have seemed to a stranger, which swept to and from Lancaster all day long, hunting the county up and down, and regularly subsiding back into silence about sunset, could not fail (when united with this permanent distinction of Lancashire as the very metropolis and citadel of labour) to point the thoughts pathetically upon that counter-vision of rest, of saintly repose from strife and sorrow, towards which, as to their secret haven, the profounder aspirations of man's heart are in solitude continually travelling. Obliquely upon our left we were nearing the sea; which also must, under the present circumstances, be repeating the general state of halcyon repose. The sea, the atmosphere, the light,

---

[1] '*Twice in the year*': There were at that time only two assizes even in the most populous counties—viz. the Lent Assizes and the Summer Assizes.

[2] '*Sigh-born*': I owe the suggestion of this word to an obscure remembrance of a beautiful phrase in 'Giraldus Cambrensis'—viz. '*suspiriosæ cogitationes.*'

bore each an orchestral part in this universal lull. Moonlight and the first timid tremblings of the dawn were by this time blending; and the blendings were brought into a still more exquisite state of unity by a slight silvery mist, motionless and dreamy, that covered the woods and fields, but with a veil of equable transparency. Except the feet of our own horses,—which, running on a sandy margin of the road, made but little disturbance,—there was no sound abroad. In the clouds and on the earth prevailed the same majestic peace; and, in spite of all that the villain of a schoolmaster has done for the ruin of our sublimer thoughts, which are the thoughts of our infancy, we still believe in no such nonsense as a limited atmosphere. Whatever we may swear with our false feigning lips, in our faithful hearts we still believe, and must for ever believe, in fields of air traversing the total gulf between earth and the central heavens. Still, in the confidence of children that tread without fear *every* chamber in their father's house, and to whom no door is closed, we, in that Sabbatic vision which sometimes is revealed for an hour upon nights like this, ascend with easy steps from the sorrow-stricken fields of earth upwards to the sandals of God.

Suddenly, from thoughts like these I was awakened to a sullen sound, as of some motion on the distant road. It stole upon the air for a moment; I listened in awe; but then it died away. Once roused, however, I could not but observe with alarm the quickened motion of our horses. Ten years' experience had made my eye learned in the valuing of motion; and I saw that we were now running thirteen miles an hour. I pretend to no presence of mind. On the contrary, my fear is that I am miserably and shamefully deficient in that quality as regards action. The palsy of doubt and distraction hangs like some guilty weight of dark unfathomed remembrances upon my energies when the signal is flying for *action*. But, on the other hand, this accursed gift I have, as regards *thought*, that in the first step towards the possibility of a misfortune I see its total evolution; in the radix of the series I see too certainly and too instantly its entire expansion; in the first syllable of the dreadful sentence I read already the last. It was not that I feared for ourselves. *Us* our bulk and impetus charmed against peril in any collision. And I had ridden through too many hundreds of perils that were frightful to approach, that were matter of laughter to look back upon, the first face of which was horror, the parting face a jest—for any anxiety to rest upon *our* interests. The mail was not built, I felt assured, nor bespoke, that could betray *me* who trusted to its protection. But any carriage that we could meet would be frail and light in comparison of ourselves. And I remarked this ominous accident of our situation,—we were on the wrong side of the road. But then, it may be said, the other party, if other there was, might also be on the wrong side; and two wrongs might make a right. *That* was not likely. The same motive which had drawn *us* to the right-hand side of the road—viz. the luxury of the soft beaten sand as contrasted with the paved centre—would prove attractive to others. The two adverse carriages would therefore, to a certainty, be travelling on the same side; and from this side, as not being ours in law, the crossing over to the other would, of course, be looked for from *us*.[1] Our lamps, still lighted, would give the impression of vigilance on our part. And every creature that met us would rely upon *us* for quartering.[2] All this, and if the separate links of the anticipation had been a thousand times more, I saw, not discursively, or by effort, or by succession, but by one flash of horrid simultaneous intuition.

Under this steady though rapid anticipation of the evil which *might* be gathering ahead, ah! what a sullen mystery of fear, what a sigh of woe, was that which stole upon the air, as again the far-off sound of a wheel was heard! A whisper it was—a whisper from, perhaps, four miles off—secretly announcing a ruin that, being foreseen, was not the less inevitable: that, being known, was not therefore healed. What could be done—who was it that could do it—to check the storm-flight of these maniacal horses? Could I not seize the reins from the grasp of the slumbering coachman? You, reader, think that it would have been in *your* power to do so. And I quarrel not with your estimate of yourself. But, from the way in which the coachman's hand was viced between his upper and lower thigh, this was impossible. Easy was it? See, then, that bronze equestrian statue. The cruel rider has kept the bit in his horse's mouth for two centuries. Unbridle him for a minute, if you please, and wash his mouth with water. Easy was it? Unhorse me, then, that imperial rider; knock me those marble feet from those marble stirrups of Charlemagne.

The sounds ahead strengthened, and were now too clearly the sounds of wheels. Who and what could it be? Was it industry in a taxed cart? Was it youthful gaiety in a gig? Was it sorrow that loitered, or joy that raced? For as yet the snatches of sound were too intermitting, from distance, to decipher the character of the motion. Whoever were the travellers, something must be done to warn them. Upon the other party rests the active responsibility, but upon *us* —and, woe is me! that *us* was reduced to my frail opium-shattered self—rests the responsibility of warning. Yet, how should this be accomplished? Might I not sound the guard's horn? Already, on the first thought, I was making my

---

[1] It is true that, according to the law of the case as established by legal precedents, all carriages were required to give way before royal equipages, and therefore before the mail as one of them. But this only increased the danger, as being a regulation very imperfectly made known, very unequally enforced, and therefore often embarrassing the movements on both sides.

[2] '*Quartering*': This is the technical word, and, I presume, derived from the French *cartayer*, to evade a rut or any obstacle.

way over the roof to the guard's seat. But this, from the accident which I have mentioned, of the foreign mails being piled upon the roof, was a difficult and even dangerous attempt to one cramped by nearly three hundred miles of out-side travelling. And, fortunately, before I had lost much time in the attempt, our frantic horses swept round an angle of the road which opened upon us that final stage where the collision must be accomplished and the catastrophe sealed. All was apparently finished. The court was sitting; the case was heard; the judge had finished; and only the verdict was yet in arrear.

Before us lay an avenue straight as an arrow, six hundred yards, perhaps, in length; and the umbrageous trees, which rose in a regular line from either side meeting high overhead, gave to it the character of a cathedral aisle. These trees lent a deeper solemnity to the early light; but there was still light enough to perceive, at the further end of this Gothic aisle, a frail reedy gig, in which were seated a young man, and by his side a young lady. Ah, young sir! what are you about? If it is requisite that you should whisper your communications to this young lady—though really I see nobody, at an hour and on a road so solitary, likely to overhear you—is it therefore requisite that you should carry your lips forward to hers? The little carriage is creeping on at one mile an hour; and the parties within it, being thus tenderly engaged, are naturally bending down their heads. Between them and eternity, to all human calculation, there is but a minute and a-half. Oh heavens! what is it that I shall do? Speaking or acting, what help can I offer? Strange it is, and to a mere auditor of the tale might seem laughable, that I should need a suggestion from the *Iliad* to prompt the sole resource that remained. Yet so it was. Suddenly I remembered the shout of Achilles, and its effect. But could I pretend to shout like the son of Peleus, aided by Pallas? No: but then I needed not the shout that should alarm all Asia militant; such a shout would suffice as might carry terror into the heart of two thoughtless young people and one gig-horse. I shouted—and the young man heard me not. A second time I shouted—and now he heard me, for now he raised his head.

Here, then, all had been done that, by me, *could* be done; more on *my* part was not possible. Mine had been the first step; the second was for the young man; the third was for God. If, said I, this stranger is a brave man, and if indeed he loves the young girl at his side—or, loving her not, if he feels the obligation, pressing upon every man worthy to be called a man, of doing his utmost for a woman confided to his protection—he will at least make some effort to save her. If *that* fails, he will not perish the more, or by a death more cruel, for having made it; and he will die as a brave man should, with his face to the danger, and with his arm about the woman that he sought in vain to save. But, if he makes no effort,—shrinking without a struggle from his duty,—he himself will not the less certainly perish for this baseness of poltroonery. He will die no less: and why not? Wherefore should we grieve that there is one craven less in the world? No; *let* him perish, without a pitying thought of ours wasted upon him; and, in that case, all our grief will be reserved for the fate of the helpless girl who now, upon the least shadow of failure in *him*, must by the fiercest of translations—must without time for a prayer—must within seventy seconds—stand before the judgment-seat of God.

But craven he was not: sudden had been the call upon him, and sudden was his answer to the call. He saw, he heard, he comprehended, the ruin that was coming down; already its gloomy shadow darkened above him; and already he was measuring his strength to deal with it. Ah! what a vulgar thing does courage seem when we see nations buying it and selling it for a shilling a-day: ah! what a sublime thing does courage seem when some fearful summons on the great deeps of life carries a man, as if running before a hurricane, up to the giddy crest of some tumultuous crisis from which lie two courses, and a voice says to him audibly, 'One way lies hope; take the other, and mourn for ever!' How grand a triumph if, even then, amidst the raving of all around him, and the frenzy of the danger, the man is able to confront his situation—is able to retire for a moment into solitude with God, and to seek his counsel from *Him*!

For seven seconds, it might be, of his seventy, the stranger settled his countenance stedfastly upon us, as if to search and value every element in the conflict before him. For five seconds more of his seventy he sat immovably, like one that mused on some great purpose. For five more, perhaps, he sat with eyes upraised, like one that prayed in sorrow, under some extremity of doubt, for light that should guide him to the better choice. Then suddenly he rose; stood upright; and, by a powerful strain upon the reins, raising his horse's fore-feet from the ground, he slewed him round on the pivot of his hind-legs, so as to plant the little equipage in a position nearly at right angles to ours. Thus far his condition was not improved; except as a first step had been taken towards the possibility of a second. If no more were done, nothing was done; for the little carriage still occupied the very centre of our path, though in an altered direction. Yet even now it may not be too late: fifteen of the seventy seconds may still be unexhausted; and one almighty bound may avail to clear the ground. Hurry, then, hurry! for the flying moments—*they* hurry. Oh, hurry, hurry, my brave young man! for the cruel hoofs of our horses—*they* also hurry! Fast are the flying moments, faster are the hoofs of our horses. But fear not for *him*, if human energy can suffice; faithful was he that drove to his terrific duty; faithful was the horse to *his* command. One blow, one impulse given with voice and hand, by the stranger, one rush from the horse, one bound as if in the act of rising to a fence, landed the docile creature's fore-feet upon the crown or arching centre of the road. The larger half of the little equipage had then cleared our over-towering shadow: *that* was evident even to my own agitated sight. But it mattered little that one wreck should float off in safety if upon the wreck that perished were embarked the human freightage. The rear part of the carriage —was *that* certainly beyond the line of absolute ruin? What power could answer the question? Glance of eye, thought of man, wing of angel, which of these had speed enough to sweep between the question and the answer, and divide the one from the other? Light does not tread upon the steps of light more indivisibly than did our all-conquering arrival upon the escaping efforts of the gig. *That* must the young man have felt too plainly. His back was now turned to us; not by sight could he any longer communicate with the peril; but, by the dreadful rattle of our harness, too truly had his ear been instructed that all was finished as regarded any effort of *his*. Already in resignation he had rested from his struggle; and perhaps in his heart he was whispering, 'Father, which art in heaven, do Thou finish above what I on earth have attempted.' Faster than ever mill-race we ran past them in our inexorable flight. Oh, raving of hurricanes that must have sounded in their young ears at the moment of our transit! Even in that moment the thunder of collision spoke aloud. Either with the swingle-bar, or with the haunch of our near leader, we had struck the off-wheel of the little gig; which stood rather obliquely, and not quite so far advanced as to be accurately parallel with the near-wheel. The blow, from the fury of our passage, resounded terrifically. I rose in horror, to gaze upon the ruins we might have caused. From my elevated station I looked down, and looked back upon the scene; which in a moment told its own tale, and wrote all its records on my heart for ever.

Here was the map of the passion that now had finished. The horse was planted immovably, with his fore-feet upon the paved crest of the central road. He of the whole party might be supposed untouched by the passion of death. The little cany carriage—partly, perhaps, from the violent torsion of the wheels in its recent movement, partly from the thundering blow we had given to it—as if it sympathised with human horror, was all alive with tremblings and shiverings. The young man trembled not, nor shivered. He sat like a rock. But *his* was the steadiness of agitation frozen into rest by horror. As yet he dared not to look round; for he knew that, if anything remained to do, by him it could no longer be done. And as yet he knew not for certain if their safety were accomplished. But the lady——

But the lady——! Oh, heavens! will that spectacle ever depart from my dreams, as she rose and sank upon her seat, sank and rose, threw up her arm wildly to heaven, clutched at some visionary object in the air, fainting, praying, raving, despairing? Figure to yourself, reader, the elements of the case; suffer me to recall before your mind the circumstances of that unparalleled situation. From the silence and deep peace of this saintly summer night—from the pathetic blending of this sweet moonlight, dawnlight, dreamlight—from the manly tenderness of this flattering, whispering, murmuring love—suddenly as from the woods and fields—suddenly as from the chambers of the air opening in revelation—suddenly as from the ground yawning at her feet, leaped upon her, with the flashing of cataracts, Death the crowned phantom, with all the equipage of his terrors, and the tiger roar of his voice.

The moments were numbered; the strife was finished; the vision was closed. In the twinkling of an eye, our flying horses had carried us to the termination of the umbrageous aisle; at the right angles we wheeled into our former direction; the turn of the road carried the scene out of my eyes in an instant, and swept it into my dreams for ever.

'The English Mail Coach': *Blackwood's Magazine*, Dec. 1849; Masson XIII.

Pursuit and Escape

About five miles out of the town their road was crossed by a torrent, over which they could not hit the bridge. 'Forward!' cried the lady, 'Oh, heavens! forward!'; and, Kate repeating the word to the horse, the docile creature leaped down into the water. They were all sinking at first; but, having its head free, the horse swam clear of all obstacles through midnight darkness, and scrambled out on the opposite bank. The two riders were dripping from the shoulders downward. But, seeing a light twinkling from a cottage window, Kate rode up, obtaining a little refreshment, and the benefit of a fire, from a poor labouring man. From this man she also bought a warm mantle for the lady; who besides her torrent bath, was dressed in a light evening robe, so that but for the horseman's cloak of Kate she would have perished. But there was no time to lose. They had already lost two hours from the consequences of their cold bath. Cuzco was still eighteen miles distant; and the alcalde's shrewdness would at once divine this to be his wife's mark. They remounted: very soon the silent night echoed the hoofs of a pursuing rider; and now commenced the most frantic race, in which each party rode as if the whole game of life were staked upon the issue. The pace was killing; and Kate has delivered it as her opinion, in the memoirs which she wrote, that the alcalde was the better mounted. This may be doubted. And certainly Kate had ridden too many years in the Spanish cavalry to have any fear of his worship's horsemanship; but it was a prodigious disadvantage that *her* horse had to carry double, while the horse ridden by her opponent was one of those belonging to the murdered Don Antonio, and known to Kate as a powerful animal. At length they had come within three miles of Cuzco. The road after this descended the whole way to the city, and in some places rapidly, so as to require a cool rider. Suddenly a deep trench appeared, traversing the whole extent of a broad heath. It was useless to evade it. To have hesitated was to be lost. Kate saw the necessity of clearing it; but she doubted much whether her poor exhausted horse, after twenty-one miles of work so severe, had strength for the effort. However, the race was nearly finished; a score of dreadful miles had been accomplished; and Kate's maxim, which never yet had failed, both figuratively for life, and literally for the saddle, was—to ride at everything that showed a front of resistance. She did so now. Having come upon the trench rather too suddenly, she wheeled round for the advantage of coming down upon it with more impetus, rode resolutely at it, and gained the opposite bank. The hind feet of her horse were sinking back from the rottenness of the ground; but the strong supporting bridlehand of Kate carried him forward; and in ten minutes more they would be in Cuzco. This being seen by the vengeful alcalde, who had built great hopes on the trench, he unslung his carbine, pulled up, and fired after the bonny black horse and its two bonny riders. But this vicious manoeuvre would have lost his worship any bet that he might have had depending on this admirable steeplechase. For the bullets, says Kate in her memoirs, whistled round the poor clinging lady *en croupe*—luckily none struck *her*; but one wounded the horse. And that settled the odds. Kate now planted herself well in her stirrups to enter Cuzco, almost dangerously a winner; for the horse was so maddened by the wound, and the road so steep, that he went like blazes; and it really became difficult for Kate to guide him with any precision through narrow episcopal[1] paths. Henceforwards the wounded horse required unintermitting attention; and yet, in the mere luxury of strife, it was impossible for Kate to avoid turning a little in her saddle to see the alcalde's performance on this tight-rope of the trench. His worship's horsemanship, being, perhaps, rather rusty, and he not perfectly acquainted with his horse, it would have been agreeable for *him* to compromise the case by riding round, or dismounting. But all *that* was impossible. The job must be done. And I am happy to report, for the reader's satisfaction, the sequel—so far as Kate could attend the performance. Gathering himself up for mischief, the alcalde took a mighty sweep, as if ploughing out the line of some vast encampment, or tracing the *pomœrium* for some future Rome; then, like thunder and lighting, with arms flying aloft in the air, down he came upon the trembling trench. But the horse refused the leap; to take the leap was impossible; abso-

[1] '*Episcopal*': The roads around Cuzco were made, and maintained, under the patronage and control of the bishop.

lutely to refuse it, the horse felt, was immoral; and therefore, as the only compromise that *his* unlearned brain could suggest, he threw his worship right over his ears, lodging him safely in a sand-heap, that rose with clouds of dust and screams of birds into the morning air. Kate had now no time to send back her compliments in a musical halloo. The alcalde missed breaking his neck on this occasion very narrowly; but his neck was of no use to him in twenty minutes more, as the reader will find. Kate rode right onwards; and, coming in with a lady behind her, horse bloody, and pace such as no hounds could have lived with, she ought to have made a great sensation in Cuzco. But, unhappily, the people of Cuzco, the spectators that *should* have been, were fast asleep in bed.

The steeplechase into Cuzco had been a fine headlong thing, considering the torrent, the trench, the wounded horse, the lovely Andalusian lady, with her agonising fears, mounted behind Kate, together with the meek dove-like dawn; but the finale crowded together the quickest succession of changes that out of a melodrama ever *can* have been witnessed. Kate reached the convent in safety; carried into the cloisters, and delivered like a parcel, the fair Andalusian. But to rouse the servants and obtain admission to the convent caused a long delay; and, on returning to the street through the broad gateway of the convent, whom should she face but the alcalde! How he had escaped the trench who can tell? He had no time to write memoirs; his horse was too illiterate. But he *had* escaped; temper not at all improved by that adventure, and now raised to a hell of malignity by seeing that he had lost his prey. The morning light showed him how to use his sword, and whom he had before him; and he attacked Kate with fury. Both were exhausted; and Kate, besides that she had no personal quarrel with the alcalde, having now accomplished her sole object in saving the lady, would have been glad of a truce. She could with difficulty wield her sword; and the alcalde had so far the advantage that he wounded Kate severely. That roused her ancient Biscayan blood; and she turned on him now with deadly determination. At that moment in rode two servants of the alcalde, who took part with their master. These odds strengthened Kate's resolution, but weakened her chances. Just then, however, rode in, and ranged himself on Kate's side, the servant of the murdered Don Calderon. In an instant Kate had pushed her sword through the alcalde; who died upon the spot. In an instant, the servant of Calderon had fled. In an instant the alguazils had come up. They and the servants of the alcalde pressed furiously on Kate, who was again fighting for her life with persons not even known to her by sight. Against such odds, she was rapidly losing ground; when in an instant, on the opposite side of the street, the great gates of the Episcopal Palace rolled open. Thither it was that Calderon's servant had fled. The bishop and his attendants hurried across. 'Senor Caballero,' said the bishop, 'In the name of the Virgin, I enjoin you to surrender your sword.'—'My lord,' said Kate, 'I dare not do it with so many enemies about me.'—'But I,' replied the bishop, 'become answerable to the law for your safe keeping.' Upon which, with filial reverence, all parties dropped their swords. Kate being severely wounded, the bishop led her into his palace. In another instant came the catastrophe: Kate's discovery could no longer be delayed; the blood flowed too rapidly; and the wound was in her bosom. She requested a private interview with the bishop: all was known in a moment; surgeons and attendants were summoned hastily; and Kate had fainted. The good bishop pitied her, and had her attended in his palace; then removed to a convent; then to a second convent at Lima; and, after many months had passed, his report of the whole extraordinary case in all its details to the supreme government at Madrid drew from the king, Philip IV, and from the papal legate, an order that the nun should be transferred to Spain.

'The Spanish Military Nun': *Tait's Magazine*, 1847; Masson XIII.

Portraits of Contemporaries

Samuel Taylor Coleridge

Preliminary

It was, I think, in the month of August, but certainly in the summer season, and certainly in the year 1807, that I first saw this illustrious man. My knowledge of him as a man of most original genius began about the year 1799. A little before that time Wordsworth had published the first edition (in a single volume) of the 'Lyrical Ballads,' and into this had been introduced Mr. Coleridge's poem of the 'Ancient Mariner,' as the contribution of an anonymous friend. It would be directing the reader's attention too much to myself if I were to linger upon this, the greatest event in the unfolding of my own mind. Let me say, in one word, that, at a period when neither the one nor the other writer was valued by the public—both having a long warfare to accomplish of contumely and ridicule before they could rise into their present estimation—I found in these poems 'the ray of a new morning,' and an absolute revelation of untrodden worlds teeming with power and beauty as yet unsuspected amongst men.

Tait's Magazine, Oct. 1834–Jan. 1835; Masson II.

General Portrait. His Philosophy

Two or three days had slipped away in waiting for Coleridge's re-appearance at Nether Stowey, when suddenly Lord Egmont called upon Mr. Poole, with a present for Coleridge: it was a canister of peculiarly fine snuff, which Coleridge now took profusely. Lord Egmont, on this occasion, spoke of Coleridge in the terms of excessive admiration, and urged Mr. Poole to put him upon undertaking some great monumental work, that might furnish a sufficient arena for the display of his various and rare accomplishments; for his multiform erudition on the one hand, for his splendid power of theorizing and combining large and remote notices of facts on the other. And he suggested, judiciously enough, as one theme which offered a field at once large enough and indefinite enough to suit a mind that could not show its full compass of power unless upon very plastic materials—a History of Christianity, in its progress and in its chief divarications into Church and Sect, with a continual reference to the relations subsisting between Christianity and the current philosophy; their occasional connexions or approaches, and their constant mutual repulsions. 'But, at any rate, let him do something,' said Lord Egmont; 'for at present he talks very much like an angel, and does nothing at all.' Lord Egmont I understood from everybody to be a truly good and benevolent man; and on this occasion he spoke with an earnestness which agreed with my previous impression. Coleridge, he said, was now in the prime of his powers—uniting something of youthful vigour with sufficient experience of life; having the benefit, beside, of vast meditation, and of reading unusually discursive. No man had ever been better qualified to revive the heroic period of literature in England, and to give a character of weight to the philosophic erudition of the country upon the Continent. 'And what a pity,' he added, 'if this man were, after all, to vanish like an apparition, and you, I, and a few others, who have witnessed his grand *bravuras* of display, were to have the usual fortune of ghost-seers, in meeting no credit for any statements that we might vouch on his behalf!'

On this occasion we learned, for the first time, that Lord Egmont's carriage had, some days before, conveyed Coleridge to Bridgewater, with a purpose of staying one single day at that place, and then returning to Mr. Poole's. From the sort of laugh with which Lord Egmont taxed his own simplicity, in having confided at all in the stability of any Coleridgian plan, I now gathered that procrastination in excess was, or had become, a marking feature in Coleridge's daily life. Nobody who knew him ever thought of depending on any appointment he might make: spite of his uniformly honourable intentions, nobody attached any weight to his assurances *in re futura*: those who asked him to dinner or any other party, as a matter of course, sent a carriage for him, and went personally or by proxy to fetch him; and, as to letters, unless the address were in some female hand that commanded his affectionate esteem, he tossed them all into one general *deadletter bureau*, and rarely, I believe, opened them at all. Bourrienne mentions a mode of abridging the trouble attached to a very extensive correspondence, by which infinite labour was saved to himself, and to Napoleon, when First Consul. Nine out of ten letters, supposing them letters of business with official applications of a special kind, he contends, answer themselves: in other words, time alone must soon produce events which virtually contain the answer. On this principle the letters were opened periodically, after intervals, suppose, of six weeks; and, at the end of that time, it was found that not many remained to require any further more particular answer. Coleridge's plan, however, was shorter: he opened none, I understood, and answered none. At least such was his habit at that time. But, on that same day, all this, which I heard now for the first time, and with much concern, was fully explained; for already he was under the full dominion of opium, as he himself revealed to me, and with a deep expression of horror at the hideous bondage, in a private walk of some length which I took with him about sunset.

Lord Egmont's information, and the knowledge now gained of Coleridge's habits, making it very uncertain when I might see him in my present hospitable quarters, I immediately took my leave of Mr. Poole, and went over to Bridgewater. I had received directions for finding out the house where Coleridge was visiting; and, in riding down a main street of Bridgewater, I noticed a gateway corresponding to the description given me. Under this was standing, and gazing about him, a man whom I will describe. In height he might seem to be about five feet eight (he was, in reality, about an inch and a-half taller, but his figure was of an order which drowns the height); his person was broad and full, and tended even to corpulence; his complexion was fair, though not what painters technically style fair, because it was associated with black hair; his eyes were large, and soft in their expression; and it was from the peculiar appearance of haze or dreaminess which mixed with their light that I recognised my object. This was Coleridge. I examined him steadfastly for a minute or more; and it struck me that he saw neither myself nor any other object in the street. He was in a deep reverie; for I had dismounted, made two or three trifling arrangements at an inn-door, and advanced close to him, before he had apparently become conscious of my presence. The sound of my voice, announcing my own name, first awoke him; he started, and for a moment seemed at a loss to understand my purpose or his own situation; for he repeated rapidly a number of words which had no relation to either of us. There was no *mauvaise honte* in his manner, but simple perplexity, and an apparent difficulty in recovering his position amongst daylight realities. This little scene over, he received me with a kindness of manner so marked that it might be called gracious. The hospitable family with whom he was domesticated were distinguished for their amiable manners and enlightened understandings: they were descendants from Chubb, the philosophic writer, and bore the same name. For Coleridge they all testified deep affection and esteem—sentiments in which the whole town of Bridgewater seemed to share; for in the evening, when the heat of the day had declined, I walked out with him; and rarely, perhaps never, have I seen a person so much interrupted in one hour's space as Coleridge, on this occasion, by the courteous attentions of young and old. ...

Coleridge led me to a drawing-room, rang the bell for refreshments, and omitted no point of a courteous reception. He told me that there would be a very large dinner party on that day, which, perhaps, might be disagreeable to a perfect stranger; but, if not, he could assure me of a most hospitable welcome from the family. I was too anxious to see him under all aspects to think of declining this invitation. That point being settled, Coleridge, like some great river, the Orellana, or the St. Lawrence, that, having been checked and fretted by rocks or thwarting islands, suddenly recovers its volume of waters and its mighty music, swept at once, as if returning to his natural business, into a continuous strain of eloquent dissertation, certainly the most novel, the most finely illustrated, and traversing the most spacious fields of thought by transitions the most just and logical, that it was possible to conceive. What I mean by saying that his transitions were 'just' is by way of contradistinction to that mode of conversation which courts variety through links of *verbal* connexions. Coleridge, to many people, and often I have heard the complaint, seemed to wander; and he seemed then to wander the most when in fact, his resistance to the wandering instinct was greatest—viz., when the compass and huge circuit by which his illustrations moved travelled farthest into remote regions before they began to revolve. Long before this coming round commenced most people had lost him, and naturally enough supposed that he had lost himself. They continued to admire the separate beauty of the thoughts, but did not see their relations to the dominant theme. Had the conversation been thrown upon paper, it might have been easy to trace the continuity of the links; just as in Bishop Berkeley's 'Siris,' from a pedestal so low and abject, so culinary, as Tar Water, the method of preparing it, and its medicinal effects, the dissertation ascends, like Jacob's ladder, by just gradations, into the Heaven of Heavens and the thrones of the Trinity. But Heaven is there connected with earth by the Homeric chain of gold; and, being subject to steady examination, it is easy to trace the links; whereas, in conversation, the loss of a single word may cause the whole cohesion to disappear from view. However, I can assert, upon my long and intimate knowledge of Coleridge's mind, that logic the most severe was as inalienable from his modes of thinking as grammar from his language.

On the present occasion, the original theme, started by myself, was Hartley and the Hartleian theory. I had carried as a little present to Coleridge a scarce Latin pamphlet, 'De Ideis,' written by Hartley about 1746,—that is, about three years earlier than the publication of his great work. He had also preluded to this great work in a little English medical tract upon Joanna Stephens's medicine for the stone; for indeed Hartley was the person upon whose evidence the House of Commons had mainly relied in giving to that same Joanna a reward of £5000 for her idle medicines—an application of public money not without its use, in so far as it engaged men by selfish motives to cultivate the public service, and to attempt public problems of very difficult solution; but else, in that particular instance, perfectly idle, as the groans of three generations since Joanna's era have too feelingly established. It is known to most literary people that Coleridge was, in early life, so passionate an admirer of the Hartleian philosophy that 'Hartley' was the sole baptismal name which he gave to his eldest child; and in an early poem, entitled 'Religious Musings,' he has characterized Hartley as

> '*Him of mortal kind*
> *Wisest, him first who mark'd the ideal tribes*
> *Up the fine fibres through the sentient brain*
> *Pass in fine surges.*'

But at present (August 1807) all this was a forgotten thing. Coleridge was so profoundly ashamed of the shallow Unitarianism of Hartley, and so disgusted to think that he could at any time have countenanced that creed, that he would scarcely allow to Hartley the reverence which is undoubtedly his due; for I must contend that, waiving all question of the extent to which Hartley would have pushed it (as though the law of association accounted not only for our complex pleasures and pains, but also might be made to explain the act of ratiocination), —waiving also the physical substratum of nervous vibrations and miniature vibrations to which he has chosen to marry his theory of association; —all this apart, I must contend that the 'Essay on Man, his Frame, his Duty, and his Expectations' stands forward as a specimen almost unique of elaborate theorizing, and a monument of absolute beauty in the impression left of its architectural grace. In this respect it has, to my mind, the spotless beauty and the ideal proportions of some Grecian statue. However, I confess that, being myself, from my earliest years, a reverential believer in the doctrine of the Trinity, simply because I never attempted to bring all things within the mechanic understanding, and because, like Sir Thomas Browne, my mind almost demanded mysteries in so mysterious a system of relations as those which connect us with another world, and also because the farther my understanding opened the more I perceived of dim analogies to strengthen my creed, and because nature herself, mere physical nature, has mysteries no less profound; for these, and for many other '*becauses*,' I could not reconcile with my general reverence for Mr. Coleridge the fact, so often reported to me, that he was a Unitarian. But, said some Bristol people to me, not only is he a Unitarian —he is also a Socinian. In that case, I replied, I cannot hold him a Christian. I am a liberal man, and have no bigotry or hostile feelings towards a Socinian; but I can never think that man a Christian who has blotted out of his scheme the very powers by which only the great offices and functions of Christianity can be sustained; neither can I think that any man, though he make himself a marvellously clever disputant, ever could tower upwards into a very great philosopher unless he should begin or should end with Christianity. Kant is a dubious exception. Not that I mean to question his august pretensions, so far as they went, and in his proper line. Within his own circle none durst tread but he.

But that circle was limited. He was called, by one who weighed him well, the *alles-zermalmender*, the world-shattering Kant. He could destroy—his intellect was essentially destructive. He was the Gog and he was the Magog of Hunnish desolation to the existing schemes of Philosophy. He probed them; he showed the vanity of vanities which beseiged their foundations—the rottenness below, the hollowness above. But he had no instincts of creation or restoration within his Apollyon mind; for he had no love, no faith, no self-distrust, no humility, no childlike docility; all which qualities belonged essentially to Coleridge's mind, and waited only for manhood and for sorrow to bring them forward.

Ibid.

His Marriage

For about three hours he had continued to talk, and in the course of this performance he had delivered many most striking aphorisms, embalming more weight of truth, and separately more deserving to be themselves embalmed, than would easily be found in a month's course of select reading. In the midst of our conversation, if that can be called conversation which I so seldom sought to interrupt, and which did not often leave openings for contribution, the door opened, and a lady entered. She was in person full and rather below the common height; whilst her face showed to my eye some prettiness of rather a commonplace order. Coleridge paused upon her entrance; his features, however, announced no particular complacency, and did not relax into a smile. In a frigid tone he said, whilst turning to me, 'Mrs Coleridge'; in some slight way he then presented me to her: I bowed; and the lady almost immediately retired. From this short but ungenial scene, I gathered, what I afterwards learned redundantly, that Coleridge's marriage had not been a very happy one. But let not the reader misunderstand me. Never was there a baser insinuation, viler in the motive, or more ignoble in the manner, than that passage in some lampoon of Lord Byron's, where, by way of vengeance on Mr. Southey (who was the sole delinquent), he described both him and Coleridge as having married 'two milliners from Bath.' Everybody knows what is *meant* to be conveyed in that expression, though it would be hard, indeed, if, even at Bath, there should be any class under such a fatal curse, condemned so irretrievably, and so hopelessly prejudged, that ignominy must, at any rate, attach, in virtue of a mere name or designation, to the mode by which they gained their daily bread, or possibly supported the declining years of a parent. However, in this case, the whole sting of the libel was a pure falsehood of Lord Byron's. Bath was not the native city, nor at any time the residence, of the ladies in question, but Bristol. As to the other word, '*milliners*,' that is not worth inquiring about. Whether they, or any one of their family, ever *did* exercise this profession, I do not know; they were, at all events, too young, when removed by marriage from Bristol, to have been much tainted by the worldly feelings which may beset such a mode of life. But, what is more to the purpose, I heard, at this time, in Bristol, from Mr. Cottle, the author, a man of high principle, as also from his accomplished sisters,—from the ladies, again, who had succeeded Mrs. Hannah More in her school, and who enjoyed her entire confidence,—that the whole family of four or five sisters had maintained an irreproachable character, though naturally exposed, by their personal attractions, to some peril, and to the malevolence of envy. This declaration, which I could strengthen by other testimony equally disinterested, if it were at all necessary, I owe to truth; and I must also add, upon a knowledge more personal, that Mrs. Coleridge was, in all circumstances of her married life, a virtuous wife and a conscientious mother; and, as a mother, she showed at times a most meritorious energy. In particular, I remember that, wishing her daughter to acquire the Italian language, and having in her retirement at Keswick no means of obtaining a master, she set to work resolutely, under Mr. Southey's guidance, to learn the language herself, at a time of life when such attainments are not made with ease or pleasure. She became mistress of the language in a very respectable extent, and then communicated her new accomplishment to her most interesting daughter.

I go on, therefore, to say, that Coleridge afterwards made me, as doubtless some others, a confidant in this particular. What he had to complain of was simply incompatibility of temper and disposition. Wanting all cordial admiration, or indeed comprehension, of her husband's intellectual powers, Mrs. Coleridge wanted the original basis for affectionate patience and candour. Hearing from everybody that Coleridge was a man of most extraordinary endowments, and attaching little weight, perhaps, to the distinction between popular talents and such as by their very nature are doomed to a slower progress in the public esteem, she naturally looked to see, at least, an ordinary measure of worldly consequence attend upon their exercise. Now, had Coleridge been as persevering and punctual as the great mass of professional men, and had he given no reason to throw the *onus* of the different result upon his own different habits, in that case this result might, possibly and eventually, have been set down to the peculiar constitution of his powers, and their essential mal-adaptation to the English market. But, this trial having never fairly been made, it was natural to impute his non-success exclusively to his own irregular application, and to his carelessness in forming judicious connexions. In circumstances such as these, however, no matter how caused or how palliated, was laid a sure ground of discontent and fretfulness in any woman's mind, not unusually indulgent or unusually magnanimous. Coleridge, besides, assured me that his marriage was not his own deliberate act, but was in a manner forced upon his sense of honour by the scrupulous Southey, who insisted that he had gone too far in his attentions to Miss Fricker for any honourable retreat. On the other hand, a neutral spectator of the parties protested to me, that, if ever in his life he had seen a man under deep fascination, and what he would have called desperately in love, Coleridge, in relation to Miss F., was that man. Be that as it might, circumstances occurred soon after the marriage which placed all the parties in a trying situation for their candour and good temper. I had a full outline of the situation from two of those who were chiefly interested, and a partial one from a third: nor can it be denied that all the parties offended in point of prudence. A young lady became a neighbour, and a daily companion of Coleridge's walks, whom I will not describe more particularly than by saying that intellectually she was very superior to Mrs. Coleridge. That superiority alone, when made conspicuous by its effects in winning Coleridge's regard and society, could not but be deeply mortifying to a young wife. However, it was moderated to her feelings by two considerations:—1. That the young lady was much too kind-hearted to have designed any annoyance in this triumph, or to express any exultation; 2. That no shadow of suspicion settled upon the moral conduct or motives of either party: the young lady was always attended by her brother; she had no personal charms; and it was manifest that mere intellectual sympathies, in reference to literature and natural scenery, had associated them in their daily walks.

Still, it is a bitter trial to a young married woman to sustain any sort of competition with a female of her own age for any part of her husband's regard, or any share of his company. Mrs. Coleridge, not having the same relish for long walks or rural scenery, and their residence being, at this time, in a very sequestered village, was condemned to a daily renewal of this trial. Accidents of another kind embittered it still further; often it would happen that the walking party returned drenched with rain; in which case, the young lady, with a laughing gaiety, and evidently unconscious of any liberty that she was taking, or any wound that she was inflicting, would run up to Mrs. Coleridge's wardrobe, array herself, without leave asked, in Mrs. Coleridge's dresses, and make herself merry with her own unceremoniousness and Mrs. Coleridge's gravity. In all this, she took no liberty that she would not most readily have granted in return; she confided too unthinkingly in what she regarded as the natural privileges of friendship; and as little thought that she had been receiving or exacting a favour, as, under an exchange of their relative positions, she would have claimed to confer one. But Mrs. Coleridge viewed her freedoms with a far different eye:

she felt herself no longer the entire mistress of her own house; she held a divided empire; and it barbed the arrow to her womanly feelings that Coleridge treated any sallies of resentment which might sometimes escape her as narrow-mindedness; whilst, on the other hand, her own female servant, and others in the same rank of life, began to drop expressions which alternately implied pity for her as an injured woman, or contempt for her as a very tame one.

The reader will easily apprehend the situation, and the unfortunate results which it boded to the harmony of a young married couple, without further illustration. Whether Coleridge would not, under any circumstances, have become indifferent to a wife not eminently capable of enlightened sympathy with his own ruling pursuits, I do not undertake to pronounce. My own impression is, that neither Coleridge nor Lord Byron could have failed, eventually, to quarrel with *any* wife, though a Pandora sent down from heaven to bless him. But, doubtless, this consummation must have been hastened by a situation which exposed Mrs. Coleridge to an invidious comparison with a more intellectual person; as, on the other hand, it was most unfortunate for Coleridge himself to be continually compared with one so ideally correct and regular in his habits as Mr. Southey. Thus was their domestic peace prematurely soured: embarrassments of a pecuniary nature would be likely to demand continual sacrifices; no depth of affection existing, these would create disgust or dissension; and at length each would believe that their union had originated in circumstances overruling their own deliberate choice.

Ibid.

The Lake Poets

About the close of the first revolutionary war it must have been, or in the brief interval of peace, that Coleridge resorted to the English Lakes as a place of residence.[1] Wordsworth had a natural connexion with that region, by birth, breeding, and family alliances. Wordsworth must have attracted Coleridge to the Lakes; and Coleridge, through his affinity to Southey, eventually attracted *him.* Southey, as is known to all who take an interest in the Lake colony, married a sister of Mrs. Coleridge's; and, as a singular eccentricity in the circumstances of that marriage, I may mention that, on his wedding-day, and from the very portico of the church, Southey left his bride to embark for Lisbon. His uncle, Dr. Herbert, was chaplain to the English factory in that city; and it was

[1] It was in 1800 that Coleridge removed from London to Keswick, Wordsworth being then at Grasmere.—M.

to benefit by the facilities in that way opened to him for seeing Portugal that Southey now went abroad. He extended his tour to Spain; and the result of his notices was communicated to the world in a volume of travels. By such accidents of personal or family connexion as I have mentioned was the Lake colony gathered; and the critics of the day, unaware of the real facts, supposed them to have assembled under common views in literature—particularly with regard to the true functions of poetry, and the true theory of poetic diction. Under this original blunder, laughable it is to mention that they went on to *find* in their writings all the agreements and common characteristics which their blunder had presumed; and they incorporated the whole community under the name of the *Lake School*. Yet Wordsworth and Southey never had one principle in common; their hostility was even flagrant. Indeed, Southey troubled himself little about abstract principles in anything; and, so far from agreeing with Wordsworth to the extent of setting up a separate school in poetry, he told me himself (August 1812) that he highly disapproved both of Mr. Wordsworth's theories and of his practice. It is very true that one man may sympathize with another, or even follow his leading, unconscious that he does so; or he may go so far as, in the very act of virtual imitation, to deem himself in opposition; but this sort of blind agreement could hardly be supposed of two men so discerning and so self-examining as Wordsworth and Southey. And, in fact, a philosophic investigation of the difficult questions connected with this whole slang about schools, Lake schools, &c., would show that Southey has not, nor ever had, any *peculiarities* in common with Wordsworth, beyond that of exchanging the old prescriptive diction of poetry, introduced between the periods of Milton and Cowper, for the simpler and profounder forms of daily life in some instances, and of the Bible in others. The bold and uniform practice of Wordsworth was here adopted, on perfectly independent views, by Southey. In this respect, however, Cowper had already begun the reform; and his influence, concurring with the now larger influence of Wordsworth, has operated so extensively as to make their own original differences at this day less perceptible.

By the way, the word *colony* reminds me that I have omitted to mention in its proper place some scheme for migrating to America which had been entertained by Coleridge and Southey about the year 1794-95, under the learned name of *Pantisocracy*. So far as I ever heard, it differed little, except in its Grecian name, from any other scheme for mitigating the privations of a wilderness by settling in a cluster of families, bound together by congenial tastes and uniform principles, rather than in self-depending, insulated households. Steadily pursued, it might, after all, have been a fortunate plan for Coleridge. 'Soliciting my food from daily toil,' a line in which Coleridge alludes to the scheme, implies a condition of life that would have upheld Coleridge's health and happiness somewhat better than the habits of luxurious city life as now constituted in Europe. But, returning to the Lakes, and to the Lake colony of poets: So little were Southey and Wordsworth connected by any personal intercourse in those days, and so little disposed to be connected, that, whilst the latter had a cottage in Grasmere, Southey pitched his tent at Greta Hall, on a little eminence rising immediately from the river Greta and the town of Keswick. Grasmere is in Westmorland; Keswick in Cumberland; and they are thirteen good miles apart. Coleridge and his family were domiciliated in Greta Hall; sharing that house, a tolerably large one, on some principle of amicable division, with Mr. Southey. But Coleridge personally was more often to be found at Grasmere— which presented the threefold attractions of loveliness so complete as to eclipse even the scenery of Derwentwater; a pastoral state of society, free from the deformities of a little town like Keswick; and, finally, for Samuel Taylor Coleridge, the society of Wordsworth. Not before 1815 or 1816 could it be said that Southey and Wordsworth were even upon friendly terms; so entirely is it untrue that they combined to frame a school of poetry. Up to that time, they viewed each other with mutual respect, but also with mutual dislike; almost, I might say, with mutual disgust. Wordsworth disliked in Southey the want of depth, or the apparent want, as regards the power of philosophic abstraction. Southey disliked in Wordsworth the air of dogmatism, and the unaffable haughtiness of his manner. Other more trivial reasons combined with these.

Ibid.

His Lectures

It was not long after this event[1] that my own introduction to Coleridge occurred. At that time some negotiation was pending between him and the Royal Institution, which ended in their engaging him to deliver a course of lectures on Poetry and the Fine Arts during the ensuing winter. For this series (twelve or sixteen, I think) he received a sum of one hundred guineas. And, considering the slightness of the pains which he bestowed upon them, he was well remunerated. I fear that they did not increase his reputation; for never did any man treat his audience with less respect, or his task with less careful attention. I was in London for part of the time, and can report the circumstances, having made a point of attending duly at the appointed hours. Coleridge was at that time living uncomfortably enough at the 'Courier' office, in the Strand. In such a situation,

[1] Coleridge's return from Malta.—B.D.

annoyed by the sound of feet passing his chamber-door continually to the printing-rooms of this great establishment, and with no gentle ministrations of female hands to sustain his cheerfulness, naturally enough his spirits flagged; and he took more than ordinary doses of opium. I called upon him daily, and pitied his forlorn condition. There was no bell in the room; which for many months answered the double purpose of bedroom and sitting-room. Consequently, I often saw him, picturesquely enveloped in nightcaps, surmounted by handkerchiefs indorsed upon handkerchiefs, shouting from the attics of the 'Courier' office, down three or four flights of stairs, to a certain 'Mrs. Brainbridge,' his sole attendant, whose dwelling was in the subterranean regions of the house. There did I often see the philosopher, with the most lugubrious of faces, invoking with all his might this uncouth name of 'Brainbridge,' each syllable of which he intonated with long-drawn emphasis, in order to overpower the hostile hubbub coming downwards from the creaking press, and the roar from the Strand, which entered at all the front windows. 'Mistress Brainbridge! I say, Mistress Brainbridge!' was the perpetual cry, until I expected to hear the Strand, and distant Fleet Street, take up the echo of 'Brainbridge!' Thus unhappily situated, he sank more than ever under the dominion of opium; so that, at two o'clock, when he should have been in attendance at the Royal Institution, he was too often unable to rise from bed. Then came dismissals of audience after audience, with pleas of illness; and on many of his lecture days I have seen all Albemarle Street closed by a 'lock' of carriages, filled with women of distinction, until the servants of the Institution or their own footmen advanced to the carriage-doors with the intelligence that Mr. Coleridge had been suddenly taken ill. This plea, which at first had been received with expressions of concern, repeated too often, began to rouse disgust. Many in anger, and some in real uncertainty whether it would not be trouble thrown away, ceased to attend. And we that were more constant too often found reason to be disappointed with the quality of his lecture. His appearance was generally that of a person struggling with pain and overmastering illness. His lips were baked with feverish heat, and often black in colour; and, in spite of the water which he continued drinking through the whole course of his lecture, he often seemed to labour under an almost paralytic inability to raise the upper jaw from the lower. In such a state, it is clear that nothing could save the lecture itself from reflecting his own feebleness and exhaustion, except the advantage of having been pre-composed in some happier mood. But that never happened: most unfortunately he relied upon his extempore ability to carry him through. Now, had he been in spirits, or had he gathered animation, and kindled by his own motion, no written lecture could have been more effectual than one of his unpremeditated colloquial harangues. But either he was depressed originally below the point from which any re-ascent was possible, or else this re-action was intercepted by continual disgust from looking back upon his own ill-success; for, assuredly, he never once recovered that free and eloquent movement of thought which he could command at any time in a private company. The passages he read, moreover, in illustrating his doctrines, were generally unhappily chosen, because chosen at haphazard, from the difficulty of finding at a moment's summons those passages which his purpose required. Nor do I remember any that produced much effect, except two or three, which I myself put ready marked into his hands, among the Metrical Romances edited by Ritson.

Generally speaking, the selections were as injudicious and as inappropriate as they were ill delivered; for, amongst Coleridge's accomplishments, good reading was not one; he had neither voice (so, at least, *I* thought) nor management of voice. This defect is unfortunate in a public lecturer; for it is inconceivable how much weight and effectual pathos can be communicated by sonorous depth and melodious cadences of the human voice to sentiments the most trivial; nor, on the other hand, how the grandest are emasculated by a style of reading which fails in distributing the lights and shadows of a musical intonation. However, this defect chiefly concerned the immediate impression; the most afflicting to a friend of Coleridge's was the entire absence of his own peculiar and majestic intellect; no heart, no soul, was in anything he said; no strength of feeling in recalling universal truths; no power of originality or compass of moral relations in his novelties; all was a poor faint reflection from jewels once scattered in the highway by himself in the prodigality of his early opulence—a mendicant dependence on the alms dropped from his own overflowing treasury of happier times.

The next opportunity I had of seeing Coleridge was at the Lakes, in the winter of 1809, and up to the autumn of the following year. During this period it was that he carried on the original publication of 'The Friend'[1]; and for much the greater part of the time I saw him daily. He lived as a visitor in the house occupied by Mr. Wordsworth. This house (Allan Bank by name) was in Grasmere; and in another part of the same vale, at a distance of barely one mile, I myself had a cottage, and a considerable library. Many of my books being German, Coleridge borrowed them in great numbers. Having a general license from me to use them as he would, he was in the habit of accumulating them so largely at Allan Bank (the name of Mr. Wordsworth's house) that sometimes as many as five hundred were absent at once: which I mention in order to

[1] The first number of this celebrated but unfortunate periodical, 'printed on stamped paper by a printer of the name of Brown at Penrith,' was issued, the already cited memoir of Coleridge informs us, on Thursday, 1st June 1809, and the last on 15th March 1810.—M.

notice a practice of Coleridge's, indicating his very scrupulous honour in what regarded the rights of ownership. Literary people are not always so strict in respecting property of this description; and I know more than one celebrated man who professes as a maxim that he holds it no duty of honour to restore a borrowed book; not to speak of many less celebrated persons, who, without openly professing such a principle, do however, in fact, exhibit a lax morality in such cases. The more honourable it was to poor Coleridge, who had means so trifling of buying books for himself, that, to prevent my flocks from mixing and being confounded with the flocks already folded at Allan Bank (his own and Wordsworth's), or rather that they *might* mix without danger, he duly inscribed my name in the blank leaves of every volume; a fact which became rather painfully made known to me; for, as he had chosen to dub me *Esquire*, many years after this it cost myself and a female friend some weeks of labour to hunt out these multitudinous memorials and to erase this heraldic addition; which else had the appearance to a stranger of having been conferred by myself.

Ibid.

After the Lakes

In the autumn of 1810, Coleridge left the Lakes; and, so far as I am aware, for ever. I once, indeed, heard a rumour of his having passed through with some party of tourists—some reason struck me at the time for believing it untrue—but, at all events, he never returned to them as a resident. What might be his reason for this eternal self-banishment from scenes which he so well understood in all their shifting forms of beauty, I can only guess. Perhaps it was the very opposite reason to that which is most obvious: not, possibly, because he had become indifferent to their attractions, but because his undecaying sensibility to their commanding power had become associated with too afflicting remembrances, and flashes of personal recollections, suddenly restored and illuminated —recollections which will

> '*Sometimes leap*
> *From hiding-places ten years deep,*'

and bring into collision the present with some long-forgotten past, in a form too trying and too painful for endurance. I have a brilliant Scotch friend, who cannot walk on the seashore—within sight of its ἀνήριθμον γέλασμα, the multitudinous laughter of its waves, or within hearing of its resounding uproar, because they bring up, by links of old association, too insupportably to his mind the agitations of his glittering, but too fervid youth. There is a feeling—morbid, it may be, but for which no anodyne is found in all the schools from Plato to Kant—to which the human mind is liable at times: it is best described in a little piece by Henry More, the 'Platonist.' He there represents himself as a martyr to his own too passionate sense of beauty, and his consequent too pathetic sense of its decay. Everywhere—above, below, around him, in the earth, in the clouds, in the fields, and in their 'garniture of flowers'—he beholds a beauty carried to excess; and this beauty becomes a source of endless affliction to him, because everywhere he sees it liable to the touch of decay and mortal change. During one paroxysm of this sad passion, an angel appears to comfort him; and, by the sudden revelation of her immortal beauty, does, in fact, suspend his grief. But it is only a suspension; for the sudden recollection that her privileged condition, and her exemption from the general fate of beauty, is only by way of exception to a universal rule, restores his grief: 'And thou thyself,' he says to the angel—

> *'And thou thyself, that com'st to comfort me,*
> *Wouldst strong occasion of deep sorrow bring,*
> *If thou wert subject to mortality!'*

Every man who has ever dwelt with passionate love upon the fair face of some female companion through life must have had the same feeling, and must often, in the exquisite language of Shakspere's sonnets, have commanded and adjured all-conquering Time, there, at least, and upon that one tablet of his adoration,

> *'To write no wrinkle with his antique hand.'*

Vain prayer! Empty adjuration! Profitless rebellion against the laws which season all things for the inexorable grave! Yet not the less we rebel again and again; and, though wisdom counsels resignation, yet our human passions, still cleaving to their object, force us into endless rebellion. Feelings the same in kind as these attach themselves to our mental power, and our vital energies. Phantoms of lost power, sudden intuitions, and shadowy restorations of forgotten feelings, sometimes dim and perplexing, sometimes by bright but furtive glimpses, sometimes by a full and steady revelation, overcharged with light—throw us back in a moment upon scenes and remembrances that we have left full thirty years behind us. In solitude, and chiefly in the solitudes of nature, and, above all, amongst the great and *enduring* features of nature, such as mountains, and quiet dells, and the lawny recesses of forests, and the silent shores of lakes, features with which (as being themselves less liable to change) our feelings have a more abiding association—under these circumstances it is that such evanescent hauntings of our past and forgotten selves are most apt to startle and to waylay us. These are *positive* torments from which the agitated mind shrinks in fear; but there are others *negative* in their nature—that is, blank mementoes of powers extinct, and of faculties burnt out within us. And from both forms of anguish—from this twofold scourge—poor Coleridge fled, perhaps, in flying from the beauty of external nature. In alluding to this latter, or negative form of suffering—that form, I mean, which presents not the too fugitive glimpses of past power, but its blank annihilation—Coleridge himself most beautifully insists upon and illustrates the truth that all which we find in Nature must be created by our selves; and that alike whether Nature is so gorgeous in her beauty as to seem apparelled in her wedding-garment or so powerless and extinct as to seem palled in her shroud. In either case,

> '*O, Lady, we receive but what we give,*
> *And in our life alone does nature live;*
> *Ours is her wedding-garment, ours her shroud.*

> *It were a vain endeavour,*
> *Though I should gaze for ever*
> *On that green light that lingers in the west:*
> *I may not hope from outward forms to win*
> *The passion and the life whose fountains are within.*'

This was one, and the most common, shape of extinguished power from which Coleridge fled to the great city. But sometimes the same decay came back upon his heart in the more poignant shape of intimations and vanishing glimpses, recovered for one moment from the paradise of youth, and from fields of joy and power, over which, for him, too certainly, he felt that the cloud of night was settling for ever. Both modes of the same torment exiled him from nature; and for the same reasons he fled from poetry and all commerce with his own soul; burying himself in the profoundest abstractions from life and human sensibilities.

> '*For not to think of what I needs must feel,*
> *But to be still and patient all I can;*
> *And haply* by abstruse research to steal,
> From my own nature, all the natural man;
> *This was my sole resource, my only plan;*
> *Till that, which suits a part, infects the whole,*
> *And now is almost grown the habit of my soul.*'

Such were, doubtless, the true and radical causes which, for the final twenty-four years of Coleridge's life, drew him away from these scenes of natural beauty in which only, at an earlier stage of life, he found strength and restoration. Those scenes still survived; but their power was gone, because *that* had been derived from himself, and his ancient self had altered. Such were the *causes*; but the immediate *occasion* of this departure from the Lakes, in the autumn of 1810, was the favourable opportunity then presented to him of migrating in a pleasant way. Mr. Basil Montagu, the Chancery barrister, happened at that time to be returning to London, with Mrs. Montagu, from a visit to the Lakes, or to Wordsworth.[1] His travelling carriage was roomy enough to allow of his offering Coleridge a seat in it; and his admiration of Coleridge was just then fervent enough to prompt a friendly wish for that sort of close connexion (viz. by domestication as a guest under Mr. Basil Montagu's roof) which is the most trying to friendship, and which in this instance led to a perpetual rupture of it. The domestic habits of eccentric men of genius, much more those of a man so irreclaimably irregular as Coleridge, can hardly be supposed to promise very auspiciously for any connexion so close as this. A very extensive house and household, together with the unlimited licence of action which belongs to the *ménage* of some great Dons amongst the nobility, could alone have made Coleridge an inmate perfectly desirable. Probably many little jealousies and offences had been mutually suppressed; but the particular spark which at length fell amongst the combustible materials already prepared, and thus produced the final explosion, took the following shape:—Mr. Montagu had published a book against the use of wine and intoxicating liquors of every sort.[2] Not out of parsimony or under any suspicion of inhospitality, but in mere self-consistency and obedience to his own conscientious scruples, Mr. Montagu would not countenance the use of wine at his own table. So far all was right. But doubtless, on such a system, under the known habits of modern life, it should have been made a rule to ask no man to dinner: for to force men, without warning, to a *single* (and, therefore, thoroughly useless) act of painful abstinence, is what neither I nor any man can have a right to do. In point of sense, it is, in fact, precisely the freak of Sir Roger de Coverley, who drenches his friend the 'Spectator' with a hideous decoction: not, as his confiding visitor had supposed, for some certain and immediate benefit to follow, but simply as having a *tendency* (if well supported by many years' continuance of similar drenches) to abate the remote contingency of the stone. Hear this, ye Gods of the Future!

---

[1] Basil Montagu (1770–1851) and his wife were celebrities in London society for many years. Among his publications, besides legal treatises, were an edition of Bacon's Works and a volume of selections from the older English Prose-writers.

[2] *Inquiry into the Effects of Fermented Liquors. By a Water-drinker.* London, 1814.—M.

I am required to perform a most difficult sacrifice; and forty years hence I *may*, by persisting so long, have some dim chance of reward. One day's abstinence could do no good on *any* scheme: and no man was likely to offer himself for a second. However, such being the law of the castle, and that law well known to Coleridge, he nevertheless, thought fit to ask to dinner Colonel (then Captain) Pasley, of the Engineers, well known in those days for his book on the 'Military Policy of England,' and since for his 'System of Professional Instruction.' Now, where or in what land abides that

> '*Captain, or Colonel, or Knight-in-arms,*'

to whom wine in the analysis of dinner is a neutral or indifferent element? Wine, therefore, as it was not of a nature to be omitted, Coleridge took care to furnish at his own private cost. And so far, again, all was right. But why must Coleridge give his dinner to the captain in Mr. Montagu's house? There lay the affront; and, doubtless, it was a very inconsiderate action on the part of Coleridge. I report the case simply as it was then generally borne upon the breath, not of scandal, but of jest and merriment. The result, however, was no jest; for bitter words ensued—words that festered in the remembrance; and a rupture between the parties followed, which no reconciliation has ever healed.

Meantime, on reviewing this story, as generally adopted by the learned in literary scandal, one demur rises up. Dr. Parr, a lisping Whig pedant, without personal dignity or conspicuous power of mind, was a frequent and privileged inmate at Mr. Montagu's. Him now—this Parr—there was no conceivable motive for enduring; that point is satisfactorily settled by the pompous inanities of his works. Yet, on the other hand, his habits were in their own nature far less endurable than Samuel Taylor Coleridge's; for the monster smoked;—and how? How did the 'Birmingham Doctor'[1] smoke? Not as you, or I, or other civilized people smoke, with a gentle cigar—but with the very coarsest tobacco. And those who know how that abomination lodges and nestles in the draperies of window-curtains will guess the horror and detestation in which the old

---

[1] '*Birmingham Doctor*':—This was a *sobriquet* imposed on Dr. Parr by 'The Pursuits of Literature,' that most popular of satires at the end of the eighteenth and opening of the nineteenth centuries. The name had a mixed reference to the Doctor's personal connexion with Warwickshire, but chiefly to the Doctor's spurious and windy imitation of Dr. Johnson. He was viewed as the Birmingham (or mock) Dr. Johnson. Why the word *Birmingham* has come for the last sixty or seventy years to indicate in every class of articles the spurious in opposition to the genuine, I suppose to have arisen from the Birmingham habit of reproducing all sorts of London or Paris trinkets, *bijouterie*, &c., in cheaper materials and with inferior workmanship.

Whig's memory is held by all enlightened women. Surely, in a house where the Doctor had any toleration at all, Samuel Taylor Coleridge might have enjoyed an unlimited toleration.

Ibid.

His Talk

Above all things, I shunned, as I would shun a pestilence, Coleridge's capital error, which through life he practised, of keeping the audience in a state of passiveness. Unjust this was to others, but most of all to himself. This eternal stream of talk which never for one instant intermitted, and allowed no momentary opportunity of reaction to the persecuted and baited auditor, was absolute ruin to the interests of the talker himself. Always passive, always acted upon, never allowed to react, into what state did the poor afflicted listener—he that played the *rôle* of listener—collapse? He returned home in the exhausted condition of one that has been drawn up just before death from the bottom of a well occupied by foul gases; and, of course, hours before he had reached that perilous point of depression, he had lost all power of distinguishing, under-standing, or connecting. I, for my part, without needing to think of the unami-able arrogance involved in such a habit, simply on principles of deadliest selfish-ness, should have avoided thus incapacitating my hearer from doing any justice to the rhetoric or the argument with which I might address him.

Confessions, 1853; Masson III.

His Interminable Talk

As Madame de Stael observed, Coleridge talked and *could* talk, only by mono-logue. Such a mode of systematic trespass upon the conversational rights of a whole party gathered together under pretence of amusement is fatal to every purpose of social intercourse, whether that purpose be connected with direct use and the service of the intellect, or with the general graces and amenities of life. The result is the same under whatever impulse such an outrage is practised; but the impulse is not always the same; it varies, and so far the criminal in-tention varies. In some people this gross excess takes its rise in pure arrogance. They are fully aware of their own intrusion upon the general privileges of the company; they are aware of the temper in which it is likely to be received; but they persist wilfully in the wrong, as a sort of homage levied compulsorily upon those who may wish to resist it, but hardly *can* do so without a violent interruption, wearing the same shape of indecorum as that which they resent. In most people, however, it is not arrogance which prompts this capital offence against social rights, but a blind selfishness, yielding passively to its own instincts, without being distinctly aware of the degree in which this self-indulgence trespasses on the rights of others. We see the same temper illustrated at times in travelling. A brutal person, as we are disposed at first to pronounce him, but more frequently one who yields unconsciously to a lethargy of selfishness, plants himself at the public fireplace, so as to exclude his fellow-travellers from all but a fraction of the warmth. Yet he does not do this in a spirit of wilful aggression upon others; he has but a glimmering suspicion of the odious shape which his own act assumes to others, for the luxurious torpor of self-indulgence has extended its mists to the energy and clearness of his perceptions. Meantime, Coleridge's habit of soliloquizing through a whole evening of four or five hours had its origin neither in arrogance nor in absolute selfishness. The fact was that he *could* not talk unless he were uninterrupted, and unless he were able to count upon this concession from the company. It was a silent contract between him and his hearers that nobody should speak but himself. If any man objected to this arrangement, why did he come ? For, the custom of the place, the *lex loci*, being notorious, by coming at all he was understood to profess his allegiance to the autocrat who presided. It was not, therefore, by an insolent usurpation that Coleridge persisted in monology through his whole life, but in virtue of a concession from the kindness and respect of his friends. You could not be angry with him for using his privilege, for it was a privilege conferred by others, and a privilege which he was ready to resign as soon as any man demurred to it. But, though reconciled to it by these considerations, and by the ability with which he used it, you could not but feel that it worked ill for all parties. Himself it tempted oftentimes into pure garrulity of egotism, and the listeners it reduced to a state of debilitated sympathy or of absolute torpor. Prevented by the custom from putting questions, from proposing doubts, from asking for explanations, reacting by no mode of mental activity, and condemned also to the mental distress of hearing opinions or doctrines stream past them by flights which they must not arrest for a moment so as even to take a note of them, and which yet they could not often understand, or, seeming to understand, could not always approve, the audience sank at times into a listless condition of inanimate vacuity. To be acted upon for ever, but never to react, is fatal to the very powers by which sympathy must grow, or by which intelligent admiration can be evoked. For his own sake, it was Coleridge's interest to have forced his hearers into the active commerce of question and answer, of objection and demur. Not otherwise was it possible that even the attention could be kept from drooping, or the coherency and dependency of the arguments be forced into light.

'Conversation', *Tait's Magazine*, Oct. 1847; Masson X.

Wordsworth and his Family

Portrait of Wordsworth. First Meeting

I was ushered up a little flight of stairs, fourteen in all, to a little drawing-room, or whatever the reader chooses to call it. Wordsworth himself has described the fireplace of this room as his

> *'Half-kitchen and half-parlour fire.'*

It was not fully seven feet six inches high, and, in other respects, pretty nearly of the same dimensions as the rustic hall below. There was, however, in a small recess, a library of perhaps three hundred volumes, which seemed to consecrate the room as the poet's study and composing room; and such occasionally it was. But far oftener he both studied, as I found, and composed, on the high road. I had not been two minutes at the fireside, when in came Wordsworth, returning from his friendly attentions to the travellers below, who, it seemed, had been over-persuaded by hospitable solicitations to stay for this night in Grasmere, and to make out the remaining thirteen miles of their road to Keswick on the following day. Wordsworth entered. And *'whatlike'*—to use a Westmoreland as well as a Scottish expression—*'what-like'* was Wordsworth? A reviewer in 'Tait's Magazine,' noticing some recent collection of literary portraits, gives it as his opinion that Charles Lamb's head was the finest among them. This remark may have been justified by the engraved portraits; but, certainly, the critic would have cancelled it, had he seen the original heads—at least, had he seen them in youth or in maturity; for Charles Lamb bore age with less disadvantage to the intellectual expression of his appearance than Wordsworth, in whom a sanguine complexion had, of late years, usurped upon the original bronze-tint; and this change of hue, and change in the quality of skin, he had made fourfold more conspicuous, and more unfavourable in its general effect, by the harsh contrast of grizzled hair which had displaced the original brown. No change in personal appearance ever can have been so unfortunate; for, generally speaking, whatever other disadvantages old age may bring along with it, one effect, at least in male subjects, has a compensating tendency—that it removes any tone of vigour too harsh, and mitigates the expression of power too unsubdued. But, in Wordsworth, the effect of the change has been to substitute an air of animal vigour, or, at least, hardiness, as if derived from constant exposure to the wind and weather, for the fine sombre complexion which he once wore, resembling that of a Venetian senator or a Spanish monk.

Here, however, in describing the personal appearance of Wordsworth, I go back, of course, to the point of time at which I am speaking. He was, upon the whole, not a well-made man. His legs were pointedly condemned by all female connoisseurs in legs; not that they were bad in any way which *would* force itself upon your notice—there was no absolute deformity about them; and undoubtedly they had been serviceable legs beyond the average standard of human requisition; for I calculate, upon good data, that with these identical legs Wordsworth must have traversed a distance of 175,000 to 180,000 English miles —a mode of exertion which, to him, stood in the stead of alcohol and all other stimulants whatsoever to the animal spirits; to which, indeed, he was indebted for a life of unclouded happiness, and we for much of what is most excellent in his writings. But, useful as they have proved themselves, the Wordsworthian legs were certainly not ornamental; and it was really a pity, as I agreed with a lady in thinking, that he had not another pair for evening dress parties—when no boots lend their friendly aid to mask our imperfections from the eyes of female rigorists—those *elegantes formarum spectatrices*. A sculptor would certainly have disapproved of their contour. But the worst part of Wordsworth's person was the bust; there was a narrowness and a droop about the shoulders which became striking, and had an effect of meanness, when brought into close juxtaposition with a figure of a more statuesque build. Once on a summer evening, walking in the Vale of Langdale with Wordsworth, his sister, and Mr. J.——, a native Westmoreland clergyman, I remember that Miss Wordsworth was positively mortified by the peculiar illustration which settled upon this defective conformation. Mr. J——, a fine towering figure, six feet high, massy and columnar in his proportions, happened to be walking, a little in advance, with Wordsworth; Miss Wordsworth and myself being in the rear; and from the nature of the conversation which then prevailed in our front rank, something or other about money, devises, buying and selling, we of the rear-guard thought it requisite to preserve this arrangement for a space of three miles or more; during which time, at intervals, Miss Wordsworth would exclaim, in a tone of vexation, 'Is it possible,—can that be William? How very mean he looks!' And she did not conceal a mortification that seemed really painful, until I, for my part, could not forbear laughing outright at the serious interest which she carried into this trifle. She was, however, right, as regarded the mere visual judgment. Wordsworth's figure, with all its defects, was brought into powerful relief by one which had been cast in a more square and massy mould; and in such a case it impressed a spectator with a sense of absolute meanness, more especially when viewed from behind and not counteracted by his countenance; and yet Wordsworth was of a good height (five feet ten), and not a slender man; on the contrary, by the side of Southey, his limbs looked thick, almost in a disproportionate degree. But the total effect of Wordsworth's person was always worst in a state of motion. Meantime, his face—that was one which would have made amends for greater defects of figure. Many such, and finer, I have seen amongst the portraits of Titian, and, in a later period, amongst those of Vandyke, from the great era of Charles I, as also from the court of Elizabeth and of Charles II, but none which has more impressed me in my own time.

Haydon, in his great picture of 'Christ's Entry into Jerusalem,' has introduced Wordsworth in the character of a disciple attending his Divine Master, and Voltaire in the character of a sneering Jewish elder. This fact is well known; and as the picture itself is tolerably well known to the public eye, there are multitudes now living who will have seen a very impressive likeness of Wordsworth —some consciously, some not suspecting it. There will, however, always be many who have *not* seen any portrait at all of Wordsworth; and therefore I will describe its general outline and effect. It was a face of the long order, often falsely classed as oval: but a greater mistake is made by many people in supposing the long face which prevailed so remarkably in the Elizabethan and Carolinian periods to have become extinct in our own. Miss Ferrier, in one of her novels ('Marriage,' I think), makes a Highland girl protest that 'no Englishman *with his round face*' shall ever wean her heart from her own country; but England is not the land of round faces; and those have observed little, indeed, who think so: France it is that grows the round face, and in so large a majority of her provinces that it has become one of the national characteristics. And the remarkable impression which an Englishman receives from the eternal recurrence of the orbicular countenance proves of itself, without any *conscious* testimony, how the fact stands; in the blind sense of a monotony, not felt elsewhere, lies involved an argument that cannot be gainsaid. Besides, even upon an *a priori* argument, how is it possible that the long face so prevalent in England, by all confession, in certain splendid eras of our history, should have had time, in some five or six generations, to grow extinct? Again, the character of face varies essentially in different provinces. Wales has no connexion in this respect with Devonshire, nor Kent with Yorkshire, nor either with Westmoreland. England, it is true, tends, beyond all known examples, to a general amalgamation of differences, by means of its unrivalled freedom of intercourse. Yet, even in England, law and necessity have opposed as yet such and so many obstacles to the free diffusion of labour that every generation occupies, by at least five-sixths of its numbers, the ground of its ancestors.

The movable part of a population is chiefly the higher part; and it is the lower classes that, in every nation, compose the *fundus*, in which lies latent the national face, as well as the national character. Each exists here in racy purity and integrity, not disturbed in the one by alien intermarriages, nor in the other by novelties of opinion, or other casual effects, derived from education and reading. Now, look into this *fundus*, and you will find, in many districts, no such prevalence of the round orbicular face as some people erroneously suppose; and in Westmoreland, especially, the ancient long face of the Elizabethan period, powerfully resembling in all its lineaments the ancient Roman face, and often (though not so uniformly) the face of northern Italy in modern times. The face of Sir Walter Scott, as Irving, the pulpit orator, once remarked to me, was the indigenous face of the Border: the mouth, which was bad, and the entire lower part of the face, are seen repeated in thousands of working-men; or, as Irving chose to illustrate his position, 'in thousands of Border horse-jockeys.' In like manner, Wordsworth's face was, if not absolutely the indigenous face of the Lake district, at any rate a variety of that face, a modification of that original type. The head was well filled out; and there, to begin with, was a great advantage over the head of Charles Lamb, which was absolutely truncated in the posterior region—sawn off, as it were, by no timid sawyer. The forehead was not remarkably lofty—and, by the way, some artists, in their ardour for realizing their phrenological preconceptions, not suffering nature to surrender quietly and by slow degrees her real alphabet of signs and hieroglyphic characters, but forcing her language prematurely into conformity with their own crude speculations, have given to Sir Walter Scott a pile of forehead which is unpleasing and cataphysical, in fact, a caricature of anything that is ever seen in nature, and would (if real) be esteemed a deformity; in one instance—that which was introduced in some annual or other—the forehead makes about two-thirds of the entire face. Wordsworth's forehead is also liable to caricature misrepresentations in these days of phrenology: but, whatever it may appear to be in any man's fanciful portrait, the real living forehead, as I have been in the habit of seeing it for more than five-and-twenty years, is not remarkable for its height; but it *is*, perhaps, remarkable for its breadth and expansive development. Neither are the eyes of Wordsworth 'large,' as is erroneously stated somewhere in 'Peter's Letters'[1]; on the contrary, they are (I think) rather small; but *that* does

---

[1] Lockhart's famous publication of 1819 under the name of *Peter's Letters to his Kinsfolk.*—M.

not interfere with their effect, which at times is fine, and suitable to his intellectual character. At times, I say, for the depth and subtlety of eyes, even their colouring (as to condensation or dilation), varies exceedingly with the state of the stomach; and, if young ladies were aware of the magical transformations which can be wrought in the depth and sweetness of the eye by a few weeks' walking exercise, I fancy we should see their habits in this point altered greatly for the better. I have seen Wordsworth's eyes oftentimes affected powerfully in this respect; his eyes are not, under any circumstances, bright, lustrous, or piercing; but, after a long day's toil in walking, I have seen them assume an appearance the most solemn and spiritual that it is possible for the human eye to wear. The light which resides in them is at no time a superficial light; but, under favourable accidents, it is a light which seems to come from unfathomed depths: in fact, it is more truly entitled to be held 'the light that never was on land or sea,' a light radiating from some far spiritual world, than any the most idealizing that ever yet a painter's hand created. The nose, a little arched, is large; which, by the way (according to a natural phrenology, existing centuries ago amongst some of the lowest amongst the human species), has always been accounted an unequivocal expression of animal appetites organically strong. And that expressed the simple truth: Wordsworth's intellectual passions were fervent and strong: but they rested upon a basis of preternatural animal sensibility diffused through *all* the animal passions (or appetites); and something of that will be found to hold of all poets who have been great by original force and power, not (as Virgil) by means of fine management and exquisite artifice of composition applied to their conceptions. The mouth, and the whole circumjacencies of the mouth, composed the strongest feature in Wordsworth's face; there was nothing specially to be noticed that I know of in the mere outline of the lips; but the swell and protrusion of the parts above and around the mouth are both noticeable in themselves, and also because they remind me of a very interesting fact which I discovered about three years after this my first visit to Wordsworth.

Being a great collector of everything relating to Milton, I had naturally possessed myself, whilst yet very young, of Richardson the painter's thick octavo volume of notes on the 'Paradise Lost.'[1] It happened, however, that my copy, in consequence of that mania for portrait collecting which has stripped so many English classics of their engraved portraits, wanted the portrait of Milton. Subsequently I ascertained that it ought to have had a very good like-

[1] Jonathan Richardson (born about 1665, died 1745) published in 1734 a volume of Explanatory Notes and Remarks on *Paradise Lost*, with a Life of Milton, containing particulars which Richardson had collected about Milton personally. —M.

ness of the great poet; and I never rested until I procured a copy of the book which had not suffered in this respect by the fatal admiration of the amateur. The particular copy offered to me was one which had been priced unusually high, on account of the unusually fine specimen which it contained of the engraved portrait. This, for a particular reason, I was exceedingly anxious to see; and the reason was—that, according to an anecdote reported by Richardson himself, this portrait, of all that were shown to her, was the only one acknowledged by Milton's last surviving daughter to be a strong likeness of her father. And her involuntary gestures concurred with her deliberate words:—for, on seeing all the rest, she was silent and inanimate; but the very instant she beheld that crayon drawing from which is derived the engraved head in Richardson's book, she burst out into a rapture of passionate recognition; exclaiming—'That is my father! that is my dear father!' Naturally, therefore, after such a testimony, so much stronger than any other person in the world could offer to the authentic value of this portrait, I was eager to see it.

Judge of my astonishment when, in this portrait of Milton, I saw a likeness nearly perfect of Wordsworth, better by much than any which I have since seen of those expressly painted for himself. The likeness is tolerably preserved in that by Carruthers, in which one of the little Rydal waterfalls, &c., composes a background; yet this is much inferior, as a mere portrait of Wordsworth, to the Richardson head of Milton; and this, I believe, is the last which represents Wordsworth in the vigour of his power. The rest, which I have not seen, may be better as works of art (for anything I know to the contrary), but they must labour under the great disadvantage of presenting the features when 'defeatured,' in the degree and the way I have described, by the peculiar ravages of old age, as it affects this family; for it is noticed of the Wordsworths, by those who are familiar with their peculiarities, that in their very blood and constitutional differences lie hidden causes that are able, in some mysterious way,

> '*Those shocks of passion to prepare*
> *That kill the bloom before its time,*
> *And blanch, without the owner's crime,*
> *The most resplendent hair.*'

Some people, it is notorious, live faster by much than others; the oil is burned out sooner in one constitution than another: and the cause of this may be various; but in the Wordsworths one part of the cause is, no doubt, the secret fire of a temperament too fervid; the self-consuming energies of the brain, that gnaw at the heart and life-strings for ever. In that account which 'The Excursion' presents to us of an imaginary Scotsman who, to still the tumult of his heart, when visiting the cataracts of a mountainous region, obliges himself to study the laws of light and colour as they affect the rainbow of the stormy waters, vainly attempting to mitigate the fever which consumed him by entangling his mind in profound speculations; raising a cross-fire of artillery from the subtilizing intellect, under the vain conceit that in this way he could silence the mighty battery of his impassioned heart: there we read a picture of Wordsworth and his own youth. In Miss Wordsworth every thoughtful observer might read the same self-consuming style of thought. And the effect upon each was so powerful for the promotion of a premature old age, and of a premature expression of old age, that strangers invariably supposed them fifteen to twenty years older than they were. And I remember Wordsworth once laughingly reporting to me, on returning from a short journey in 1809, a little personal anecdote, which sufficiently showed what was the spontaneous impression upon that subject of casual strangers, whose feelings were not confused by previous knowledge of the truth. He was travelling by a stage-coach, and seated outside, amongst a good half-dozen of fellow-passengers. One of these, an elderly man, who confessed to having passed the grand climacterical year (9 multiplied into 7) of 63, though he did not say precisely by how many years, said to Wordsworth, upon some anticipations which they had been mutually discussing of changes likely to result from enclosures, &c., then going on or projecting—'Ay, ay, another dozen of years will show us strange sights; but you and I can hardly expect to see them.'—'How so?' said Wordsworth. 'How so, my friend? How old do you take me to be?'—'Oh, I beg pardon,' said the other; 'I meant no offence—but what?' looking at Wordsworth more attentively—'you'll never see three-score, I'm of opinion'; meaning to say that Wordsworth *had* seen it already. And, to show that he was not singular in so thinking, he appealed to all the other passengers; and the motion passed (*nem. con.*) that Wordsworth was rather over than under sixty. Upon this he told them the literal truth—that he had not yet accomplished his thirty-ninth year. 'God bless me!' said the climacterical man; 'so then, after all, you'll have a chance to see your childer get up like, and get settled! Only to think of that!' And so closed the conversation, leaving to Wordsworth an undeniable record of his own prematurely expressed old age in this unaffected astonishment, amongst a whole party of plain men, that he could really belong to a generation of the forward-looking, who live by hope; and might reasonably expect to see a child of seven years old matured into a man. And yet, as Wordsworth lived into his 82d year, it is plain that the premature expression of decay does not argue any real decay.

'The Lake Poets', *Tait's Magazine*, 1839; Masson II.

Wordsworth and Southey

In after life, it is true—fifteen years, perhaps, from this time—many circumstances combined to bring Southey and Wordsworth into more intimate terms of friendship: agreement in politics, sorrows which had happened to both alike in their domestic relations, and the sort of tolerance for different opinions in literature, or, indeed, in anything else, which advancing years and experience are sure to bring with them. But at this period, Southey and Wordsworth entertained a mutual esteem, but did not cordially like each other. Indeed, it would have been odd if they had. Wordsworth lived in the open air: Southey in his library, which Coleridge used to call his wife. Southey had particularly elegant habits (Wordsworth called them finical) in the use of books, Wordsworth, on the other hand, was so negligent, and so self-indulgent in the same case, that, as Southey, laughing, expressed it to me some years afterwards, when I was staying at Greta Hall on a visit—'To introduce Wordsworth into one's library is like letting a bear into a tulip garden.' What I mean by self-indulgent is this: generally it happens that new books baffle and mock one's curiosity by their uncut leaves; and the trial is pretty much the same as when, in some town where you are utterly unknown, you meet the postman at a distance from your inn, with some letter for yourself from a dear, dear friend in foreign regions, without money to pay the postage. How is it with you, dear reader, in such a case? Are you not tempted (*I am* grievously) to snatch the letter from his tantalizing hand, spite of the roar which you anticipate of 'Stop thief!' and make off as fast as you can for some solitary street in the suburbs, where you may instantly effect an entrance upon your new estate before the purchase money is paid down? Such were Wordsworth's feelings in regard to new books; of which the first exemplification I had was early in my acquaintance with him, and on occasion of a book which (if any could) justified the too summary style of his advances in rifling its charms. On a level with the eye, when sitting at the tea-table in my little cottage at Grasmere, stood the collective works of Edmund Burke. The book was to me an eye-sore and an ear-sore for many a year, in consequence of the cacophonous title lettered by the bookseller upon the back—'Burke's Works.' I have heard it said, by the way, that Donne's intolerable defect of ear grew out of his own baptismal name, when harnessed to his own surname—*John Donne*. No man, it was said, who had listened to this hideous jingle from childish years, could fail to have his genius for discord, and the abominable in sound, improved to the utmost. Not less dreadful than *John Donne* was 'Burke's Works'; which, however, on the old principle, that every day's work is no day's work, continued to annoy me for twenty-one years. Wordsworth took down the volume; unfortunately it was uncut; fortunately, and by a special Providence as to him, it seemed, tea was proceeding at the time. Dry toast required butter; butter required knives; and knives then lay on the table; but sad it was for the virgin purity of Mr. Burke's as yet unsunned pages, that every knife bore upon its blade testimonies of the service it had rendered. Did *that* stop Wordsworth? Did that cause him to call for another knife? Not at all; he

> *'Look'd at the knife that caus'd his pain:*
> *And look'd and sigh'd, and look'd and sigh'd again';*

and then, after this momentary tribute to regret, he tore his way into the heart of the volume with his knife, that left its greasy honours behind it upon every page: and are they not there to this day? This personal experience first brought me acquainted with Wordsworth's habits in that particular especially, with his intense impatience for one minute's delay which would have brought a remedy; and yet the reader may believe that it is no affectation in me to say that fifty such cases could have given me but little pain, when I explain that whatever could be made good by money, at that time, I did not regard. Had the book been an old blackletter book, having a value from its rarity, I should have been disturbed in an indescribable degree; but simply with reference to the utter impossibility of reproducing that mode of value. As to the Burke, it was a common book; I had bought the book, with many others, at the sale of Sir Cecil Wray's library, for about two-thirds of the selling price: I could easily replace it; and I mention the case at all, only to illustrate the excess of Wordsworth's outrages on books, which made him, in Southey's eyes, a mere monster; for Southey's beautiful library was his estate; and this difference of habits would alone have sufficed to alienate him from Wordsworth. And so I argued in other cases of the same nature. Meantime, had Wordsworth done as Coleridge did, how cheerfully should I have acquiesced in his destruction (such as it was, in a pecuniary sense) of books, as the very highest obligation he could confer. Coleridge often spoiled a book; but, in the course of doing this, he enriched that book with so many and so valuable notes, tossing about him, with such lavish profusion, from such a cornucopia of discursive reading, and such a fusing intellect, commentaries so many-angled and so many-coloured that I have envied many a man whose luck has placed him in the way of such injuries; and that man must have been a churl (though, God knows! too often this churl *has* existed) who could have found in his heart to complain. But Wordsworth rarely, indeed, wrote on the margin of books; and, when he did, nothing could less illustrate his intellectual superiority. The comments were such as might have been made by anybody. Once, I remember, before I had ever seen Wordsworth—probably a year before—I met a person who had once enjoyed the signal honour of travelling with him to London. It was in a stage-coach. But the person in question well knew *who* it was that had been his *compagnon de voyage*. Immediately he was glorified in my eyes. 'And,' said I, to this glorified gentleman (who, *par parenthèse*, was also a donkey), 'Now, as you travelled nearly three hundred miles in the company of Mr. Wordsworth, consequently (for this was in 1805) during two nights and two days, doubtless you must have heard many profound remarks that would inevitably fall from his lips.' Nay, Coleridge had also been of the party; and, if Wordsworth *solus* could have been dull, was it within human possibilities that these *gemini* should have been so? 'Was it possible?' I said; and perhaps my donkey, who looked like one that had been immoderately threatened, at last took courage; his eye brightened; and he intimated that he *did* remember something that Wordsworth had said—an 'observe,' as the Scotch call it.

'Ay, indeed; and what was it now? What did the great man say?'

'Why, sir, in fact, and to make a long story short, on coming near to London, we breakfasted at Baldock—you know Baldock? It's in Hertfordshire. Well, now, sir, would you believe it, though we were quite in regular time, the breakfast was precisely good for nothing?'

'And Wordsworth?'

'He observed——'

'What did he observe?'

'That the buttered toast looked, for all the world, as if it had been soaked in hot water.'

Ye heavens! '*buttered toast*!' And was it *this* I waited for? Now, thought I, had Henry Mackenzie been breakfasting with Wordsworth at Baldock (and, strange enough! in years to come I *did* breakfast with Henry Mackenzie, for the solitary time I ever met him, and at Wordsworth's house in Rydal), he would have carried off one sole reminiscence from the meeting—namely, a confirmation of his creed, that we English are all dedicated, from our very cradle, to the luxuries of the palate, and peculiarly to this. *Proh pudor!* Yet, in sad sincerity, Wordsworth's pencil-notices in books were quite as disappointing. In 'Roderick Random,' for example, I found a note upon a certain luscious description, to the effect that 'such things should be left to the imagination of the reader—not expressed.' In another place, that it was 'improper'; and, in a third, that 'the principle laid down was doubtful,' or, as Sir Roger de Coverley observes, 'that much might be said on both sides.' All this, however, indicates nothing more than that different men require to be roused by different stimulants. Wordsworth, in his marginal notes, thought of nothing but delivering himself of a strong feeling, with which he wished to challenge the reader's sympathy. Coleridge imagined an audience before him; and, however doubtful that consummation might seem, I am satisfied that he never wrote a line for which he did not feel the momentary inspiration of sympathy and applause, under the confidence, that, sooner or later, all which he had committed to the chance margins of books would converge and assemble in some common reservoir of reception. Bread scattered upon the water will be gathered after many days. This, perhaps, was the consolation that supported him; and the prospect that, for a time, his Arethusa of truth would flow underground, did not, perhaps, disturb, but rather cheered and elevated, the sublime old somnambulist.[1] Meantime, Wordsworth's habits of using books,—which, I am satisfied, would in those days, alone have kept him at a distance from most men with fine libaries —were not vulgar; not the habits of those who turn over the page by means of a wet finger (though even this abomination I have seen perpetrated by a Cambridge tutor and fellow of a college; but then he had been bred up as a ploughman, and the son of a ploughman): no; but his habits were more properly barbarous and licentious, and in the spirit of audacity belonging *de jure* to no man but him who could plead an income of four or five hundred thousand per annum, and to whom the Bodleian or the Vatican would be a three years' purchase. Gross, meantime, was his delusion upon this subject. Himself he regarded as the golden mean between the too little and the too much of care for books; and, as it happened that every one of his friends far exceeded him in this point, curiously felicitous was the explanation which he gave of this superfluous care, so as to bring it within the natural operation of some known fact in the man's peculiar situation. Southey (he was by nature something of an old bachelor) had his house filled with pretty articles—*bijouterie*, and so forth; and, naturally, he wished his books to be kept up to the same level—burnished and bright for show. Sir George Beaumont—this peculiarly elegant and accomplished man— was an old and most affectionate friend of Wordsworth's. Sir George Beaumont never had any children; if he had been so blessed, they, by familiarizing him with the spectacle of books ill used—stained, torn, mutilated, &c.—would have lowered the standard of his requisitions. The short solution of the whole case was—and it illustrated the nature of his education—he had never lived in a regular family at a time when habits are moulded. From boyhood to manhood he had been *sui juris*.

Ibid.

[1] Meantime, if it did not disturb *him*, it ought to disturb *us*, his immediate successors, who are at once the most likely to retrieve these *losses* by direct efforts, and the least likely to benefit by any casual or indirect retrievals, such as will be produced by time. Surely a subscription should be set on foot to recover all books enriched by his marginal notes. I would subscribe; and I know others who would largely.

Valuation

Not, therefore, in the 'Excursion' must we look for that reversionary influence which awaits Wordsworth with posterity. It is the vulgar superstition in behalf of big books and sounding pretensions that must have prevailed upon Coleridge and others to undervalue, by comparison with the direct philosophic poetry of Wordsworth, those earlier poems which are all short, but generally scintillating with gems of far profounder truth. I speak of that truth which strengthens into solemnity an impression very feebly acknowledged previously, or truth which suddenly unveils a connexion between objects hitherto regarded as irrelate and independent. In astronomy, to gain the rank of discoverer, it is not required that you should reveal a star absolutely new: find out with respect to an old star some new affection—as, for instance, that it has an ascertainable parallax—and immediately you bring it within the verge of a human interest; or, with respect to some old familiar planet, that its satellites suffer periodical eclipses, and immediately you bring it within the verge of terrestrial uses. Gleams of steadier vision that brighten into certainty appearances else doubtful, or that unfold relations else unsuspected, are not less discoveries of truth than the downright revelations of the telescope, or the absolute conquests of the diving-bell. It is astonishing how large a harvest of new truths would be reaped simply through the accident of a man's feeling, or being made to feel, more *deeply* than other men. He sees the same objects, neither more nor fewer, but he sees them engraved in lines far stronger and more determinate: and the difference in the strength makes the whole difference between consciousness and subconsciousness. And in questions of the mere understanding we see the same fact illustrated. The author who wins notice the most is not he that perplexes men by truths drawn from fountains of absolute novelty,—truths as yet unsunned, and from that cause obscure,—but he that awakens into illuminated consciousness ancient lineaments of truth long slumbering in the mind, although too faint to have extorted attention. Wordsworth has brought many a truth into life, both for the eye and for the understanding, which previously had slumbered indistinctly for all men.

For instance, as respects the eye, who does not acknowledge instantaneously the magical strength of truth in his saying of a cataract seen from a station two miles off that it was 'frozen by distance'? In all nature there is not an object so essentially at war with the stiffening of frost as the headlong and desperate life of a cataract; and yet notoriously the effect of distance is to lock up this frenzy of motion into the most petrific column of stillness. This effect is perceived at once when pointed out; but how few are the eyes that ever *would* have perceived it for themselves! Twilight, again—who before Wordsworth ever distinctly noticed its *abstracting* power?—that power of removing, softening, harmonising, by which a mode of obscurity executes for the eye the same mysterious office which the mind so often, within its own shadowy realms, executes for itself. In the dim interspace between day and night all disappears from our earthly scenery, as if touched by an enchanter's rod, which is either mean or inharmonious, or unquiet, or expressive of temporary things. Leaning against a column of rock, looking down upon a lake or river, and at intervals carrying your eyes forward through a vista of mountains, you become aware that your sight rests upon the very same spectacle, unaltered in a single feature, which once at the same hour was beheld by the legionary Roman from his embattled camp, or by the roving Briton in his 'wolf-skin vest,' lying down to sleep, and looking

> *'Through some leafy bower,*
> *Before his eyes were closed.'*

How magnificent is the summary or abstraction of the elementary features in such a scene, as executed by the poet himself, in illustration of this abstraction daily executed by Nature through her handmaid Twilight! Listen, reader, to the closing strain, solemn as twilight is solemn, and grand as the spectacle which it describes:—

> *'By him [i.e. the roving Briton] was seen*
> *The self-same vision which we now behold,*
> *At thy meek bidding, shadowy Power, brought forth;*
> *These mighty barriers and the gulf between;*
> *The flood, the stars—a spectacle as old*
> *As the beginning of the heavens and earth.'*[1]

Another great field there is amongst the pomps of nature which, if Wordsworth did not first notice, he certainly has noticed most circumstantially. I speak of cloud-scenery, or those pageants of sky-built architecture which sometimes in summer, at noonday, and in all seasons about sunset, arrest or appal the meditative; 'perplexing monarchs' with the spectacle of armies manœuvring, or deepening the solemnity of evening by towering edifices that mimic—but which also in mimicking mock—the transitory grandeurs of man. It is singular that these gorgeous phenomena, not less than those of the *Aurora Borealis*, have been so little noticed by poets. The *Aurora* was naturally neglected by the southern

---

[1] From Wordsworth's Sonnet beginning 'Hail, Twilight.'—M.

poets of Greece and Rome, as not much seen in their latitudes.¹ But the cloud-architecture of the daylight belongs alike to north and south. Accordingly, I remember one notice of it in Hesiod,—a case where the clouds exhibited

> '*The beauteous semblance of a flock at rest.*'

Another there is, a thousand years later, in Lucan: amongst the portents which that poet notices as prefiguring the dreadful convulsions destined to shake the earth at Pharsalia, I remember some fiery coruscation of arms in the heavens; but, so far as I recollect, the appearances might have belonged equally to the workmanship of the clouds or the Aurora. Up and down the next eight hundred years are scattered evanescent allusions to these vapoury appearances; in 'Hamlet' and elsewhere occur gleams of such allusions; but I remember no distinct sketch of such an appearance before that in the 'Antony and Cleopatra' of Skakspere, beginning,

> '*Sometimes we see a cloud that's dragonish.*'

Subsequently to Shakspere, these notices, as of all phenomena whatsoever that demanded a familiarity with nature in the spirit of love, became rarer and rarer. At length, as the eighteenth century was winding up its accounts, forth stepped William Wordsworth; of whom, as a reader of all pages in nature, it may be said that, if we except Dampier, the admirable buccaneer, the gentle *flibustier*,² and some few professional naturalists, he first and he last looked at natural objects with the eye that neither will be dazzled from without nor cheated by preconceptions from within. Most men look at nature in the hurry of a confusion that distinguishes nothing; *their* error is from without. Pope, again, and many who live in towns,³ make such blunders as that of supposing the moon to

---

¹ But then, says the reader, why was it not proportionally the more noticed by poets of the north? Certainly that question is fair. And the answer, it is scarcely possible to doubt, is this:—That until the rise of Natural Philosophy in Charles II's reign *there was no name* for the appearance; on which account some writers have been absurd enough to believe that the Aurora did not exist, noticeably, until about 1690. Shakspere, in his journeys down to Stratford (always performed on horseback), must often have been belated: he must sometimes have seen, he could not but have admired, the fiery skirmishing of the Aurora. And yet, for want of a word to fix and identify the gorgeous phenomenon, how could he introduce it as an image, or even as the subject of an allusion, in his writings?

² *Flibustier*, the ordinary French term for a buccaneer in the last forty years of the seventeenth century, is supposed to be a Spanish or French mispronunciation of the word *freebooter*.

³ It was not, however, that all poets then lived in towns; neither had Pope himself generally lived in towns. But it is perfectly useless to be familiar with

tip with silver the hills *behind* which she is rising, not by erroneous use of their eyes (for they use them not at all), but by inveterate preconceptions. Scarcely has there been a poet with what could be called a learned eye, or an eye *extensively* learned, before Wordsworth. Much affectation there has been of that sort since *his* rise, and at all times much counterfeit enthusiasm; but the sum of the matter is this,—that Wordsworth had his passion for nature fixed in his blood; it was a necessity, like that of the mulberry-leaf to the silkworm; and through his commerce with nature did he live and breathe. Hence it was—viz. from the *truth* of his love—that his knowledge grew; whilst most others, being merely hypocrites in their love, have turned out merely sciolists in their knowledge. This chapter, therefore, of *sky*-scenery may be said to have been revivified amongst the resources of poetry by Wordsworth—rekindled, if not absolutely kindled. The sublime scene indorsed upon the draperies of the storm in the fourth book of the 'Excursion' —that scene again witnessed upon the passage of the Hamilton Hills in Yorkshire—the solemn 'sky prospect' from the fields of France,—are unrivalled in that order of composition; and in one of these records Wordsworth has given first of all the true key-note of the sentiment belonging to these grand pageants. They are, says the poet, speaking in a case where the appearance had occurred towards night,

> *'Meek nature's evening comment on the shows*
> *And all the fuming vanities of earth.'*

Yes, that is the secret moral whispered to the mind. These mimicries express the laughter which is in heaven at earthly pomps. Frail and vapoury are the glories of man, even as the visionary parodies of these glories are frail, even as the scenical copies of those glories are frail, which nature weaves in clouds.

As another of those natural appearances which must have haunted men's eyes since the Flood, but yet had never forced itself into *conscious* notice until arrested by Wordsworth, I may notice an effect of *iteration* daily exhibited in the habits of cattle:—

> *'The cattle are grazing,*
> *Their heads never raising;*
> *There are forty feeding like one.'*

Now, merely as a *fact*, and if it were nothing more, this characteristic appearance

nature unless there is a public trained to love and value nature. It is not what the individual sees that will fix itself as beautiful in his recollections, but what he sees under a consciousness that others will sympathise with his feelings. Under any other circumstances familiarity does but realise the adage, and 'breeds contempt.' The great despisers of rural scenery, its fixed and permanent undervaluers, are rustics.

in the habits of cows, when all repeat the action of each, ought not to have been overlooked by those who profess themselves engaged in holding up a mirror to nature. But the fact has also a profound meaning as a hieroglyphic. In all animals which live under the protection of man a life of peace and quietness, but do not share in his labours or in his pleasures, what we regard is the species, and not the individual. Nobody but a grazier ever looks at one cow amongst a field of cows, or at one sheep in a flock. But, as to those animals which are more closely connected with man, not passively connected, but actively, being partners in his toils, and perils, and recreations—such as horses, dogs, falcons—they are regarded as individuals, and are allowed the benefit of an individual interest. It is not that cows have not a differential character, each for herself; and sheep, it is well known, have all a separate physiognomy for the shepherd who has cultivated their acquaintance. But men generally have no opportunity or motive for studying the individualities of creatures, however otherwise respectable, that are too much regarded by all of us in the reversionary light of milk, and beef, and mutton. Far otherwise it is with horses, who share in man's martial risks, who sympathise with man's frenzy in hunting, who divide with man the burdens of noonday. Far otherwise it is with dogs, that share the hearths of man, and adore the footsteps of his children. These man loves; of these he makes dear, though humble, friends. These often fight for *him*; and for *them* he reciprocally will sometimes fight. Of necessity, therefore, every horse and every dog is an individual—has a sort of personality that makes him *separately* interesting—has a beauty and a character of his own. Go to Melton, therefore, on some crimson morning, and what will you see? Every man, every horse, every dog, glorying in the plenitude of life, is in a different attitude, motion, gesture, action. It is not there the sublime unity which you must seek, where forty are like one; but the sublime infinity, like that of ocean, like that of Flora, like that of nature, where no repetitions are endured, no leaf is the copy of another leaf, no absolute identity, and no painful tautologies. This subject might be pursued into profounder recesses; but in a popular discussion it is necessary to forbear.

A volume might be filled with such glimpses of novelty as Wordsworth has first laid bare, even to the apprehension of the *senses*. For the *understanding*, when moving in the same track of human sensibilities, he has done only not so much. How often (to give an instance or two) must the human heart have felt the case, and yearned for an expression of the case, when there are sorrows which descend far below the region in which tears gather; and yet who has ever given utterance to this feeling, until Wordsworth came with his immortal line:—

'*Thoughts that do often lie too deep for tears*'?

This sentiment, and others that might be adduced (such as 'The child is father to the man'), have even passed into the popular heart, and are often quoted by those who know not *whom* they are quoting. Magnificent, again, is the sentiment, and yet an echo to one which lurks amongst all hearts, in relation to the frailty of merely human schemes for working good, which so often droop and collapse through the unsteadiness of human energies—

> '*Foundations must be laid
> In heaven.*'

How? Foundations laid in realms that are *above*? But *that* is impossible; *that* is at war with elementary physics; foundations must be laid *below*. Yes; and even so the poet throws the mind yet more forcibly on the hyperphysical character— on the grandeur transcending all physics—of those spiritual and shadowy foundations which alone are enduring.

But the great distinction of Wordsworth, and the pledge of his increasing popularity, is the extent of his sympathy with what is *really* permanent in human feelings, and also the depth of this sympathy. Young and Cowper, the two earlier leaders in the province of meditative poetry, are too circumscribed in the range of their sympathies, too narrow, too illiberal, and too exclusive. Both these poets manifested the quality of their strength in the quality of their public reception. Popular in some degree from the first, they entered upon the inheritance of their fame almost at once. Far different was the fate of Wordsworth; for in poetry of this class, which appeals to what lies deepest in man, in proportion to the native power of the poet, and his fitness for permanent life, is the strength of resistance in the public taste. Whatever is too original will be hated at the first. It must slowly mould a public for itself; and the resistance of the early thoughtless judgments must be overcome by a counter-resistance to itself in a better audience slowly mustering against the first. Forty and seven years it is since William Wordsworth first appeared as an author. Twenty of those years he was the scoff of the world, and his poetry a byword of scorn. Since, then and more than once, senates have rung with acclamations to the echo of his name. Now, at this moment, whilst we are talking about him, he has entered upon his seventy-sixth year. For himself, according to the course of nature, he cannot be far from his setting; but his poetry is only now clearing the clouds that gathered about its rising. Meditative poetry is perhaps that province of literature which will ultimately maintain most power amongst the generations which are coming; but in this department, at least, there is little competition to be apprehended by Wordsworth from anything that has appeared since the death of Shakspere

'On Wordsworth's Poetry', *Tait's Magazine*, Sept. 1845; Masson XI.

Mrs. Wordsworth and Dorothy

However, I saw sufficiently to be aware of two ladies just entering the room, through a doorway opening upon a little staircase. The foremost, a tallish young woman, with the most winning expression of benignity upon her features, advanced to me, presenting her hand with so frank an air that all embarrassment must have fled in a moment before the native goodness of her manner. This was Mrs Wordsworth, cousin of the poet, and, for the last five years or more, his wife.[1] She was now mother of two children, a son and a daughter; and she furnished a remarkable proof how possible it is for a woman neither handsome nor even comely according to the rigour of criticism—nay, generally pronounced very plain—to exercise all the practical fascination of beauty, through the mere compensatory charms of sweetness all but angelic, of simplicity the most entire, womanly self-respect and purity of heart speaking through all her looks, acts, and movements. *Words*, I was going to have added; but her words were few. In reality, she talked so little that Mr. Slave-Trade Clarkson used to allege against her that should could only say '*God bless you!*' Certainly, her intellect was not of an active order; but, in a quiescent, reposing, meditative way, she appeared always to have a genial enjoyment from her own thoughts; and it would have been strange, indeed, if she, who enjoyed such eminent advantages of training, from the daily society of her husband and his sister, failed to acquire some power of judging for herself, and putting forth some functions of activity. But undoubtedly that was not her element: to feel and to enjoy in a luxurious repose of mind—there was her *forte* and her peculiar privilege; and how much better this was adapted to her husband's taste, how much more adapted to uphold the comfort of his daily life, than a blue-stocking loquacity, or even a legitimate talent for discussion, may be inferred from his verses, beginning—

> '*She was a phantom of delight,*
> *When first she gleam'd upon my sight.*'

Once for all,[2] these exquisite lines were dedicated to Mrs. Wordsworth; were understood to describe her—to have been prompted by the feminine graces of her character; hers they are, and will remain for ever. To these, therefore, I

[1] Mary Hutchinson, who became Wordsworth's wife in October 1802, had been known to him since 1777, when she was his fellow-pupil in a Dame's school at Penrith.—M.

[2] *Once for all*, I say—on recollecting that Coleridge's verses to *Sara* were made transferable to any Sara who reigned at the time. At least three Saras appropriated them; all three long since in the grave.

may refer the reader for an idea of what was most important in the partner and second self of the poet. And I will add to this abstract of her *moral* portrait these few concluding traits of her appearance in a physical sense. Her figure was tolerably good. In complexion she was fair, and there was something peculiarly pleasing even in this accident of the skin, for it was accompanied by an animated expression of health, a blessing which, in fact, she possessed uninterruptedly. Her eyes, the reader may already know, were

> *'Like stars of twilight fair:*
> *Like twilight, too, her dark brown hair;*
> *But all things else about her drawn*
> *From May-time and the cheerful dawn.'*

Yet strange it is to tell that, in these eyes of vesper gentleness, there was a considerable obliquity of vision; and much beyond that slight obliquity which is often supposed to be an attractive foible in the countenance: this *ought* to have been displeasing or repulsive; yet, in fact, it was not. Indeed all faults, had they been ten times more and greater, would have been neutralized by that supreme expression of her features to the unity of which every lineament in the fixed parts, and every undulation in the moving parts, of her countenance, concurred, viz. a sunny benignity—a radiant graciousness—such as in this world I never saw surpassed.

Immediately behind her moved a lady, shorter, slighter, and perhaps, in all other respects, as different from her in personal characteristics as could have been wished for the most effective contrast. 'Her face was of Egyptian brown'; rarely, in a woman of English birth, had I seen a more determinate gipsy tan. Her eyes were not soft, as Mrs. Wordsworth's, nor were they fierce or bold; but they were wild and startling, and hurried in their motion. Her manner was warm and even ardent; her sensibility seemed constitutionally deep; and some subtle fire of impassioned intellect apparently burned within her, which, being alternately pushed forward into a conspicuous expression by the irrepressible instincts of her temperament, and then immediately checked, in obedience to the decorum of her sex and age, and her maidenly condition, gave to her whole demeanour, and to her conversation, an air of embarrassment, and even of self-conflict, that was almost distressing to witness. Even her very utterance and enunciation often suffered, in point of clearness and steadiness, from the agitation of her excessive organic sensibility. At times, the self-counteraction and self-baffling of her feelings caused her even to stammer, and so determinately to stammer that a stranger who should have seen her and quitted her in that state of feeling would have certainly set her down for one plagued with that infirmity of speech as distressingly as Charles Lamb himself. This was Miss Wordsworth, the only sister of the poet—his 'Dorothy'; who naturally owed so much to the lifelong intercourse with her great brother in his most solitary and sequestered years; but, on the other hand, to whom he has acknowledged obligations of the profoundest nature; and, in particular, this mighty one, through which we also, the admirers and the worshippers of this great poet, are become equally her debtors—that, whereas the intellect of Wordsworth was, by its original tendency, too stern, too austere, too much enamoured of an ascetic harsh sublimity, she it was—the lady who paced by his side continually through sylvan and mountain tracks, in Highland glens, and in the dim recesses of German charcoal-burners—that first *couched* his eye to the sense of beauty, humanized him by the gentler charities, and engrafted, with her delicate female touch, those graces upon the ruder growths of his nature which have since clothed the forest of his genius with a foliage corresponding in loveliness and beauty to the strength of its boughs and the massiness of its trunks. The greatest deductions from Miss Wordsworth's attractions, and from the exceeding interest which surrounded her in right of her character, of her history, and of the relation which she fulfilled towards her brother, were the glancing quickness of her motions, and other circumstances in her deportment (such as her stooping attitude when walking), which gave an ungraceful, and even an unsexual character to her appearance when out-of-doors. She did not cultivate the graces which preside over the person and its carriage. But, on the other hand, she was a person of very remarkable endowments intellectually; and, in addition to the other great services which she rendered to her brother, this I may mention, as greater than all the rest, and it was one which equally operated to the benefit of every casual companion in a walk—viz. the exceeding sympathy, always ready and always profound, by which she made all that one could tell her, all that one could describe, all that one could quote from a foreign author, reverberate, as it were, *à plusieurs reprises*, to one's own feelings, by the manifest impression it made upon *hers*. The pulses of light are not more quick or more inevitable in their flow and undulation, than were the answering and echoing movements of her sympathizing attention. Her knowledge of literature was irregular, and thoroughly unsystematic. She was content to be ignorant of many things; but what she knew and had really mastered lay where it could not be disturbed—in the temple of her own most fervid heart.

'The Lake Poets', *Tait's Magazine*, 1839; Masson II.

Wordsworth's Married Life

To us who, in after years, were Wordsworth's friends, or, at least, intimate acquaintances—viz., to Professor Wilson and myself—the most interesting circumstance in this marriage, the one which perplexed us exceedingly, was the very possibility that it should ever have been brought to bear. For we could not conceive of Wordsworth as submitting his faculties to the humilities and devotion of courtship. That self-surrender—that prostration of mind by which a man is too happy and proud to express the profundity of his service to the woman of his heart—it seemed a mere impossibility that ever Wordsworth should be brought to feel for a single instant; and what he did not sincerely feel, assuredly he was not the person to profess. Wordsworth, I take it upon myself to say, had not the feelings within him which make this total devotion to a woman possible. There never lived a woman whom he would not have lectured and admonished under circumstances that should have seemed to require it; nor would he have conversed with her in any mood whatever without wearing an air of mild condescension to her understanding. To lie at her feet, to make her his idol, to worship her very caprices, and to adore the most unreasonable of her frowns—these things were impossible to Wordsworth; and, being so, never could he, in any emphatic sense, have been a lover.

A lover, I repeat, in any passionate sense of the word, Wordsworth could not have been. And, moreover, it is remarkable that a woman who could dispense with that sort of homage in her suitor is not of a nature to inspire such a passion. That same meekness which reconciles her to the tone of superiority and freedom in the manner of her suitor, and which may afterwards in a wife become a sweet domestic grace, strips her of that too charming irritation, captivating at once and tormenting, which lurks in feminine pride. If there be an enchantress's spell yet surviving in this age of ours, it is the haughty grace of maidenly pride—the womanly sense of dignity, even when most in excess, and expressed in the language of scorn—which tortures a man and lacerates his heart, at the same time that it pierces him with admiration:—

> 'Oh, what a world of scorn looks beautiful
> In the contempt and anger of her lip!'

And she who spares a man the agitations of this thraldom robs him no less of its divinest transports. Wordsworth, however, who never could have laid aside his own nature sufficiently to have played *his* part in such an impassioned courtship, by suiting himself to this high sexual pride with the humility of a lover, quite as little could have enjoyed the spectacle of such a pride, or have viewed it in any degree as an attraction: it would to him have been a pure vexation.

Looking down even upon the lady of his heart, as upon the rest of the world, from the eminence of his own intellectual superiority—viewing her, in fact, as a child—he would be much more disposed to regard any airs of feminine disdain she might assume as the impertinence of girlish levity than as the caprice of womanly pride; and much I fear that, in any case of dispute, he would have called even his mistress, 'Child! child!' and perhaps even (but this I do not say with the same certainty) might have bid her hold her tongue.

If, however, no lover, in a proper sense,—though, from many exquisite passages, one might conceive that at some time of his life he was, as especially from the inimitable stanzas beginning—

> '*When she I loved was strong and gay,*
> *And like a rose in June,*'

or perhaps (but less powerfully so, because here the passion, though profound, is less the *peculiar* passion of love) from the impassioned lamentation for 'the pretty Barbara,' beginning—

> '*Tis said that some have died for love:*
> *And here and there, amidst unhallow'd ground*
> *In the cold north,*' &c.,—

yet, if no lover, or (which some of us have sometimes thought) a lover disappointed at some earlier period, by the death of her he loved, or by some other fatal event (for he always preserved a mysterious silence on the subject of that 'Lucy,' repeatedly alluded to or apostrophized in his poems); at all events she made what for him turned out a happy marriage. Few people have lived on such terms of entire harmony and affection as he lived with the woman of his final choice. Indeed, the sweetness, almost unexampled, of temper, which shed so sunny a radiance over Mrs. Wordsworth's manners, sustained by the happy life she led, the purity of her conscience, and the uniformity of her good health, made it impossible for anybody to have quarrelled with *her*; and whatever fits of ill-temper Wordsworth might have—for, with all his philosophy, he had such fits—met with no fuel to support them, except in the more irritable temperament of his sister. She was all fire, and an ardour which, like that of the first Lord Shaftesbury,

> '*O'er-informed its tenement of clay*';

and, as this ardour looked out in every gleam of her wild eyes (those 'wild eyes' so finely noticed in the 'Tintern Abbey'), as it spoke in every word of her self-baffled utterance, as it gave a trembling movement to her very person and demeanour—easily enough it might happen that any apprehension of an unkind word should with her kindle a dispute. It might have happened; and yet, to the great honour of both, having such impassioned temperaments, rarely it did happen; and this was the more remarkable, as I have been assured that both were, in childhood, irritable or even ill-tempered, and they were constantly together; for Miss Wordsworth was always ready to walk out—wet or dry, storm or sunshine, night or day; whilst Mrs. Wordsworth was completely dedicated to her maternal duties, and rarely left the house, unless when the weather was tolerable, or, at least, only for short rambles. I should not have noticed this trait in Wordsworth's occasional manners, had it been gathered from domestic or confidential opportunities. But, on the contrary, the first two occasions on which, after months' domestic intercourse with Wordsworth, I became aware of his possible ill-humour and peevishness, were so public, that others, and those strangers, must have been equally made parties to the scene. This scene occurred in Kendal.

Ibid.

Dorothy Wordsworth

As to Miss Wordsworth, who will, by some people, be classed amongst the non-prosperous, I rank her amongst the most fortunate of women; or, at least, if regard be had to that period of life which is most capable of happiness. Her fortune, after its repayment by Lord Lonsdale, was, much of it, confided, with a sisterly affection, to the use of her brother John; and part of it, I have heard, perished in his ship. How much, I never felt myself entitled to ask; but certainly a part was on that occasion understood to have been lost irretrievably. Either it was that only a partial insurance had been effected; or else the nature of the accident, being in home waters (off the coast of Dorsetshire), might, by the nature of the contract, have taken the case out of the benefit of the policy. This loss, however, had it even been total, for a single sister amongst a family of flourishing brothers, could not be of any lasting importance. A much larger number of voices would proclaim her to have been unfortunate in life because she made no marriage connexion; and certainly, the insipid as well as unfeeling ridicule which descends so plentifully upon those women, who, perhaps from strength of character, have refused to make such a connexion where it promised little of elevated happiness, *does* make the state of singleness somewhat of a trial to the patience of many; and to many the vexation of this trial has proved a snare for beguiling them of their honourable resolutions. Meantime, as the opportunities are rare in which all the conditions concur for happy marriage connexions, how important it is that the dignity of high-minded women should be upheld by society in the honourable election they make of a self-dependent virgin seclusion, by preference to a heartless marriage! Such women, as Mrs. Trollope justly remarks, fill a place in society which in their default would *not* be filled, and are available for duties requiring a tenderness and a punctuality that could not be looked for from women preoccupied with household or maternal claims. If there were no regular fund (so to speak) of women free from conjugal and maternal duties, upon what body could we draw for our 'sisters of mercy,' &c.? In another point Mrs. Trollope is probably right: few women live un-married from necessity. Miss Wordsworth had several offers; amongst them, to my knowledge, one from Hazlitt; all of them she rejected decisively. And she did right. A happier life, by far, was hers in youth, coming as near as difference of scenery and difference of relations would permit to that which was promised to Ruth—the Ruth of her brother's creation[1]—by the youth who came from Georgia's shore; for, though not upon American savannah, or Canadian lakes,

> *'With all their fairy crowds*
> *Of islands, that together lie*
> *As quietly as spots of sky*
> *Amongst the evening clouds,'*

yet, amongst the loveliest scenes of sylvan England, and (at intervals) of Sylvan Germany—amongst lakes, too, far better fitted to give the *sense* of their own character than the vast inland *seas* of America, and amongst mountains more romantic than many of the chief ranges in that country—her time fleeted away like some golden age, or like the life of primeval man; and she, like Ruth, was for years allowed

> *'To run, though* not *a bride,*
> *A sylvan huntress, by the side'*

of him to whom she, like Ruth, had dedicated her days, and to whose children, afterwards, she dedicated a love like that of mothers. Dear Miss Wordsworth! How noble a creature did she seem when I first knew her!—and when, on the very first night which I passed in her brother's company, he read to me, in

[1] '*The Ruth of her brother's creation*': So I express it; because so much in the development of the story and situations necessarily belongs to the poet. Else, for the mere outline of the story, it was founded upon fact. Wordsworth himself told me, in general terms, that the case which suggested the poem was that of an American lady, whose husband forsook her at the very place of embarkation from England, under circumstances and under expectations, upon her part, very much the same as those of Ruth. I am afraid, however, that the husband was an attorney; which is intolerable; *nisi prius* cannot be harmonized with the dream-like fairy-land of Georgia.

illustration of something he was saying, a passage from Fairfax's 'Tasso,' ending pretty nearly with these words,

> *'Amidst the broad fields and the endless wood,*
> *The lofty lady kept her maidenhood,'*

I thought that, possibly, he had his sister in his thoughts. Yet 'lofty' was hardly the right word. Miss Wordsworth was too ardent and fiery a creature to maintain the reserve essential to dignity; and dignity was the last thing one thought of in the presence of one so natural, so fervent in her feelings, and so embarrassed in their utterance—sometimes, also, in the attempt to check them. It must not, however, be supposed that there was any silliness or weakness of enthusiasm about her. She was under the continual restraint of severe good sense, though liberated from that false shame which, in so many persons, accompanies all expressions of natural emotion; and she had too long enjoyed the ennobling conversation of her brother, and his admirable comments on the poets, which they read in common, to fail in any essential point of logic or propriety of thought. Accordingly, her letters, though the most careless and unelaborate— nay, the most hurried that can be imagined—are models of good sense and just feeling. In short, beyond any person I have known in this world, Miss Wordsworth was the creature of impulse; but, as a woman most thoroughly virtuous and well-principled, as one who could not fail to be kept right by her own excellent heart, and as an intellectual creature from her cradle, with much of her illustrious brother's peculiarity of mind—finally, as one who had been, in effect, educated and trained by that very brother—she won the sympathy and the respectful regard of every man worthy to approach her. Properly, and in a spirit of prophecy, was she named *Dorothy*; in its Greek meaning, *gift of God*, well did this name prefigure the relation in which she stood to Wordsworth, the mission with which she was charged—to wait upon him as the tenderest and most faithful of domestics; to love him as a sister; to sympathize with him as a confidante; to counsel him; to cheer him and sustain him by the natural expression of her feelings—so quick, so ardent, so unaffected—upon the probable effect of whatever thoughts or images he might conceive; finally, and above all other ministrations, to ingraft, by her sexual sense of beauty, upon his masculine austerity that delicacy and those graces which else (according to the grateful acknowledgments of his own maturest retrospect) it never could have had:—

> *'The blessing of my later years*
> *Was with me when I was a boy:*
> *She gave me hopes, she gave me fears,*
> *A heart the fountain of sweet tears,*
>
> . . . . . .
>
> *And love, and thought, and joy.'*

And elsewhere he describes her, in a philosophic poem, still in MS.,[1] as one who planted flowers and blossoms with her feminine hand upon what might else have been an arid rock—massy, indeed, and grand, but repulsive from the severity of its features. I may sum up in one brief abstract the amount of Miss Wordsworth's character, as a companion, by saying, that she was the very wildest (in the sense of the most natural) person I have ever known; and also the truest, most inevitable, and at the same time the quickest and readiest in her sympathy with either joy or sorrow, with laughter or with tears, with the realities of life or the larger realities of the poets!

Meantime, amidst all this fascinating furniture of her mind, won from nature, from solitude, from enlightened companionship, Miss Wordsworth was as thoroughly deficient (some would say painfully deficient—I say charmingly deficient) in ordinary female accomplishments as 'Cousin Mary' in dear Miss Mitford's delightful sketch. Of French, she might have barely enough to read a plain modern page of narrative; Italian, I question whether any; German, just enough to insult the German literati, by showing how little she had found them or their writings necessary to her heart. The 'Luise' of Voss, the 'Hermann und Dorothea' of Goethe she had begun to translate, as young ladies do 'Télémaque'; but, like them, had chiefly cultivated the first two pages[2]; with the third she had a slender acquaintance, and with the fourth she meditated an intimacy at some future day. Music, in her solitary and out-of-doors life, she could have little reason for cultivating; nor is it possible that any woman can draw the enormous energy requisite for this attainment, upon a *modern* scale of perfection, out of any other principle than that of vanity (at least of great value for social applause) or else of deep musical sensibility; neither of which belonged to Miss Wordsworth's constitution of mind. But, as everybody agrees in our days to think this accomplishment of no value whatever, and, in fact, *unproduceable*, unless existing in an exquisite state of culture, no complaint could be made on that score, nor any surprise felt. But the case in which the irregularity of Miss Wordsworth's education *did* astonish one was in that part which respected her literary knowledge. In whatever she read, or neglected to read, she had obeyed the single impulse of her own heart; where that led her, *there* she followed: where that was mute or indifferent, not a thought had she to bestow

[1] In the concluding Book of the *Prelude*.—M.

[2] Viz., 'Calypso ne savoit se consoler du départ,' &c. For how long a period (viz., nearly two centuries) has Calypso been inconsolable in the morning studies of young ladies! As Fénélon's most dreary romance always opened at one or other of these three earliest and dreary pages, naturally to my sympathetic fancy the poor unhappy goddess seemed to be eternally aground on this Goodwin Sand of inconsolability. It is amongst the standing hypocrisies of the world, that most people affect a reverence for this book, which nobody reads.

upon a writer's high reputation, or the call for some acquaintance with his works to meet the demands of society. And thus the strange anomaly arose, of a woman deeply acquainted with some great authors, whose works lie pretty much out of the fashionable beat; able, moreover, in her own person, to produce brilliant effects; able on some subjects to write delightfully, and with the impress of originality upon all she uttered; and yet ignorant of great classical works in her own mother tongue, and careless of literary history in a degree which at once exiled her from the rank and privileges of *bluestockingism*.

The reader may, perhaps, have objected silently to the illustration drawn from Miss Mitford, that 'Cousin Mary' does not effect her fascinations out of pure negations. Such negations, from the mere startling effect of their oddity in this present age, might fall in with the general current of her attractions; but Cousin Mary's undoubtedly lay in the *positive* witcheries of a manner and a character transcending, by force of irresistible nature (as in a similar case recorded by Wordsworth in 'The Excursion') all the pomp of nature and art united as seen in ordinary creatures. Now, in Miss Wordsworth, there were certainly no 'Cousin Mary' fascinations of manner and deportment, that snatch a grace beyond the reach of art: *there* she was, indeed, painfully deficient; for hurry mars and defeats even the most ordinary expression of the feminine character—viz. its gentleness: abruptness and trepidation leave often a joint impression of what seems for an instant both rudeness and ungracefulness: and the least painful impression was that of unsexual awkwardness. But the point in which Miss Wordsworth made the most ample amends for all that she wanted of more customary accomplishments, was this very originality and native freshness of intellect, which settled with so bewitching an effect upon some of her writings, and upon many a sudden remark or ejaculation, extorted by something or other that struck her eye, in the clouds, or in colouring, or in accidents of light and shade, of form or combination of form. To talk of her 'writings' is too pompous an expression, or at least far beyond any pretensions that she ever made for herself. Of poetry she has written little indeed; and that little not, in my opinion, of much merit. The verses published by her brother, and beginning, 'Which way does the wind come?', meant only as nursery lines, are certainly wild and pretty; but the other specimen is likely to strike most readers as feeble and trivial in the sentiment. Meantime, the book which is in very deed a monument to her power of catching and expressing all the hidden beauties of natural scenery, with a felicity of diction, a truth and strength, that far transcend Gilpin, or professional writers on those subjects, is her record of a *first* tour in Scotland, made about the year 1802. This MS. book (unless my recollection of it, from a period now gone by for thirty years, has deceived me greatly) is absolutely unique in its class; and, though it never could be very popular, from the minuteness of its details, intelligible only to the eye, and the luxuriation of its descriptions, yet I believe no person has ever been favoured with a sight of it that has not yearned for its publication. Its own extraordinary merit, apart from the interest which *now* invests the name of Wordsworth, could not fail to procure purchasers for one edition on its first appearance.

Ibid.

Kate Wordsworth

Among that family, and standing fourth in the series of his children, was a little girl, whose life, short as it was, and whose death, obscure and little heard of as it was amongst all the rest of the world, connected themselves with the records of my own life by ties of passion so profound, by a grief so frantic, and so memorable through the injurious effects which it produced of a physical kind, that, had I left untouched every other chapter of my own experience, I should certainly have left behind some memorandum of this, as having a permanent interest in the psychological history of human nature. Luckily the facts are not without a parallel, and in well authenticated medical books; else I should have scrupled (as what man does *not* scruple who values, above all things, the reputation for veracity?) to throw the whole stress of credibility on my own unattached narration. But all experienced physicians know well that cases similar to mine, though not common, occur at intervals in every large community.

When I first settled in Grasmere, Catherine Wordsworth was in her infancy, but, even at that age, noticed me more than any other person, excepting, of course, her mother. She had for an attendant a young girl, perhaps thirteen years old—Sarah, one of the orphan children left by the unfortunate couple, George and Sarah Green, whose tragical end in a snow-storm I have already narrated. This Sarah Green was as far removed in character as could be imagined from that elder sister who had won so much admiration in her childish days, by her premature display of energy and household virtues. She was lazy, luxurious, and sensual: one, in fact, of those nurses who, in their anxiety to gossip about young men, leave their infant or youthful charges to the protection of chance. It was, however, not in her out-of-door ramblings, but at home, that the accident occurred which determined the fortunes of little Catherine. Mr. Coleridge was at that time a visitor to the Wordsworths at Allan Bank, that house in Grasmere to which Wordsworth had removed upon quitting his cottage. One day about noon, when, perhaps, he was coming down to breakfast, Mr. Coleridge passed Sarah Green, playing after her indolent fashion with the child; and between them lay a number of carrots. He warned the girl that raw carrots were an indigestible substance for the stomach of an infant. This warning was neglected: little Catherine ate—it was never known how many; and, in a short time, was seized with strong convulsions. I saw her in this state about two P.M. No medical aid was to be had nearer than Ambleside; about six miles distant. However, all proper measures were taken; and, by sunset, she had so far recovered as to be pronounced out of danger. Her left side, however, left arm, and left leg, from that time forward, were in a disabled state: not what could be called paralysed, but suffering a sort of atony or imperfect distribution of vital power.

Catherine was not above three years old when she died; so that there could not have been much room for the expansion of her understanding, or the unfolding of her real character. But there was room enough in her short life, and too much, for love the most frantic to settle upon her. The whole vale of Grasmere is not large enough to allow of any great distances between house and house; and, as it happened that little Kate Wordsworth returned my love, she in a manner lived with me at my solitary cottage; as often as I could entice her from home, walked with me, slept with me, and was my sole companion. That I was not singular in ascribing some witchery to the nature and manners of this innocent child, you may gather from the following most beautiful lines extracted from a sketch[1] towards her portraiture, drawn by her father (with whom, however, she was noways a favourite):—

> '*And, as a faggot sparkles on the hearth,*
> *Not less if unattended and alone*
> *Than when both young and old sit gathered round*
> *And take delight in its activity;*
> *Even so this happy creature of herself*
> *Was all sufficient: solitude to her*
> *Was blithe society, who filled the air*
> *With gladness and involuntary songs.*
> *Light were her sallies as the tripping fawn's,*
> *Forth-startled from the form where she lay couch'd;*
> *Unthought of, unexpected, as the stir*
> *Of the soft breeze ruffling the meadow-flowers,*
> *Or from before it chasing wantonly*
> *The many-coloured images impressed*
> *Upon the bosom of a placid lake.*'

[1] It is entitled ' Characteristics of a Child Three Years Old '; and is dated at the foot 1811, which must be an oversight, for she was not so old until the following year. I may as well add the first six lines, though I had a reason

It was this radiant spirit of joyousness, making solitude for her blithe society, and filling from morning to night the air 'with gladness and involuntary songs,' this it was which so fascinated my heart that I became blindly, doatingly, in a servile degree, devoted to this one affection. In the spring of 1812, I went up to London; and, early in June, by a letter from Miss Wordsworth, her aunt, I learned the terrific news (for such to me it was) that she had died suddenly. She had gone to bed in good health about sunset on June 4th; was found speechless a little before midnight; and died in the early dawn, just as the first gleams of morning began to appear above Seat Sandel and Fairfield, the mightiest of the Grasmere barriers, about an hour, perhaps, before sunrise.

Never, perhaps, from the foundations of those mighty hills, was there so fierce a convulsion of grief as mastered my faculties on receiving that heart-shattering news. Over and above my excess of love for her, I had always viewed her as an impersonation of the dawn and the spirit of infancy; and this abstraction seated in her person, together with the visionary sort of connexion which, even in her parting hours, she assumed with the summer sun, by timing her immersion into the cloud of death with the rising and setting of that fountain of life,—these combined impressions recoiled so violently into a contrast or polar antithesis to the image of death that each exalted and brightened the other. I returned hastily to Grasmere; stretched myself every night, for more than two months running, upon her grave; in fact, often passed the night upon her grave; not (as may readily be supposed) in any parade of grief; on the contrary, in that quiet valley of simple shepherds, I was secure enough from observation until morning light began to return; but in mere intensity of sick, frantic yearning after neighbourhood to the darling of my heart. Many readers will have seen in Sir Walter Scott's 'Demonology.' and in Dr. Abercrombie's 'Inquiries concerning the Intellectual Powers,' some remarkable illustrations of the creative faculties awakened in the eye or other organs by peculiar states of passion; and it is worthy of a place amongst cases of that nature that, in many solitary fields, at a considerable elevation above the level of the valleys,—fields which, in the local dialect, are called 'intacks,'—my eye was haunted at times, in

for beginning the extract where it does, in order to fix the attention upon the special circumstance which had so much fascinated myself, of her all-sufficiency to herself, and the way in which she 'filled the air with gladness and involuntary songs.' The other lines are these:

> 'Loving she is and tractable, though wild;
> And Innocence hath privilege in her
> To dignify arch looks and laughing eyes;
> And feats of cunning; and the pretty round
> Of trespass, affected to provoke
> Mock-chastisement and partnership in play.'

169

broad noonday (oftener, however, in the afternoon), with a facility, but at times also with a necessity, for weaving, out of a few simple elements, a perfect picture of little Kate in the attitude and onward motion of walking. I resorted constantly to these 'intacks,' as places where I was little liable to disturbance; and usually I saw her at the opposite side of the field, which might sometimes be at a distance of a quarter of a mile, generally not so much. Always almost she carried a basket on her head; and usually the first hint upon which the figure arose commenced in wild plants, such as tall ferns, or the purple flowers of the foxglove; but, whatever might be the colours or the forms, uniformly the same little full-formed figure arose, uniformly dressed in the little blue bed-gown and black skirt of Westmoreland, and uniformly with the air of advancing motion. Through part of June, July, and part of August, in fact throughout the summer, this frenzy of grief continued. It was reasonably to be expected that nature would avenge such senseless self-surrender to passion; for, in fact, so far from making an effort to resist it, I clung to it as a luxury (which, in the midst of suffering, it really was in part). All at once, on a day at the latter end of August, in one instant of time, I was seized with some nervous sensation that, for a moment, caused sickness. A glass of brandy removed the sickness; but I felt, to my horror, a sting as it were, of some stationary torment left behind—a torment absolutely indescribable, but under which I felt assured that life could not be borne. It is useless and impossible to describe what followed: with no apparent illness discoverable to any medical eye—looking, indeed, better than usual for three months and upwards, I was under the possession of some internal nervous malady, that made each respiration which I drew an act of separate anguish. I travelled southwards immediately to Liverpool, to Birmingham, to Bristol, to Bath, for medical advice; and finally rested—in a gloomy state of despair, rather because I saw no use in further change than that I looked for any change in this place more than others—at Clifton, near Bristol. Here it was, at length, in the course of November, that, in one hour, my malady began to leave me: it was not quite so abrupt, however, in its departure, as in its first development: a peculiar sensation arose from the knee downwards, about midnight: it went forwards through a space of about five hours, and then stopped, leaving me perfectly free from every trace of the awful malady which had possessed me, but so much debilitated as with difficulty to stand or walk. Going down soon after this, to Ilfracombe, in Devonshire, where there were hot sea baths, I found it easy enough to restore my shattered strength. But the remarkable fact in this catastrophe of my illness is that all grief for little Kate Wordsworth, nay, all remembrance of her, had, with my malady, vanished from my mind. The traces of her innocent features were utterly washed away from my heart: she might have been dead for a thousand years, so entirely abolished was the last lingering image of her face or figure. The little memorials of her which her mother had given to me, as, in particular, a pair of her red morocco shoes, won not a sigh from me as I looked at them: even her little grassy grave, white with snow, when I returned to Grasmere in January, 1813, was looked at almost with indifference; except, indeed, as now become a memorial to me of that internal physical convulsion thence arising by which I had been shaken and wrenched; and, in short, a case more entirely realizing the old Pagan superstition of a nympholepsy in the first place, and, secondly, of a Lethe or river of oblivion, and the possibility, by one draught from this potent stream, of applying an everlasting ablution to all the soils and stains of human anguish, I do not suppose the psychological history of man affords.

Ibid.

Kate's Death

To Dorothy Wordsworth   Sunday evening, June 21st [1812.]
My Dear Friend

I thank you much for your long and most affecting letter. One passage in it troubled me greatly; I mean where you spoke of our dear child's bodily sufferings. Her father and I trusted that she had been insensible to pain—that being generally the case, I believe, in convulsions. But thank God! whatever were her sufferings, they were short in comparison of what she would have had in most other complaints; and now at least sweet love she is at rest and in peace. It being God's pleasure to recal [*sic*] his innocent creature to himself, perhaps in no other way could it have been done more mercifully to her, though to the bystanders for the time few could have been more affecting to behold. How much more suffering would she have had in a common fever from a cold; and what anguish to us all, if she had called upon our names in delirium—and fancied that we would not come to her relief! This I remember witnessing at my father's bedside on the morning when he died: I was but a child, and had seen too little of him to feel much at his death; but I was greatly affected at hearing him moan out to my mother a few minutes before he died—Oh Betty Betty! why will you never come and help me to raise this weight?

I was truly glad to find from your account of her funeral that those who attended were in general such as would unaffectedly partake (more or less) in your sorrow. It has been an awful employment to me—the recollecting where I was and how occupied when this solemn scene was going on. At that time I must have been in the streets of London; tired, I remember, for I had just recovered from sickness—but chearful and filled with pleasant thoughts. Ah what a mortal revulsion of heart, if any sudden revelation could have laid open to my sight what scene was passing in Grasmere vale! On the night June 3–4—I remember, from a particular circumstance, that I lay awake all night long; in serious thought, but yet as chearful as if not a dream were troubling any one that I loved! I think I heard the clock strike *five*: if so I must have been closing my eyes in sleep just about the time that my blessed Kate was closing hers for ever! Oh that I could have died for her or with her! Willingly dear friend I would have done this. I do not say it for any momentary burst of grief, but as a feeling that I have ejaculated in truth and sincerity a thousand times since I heard of her death. If I had seen her in pain, I could have done anything for her; and reason it was that I should; for she was a blessing to *me*, and gave me many and many an hour of happy thoughts that I can never have again.

You tell me to think of her with tender chearfulness; but far from that dear friend my heart grows heavier and heavier every day. I have done what I could against this oppression of spirits; twice I have passed the evening with Mr. Coleridge; and I have often endeavoured to study. But after all I find it more tolerable to let my thoughts take their natural course, than to put such constraint upon them. But let me not trouble you with complaints who have sorrow enough of your own to bear—and to witness in others.

Yesterday I heard from Mr. Wordsworth, and was grieved to hear of Mrs. Wordsworth's state of mind; but I knew it could not be otherwise. She would have borne her loss better, I doubt not, if she had been on the spot: as it is, this affliction would be doubly poignant to her—coming upon her just when her mind would be busiest with images of a delightful return to Grasmere and meeting again with her children. I think of her with the greatest compassion and love.

This afternoon—whilst I was putting up my clothes and books into a trunk—I remembered that to-day was the 21st. of June—just a quarter of a year from the day on which I left Grasmere; for I left it on Sunday, March 22nd. On this day thirteen weeks therefore I saw Kate for the last time. The last words she said to me (except that perhaps she might call out some words of farewell in company with the rest who were present)—I think were these: the children were speaking to me all at once, and I was saying one thing to one and another to another; and she, who could not speak loud enough to overpower the other voices, had got up on a chair by which I was standing; and putting her hand upon my mouth she said with sweet importunateness of voice and gesture—Kinsey, Kinsey—what a-bring Katy from London? I believe she said it twice; and I remember that her mother noticed the earnestness of her manner, and looked at me, and smiled. This was the last time I am almost certain that I heard her sweet voice and saw her sweet countenance distinctly; and I shall never hear or see anything so delightful again. Oh if I had known that it was to be the last!

I shall leave London not earlier than Tuesday, nor later than Wednesday. I have been detained in a way that I could not prevent. How soon I shall reach Grasmere—will depend on the accidents of meeting conveyances &c. I trust I shall find you all well.

Remember me most kindly to Miss Hutchinson and to the children.

I wrote a second letter to you last Monday, June 15th.

John E. Jordan, *De Quincey to Wordsworth*, University of California Press/Cambridge University Press, 1962.

Literature

Prose as an Art

For with respect to the first oversight on the claim of Herodotus as an earliest archetype of composition so much is evident: that, if prose were simply the negation of verse, were it the fact that prose had no separate laws of its own, but that to be a composer in prose meant only his privilege of being inartificial, his dispensation from the restraints of metre, then, indeed, it would be a slight nominal honour to have been the Father of Prose. But this is ignorance, though a pretty common ignorance. To walk well, it is not enough that a man abstains from dancing. Walking has rules of its own the more difficult to perceive or to practise as they are less broadly *prononcés*. To forbear singing is not, therefore, to speak well or to read well: each of which offices rests upon a separate art of its own. Numerous laws of transition, connexion, preparation, are different for a writer in verse and a writer in prose. Each mode of composition is a great art; well executed, is the highest and most difficult of arts. And we are satisfied that, one century before the age of Herodotus, the effort must have been greater to wean the feelings from a key of poetic composition to which all minds had long been attuned and prepared than at present it would be for any paragraphist in the newspapers to make the inverse revolution by *suddenly* renouncing the modesty of prose for the impassioned forms of lyrical poetry. It was a great thing to be the leader of prose composition; great even, as we all can see at other times, to be absolutely first in any one subdivision of composition: how much more in one whole bisection of literature! And, if it is objected that Herodotus was *not* the eldest of prose writers, doubtless, in an absolute sense, no man was. There must always have been short public inscriptions, not admitting of metre, as where numbers, quantities, dimensions, were concerned. It is enough that all feeble tentative explorers of the art had been too meagre in matter, too rude in manner, like Fabius Pictor amongst the Romans, to captivate the ears of men, and *thus* to insure their own propagations.

'The Philosophy of Herodotus', *Blackwood's Magazine*, Jan. 1842; Masson VI.

The Writing of Prose

The two capital secrets in the art of prose composition are these: 1st, The philosophy of transition and connection, or the art by which one step in an evolution of thought is made to arise out of another: all fluent and effective composition depends on the *connections*;—2dly, The way in which sentences are made to modify each other; for the most powerful effects in written eloquence arise out of this reverberation, as it were, from each other in a rapid succession of sentences; and, because some limitation is necessary to the length and complexity of sentences, in order to make this interdependency felt: hence it is that the Germans have no eloquence. The construction of German prose tends to such immoderate length of sentences that no effect of intermodification can ever be apparent. Each sentence, stuffed with innumerable clauses of restriction, and other parenthetical circumstances, becomes a separate section—an independent whole.

'Autobiography': *Tait's Magazine*, Feb. 1835; Masson II.

The Prose of Hazlitt and Lamb

The account given of Lamb's friends,—of those whom he endeavoured to love because he admired them, or to esteem intellectually because he loved them personally,—is too much coloured for general acquiescence by Sergeant (since Mr. Justice) Talfourd's own early prepossessions. It is natural that an intellectual man like the Sergeant, personally made known in youth to people whom from childhood he had regarded as powers in the ideal world, and in some instances as representing the eternities of human speculation, since their names had perhaps dawned upon his mind in concurrence with the very earliest suggestion of topics which they had treated, should overrate their intrinsic grandeur. Hazlitt accordingly is styled 'the great thinker.' But, had he even been such potentially, there was an absolute bar to his achievement of that station in act and consummation. No man *can* be a great thinker in our days upon large and elaborate questions without being also a great student. To think profoundly, it is indispensable that a man should have read down to his own starting-point, and have read as a collating student to the particular stage at which he himself takes up the subject. At this moment, for instance, how could Geology be treated otherwise than childishly by one who should rely upon the encyclopædias of 1800? or Comparative Physiology by the most ingenious of men unacquainted with Marshall Hall and with the apocalyptic glimpses of secrets unfolding under the hands of Professor Owen? In such a condition of undisciplined thinking, the ablest man thinks to no purpose. He lingers upon parts of the inquiry that have lost the importance which once they had under imperfect charts of the subject; he wastes his strength upon problems that have become obsolete; he loses his way in paths that are not in the line of direction upon which the improved speculation is moving; or he gives narrow conjectural solutions of difficulties that have long since received sure and comprehensive ones. It is as if a man should in these days attempt to colonize, and yet, through inertia or through ignorance, should leave behind him all modern resources of chemistry, or chemical agriculture, or of steam-power. Hazlitt had read nothing. Unacquainted with Grecian philosophy, with Scholastic philosophy, and with the recomposition of these philosophies in the looms of Germany during the last seventy and odd years, trusting merely to the untrained instincts of keen motherwit—whence should Hazlitt have had the materials for great thinking? It is through the collation of many abortive voyages to polar regions that a man gains his first chance of entering the polar basin, or of running ahead on the true line of approach to it. The very reason for Hazlitt's defect in eloquence as a lecturer is sufficient also as a reason why he could not have been a comprehensive thinker. 'He was not eloquent,' says the Sergeant, 'in the true sense of the term.' But why? Because it seems 'his thoughts were too weighty to be moved along by the shallow stream of feeling which an evening's excitement can rouse,'—an explanation which leaves us in doubt whether Hazlitt forfeited his chance of eloquence by accommodating himself to this evening's excitement, or by gloomily resisting it. Our own explanation is different. Hazlitt was not eloquent, because he was discontinuous. No man can be eloquent whose thoughts are abrupt, insulated, capricious, and (to borrow an impressive word from Coleridge) non-sequacious. Eloquence resides not in separate or fractional ideas, but in the relations of manifold ideas, and in the mode of their evolution from each other. It is not indeed enough that the ideas should be many, and their relations coherent; the main condition lies in the *key* of the evolution, in the *law* of the succession. The elements are nothing without the atmosphere that moulds, and the dynamic forces that combine. Now Hazlitt's brilliancy is seen chiefly in separate splinterings of phrase or image which throw upon the eye a vitreous scintillation for a moment, but spread no deep suffusions of colour, and distribute no masses of mighty shadow. A flash, a solitary flash, and all is gone. Rhetoric, according to its quality, stands in many degrees of relation to the permanencies of truth; and all rhetoric, like all flesh, is partly unreal, and the glory of both is fleeting. Even the mighty rhetoric of Sir Thomas Browne, or Jeremy Taylor, to whom only it has been granted to open the trumpet-stop on that great organ of passion, oftentimes leaves behind it the sense of sadness which belongs to beautiful apparitions starting out of darkness upon the morbid eye, only to be reclaimed by darkness in the instant of their birth, or which belongs to pageantries in the clouds. But, if all rhetoric is a mode of pyrotechny, and all pyrotechnics are by necessity fugitive, yet even in these frail pomps there are many degrees of frailty. Some fireworks require an hour's duration for the expansion of their glory; others, as if formed from fulminating powder, expire in the very act of birth. Precisely on that scale of duration and of power stand the glitterings of rhetoric that are not worked into the texture, but washed on from the outside. Hazlitt's thoughts were of the same fractured and discontinuous order as his illustrative images—seldom or never self-diffusive; and *that* is a sufficient argument that he had never cultivated philosophic thinking.

Not, however, to conceal any part of the truth, we are bound to acknowledge that Lamb thought otherwise on this point, manifesting what seemed to us an extravagant admiration of Hazlitt, and perhaps even in part for that very glitter which we are denouncing—at least he did so in conversation with ourselves. But, on the other hand, as this conversation travelled a little into the tone of a disputation, and *our* frost on this point might seem to justify some undue fervour by way of balance, it is very possible that Lamb did not speak his absolute and most dispassionate judgment. And yet again, if he *did*, may we, with all reverence for Lamb's exquisite genius, have permission to say that his own constitution of intellect sinned by this very habit of discontinuity. It was a habit of mind not unlikely to be cherished by his habits of life. Amongst these habits was the excess of his social kindness. He scorned so much to deny his company and his redundant hospitality to any man who manifested a wish for either by calling upon him, that he almost seemed to think it a criminality in himself if, by accident, he really *was* from home on your visit, rather than by possibility a negligence in you, that had not forewarned him of your intention. What was the consequence? All his life, from this and other causes, he must have read in the spirit of one liable to sudden interruption; like a dragoon, in fact, reading with one foot in the stirrup, when expecting momentarily a summons to mount for action. In such situations, reading by snatches, and by intervals of precarious leisure, people form inevitably the habit of seeking and unduly valuing condensations of the meaning, where in reality the truth suffers by this short-hand exhibition; or else they demand too vivid illustrations of the meaning. Lord Chesterfield, so brilliant a man by nature, already therefore making a morbid estimate of brilliancy, and so hurried throughout his life as a public man, read under this double coercion for craving instantaneous effects. At one period, his only time for reading was in the morning, whilst under the hands of his hairdresser,—who, in that age, or even thirty years later, was an artist that, more even than a tailor, ministered to respectability. Compelled to take the hastiest of flying shots at his author, naturally Lord Chesterfield demanded a very conspicuous mark to fire at. But the author could not, in so brief a space, be always sure to crowd any very prominent objects on the eye, unless by being audaciously oracular and peremptory as regarded the sentiment, or flashy in excess as regarded its expression. 'Come now, my friend,' was Lord Chesterfield's morning adjuration to his author; 'come now, cut it short—don't prose—don't hum and haw.' The author had doubtless no ambition to enter his name on the honourable and ancient roll of gentlemen-prosers; probably he conceived himself not at all tainted with the asthmatic infirmity of humming and hawing; but, as to 'cutting it short,' how could he be sure of meeting his lordship's expectations in that point, unless by dismissing all the limitations that might be requisite to fit the idea for use, or the adjuncts that might be requisite to integrate its truth, or the final consequences that might involve some deep *arrière pensée*? To be lawfully and usefully brilliant, after this rapid fashion, a man must come forward as a refresher of old truths, where *his* suppressions are supplied by the reader's memory; not as an expounder of new truths, where oftentimes a dislocated fraction of the true is not less dangerous than the false itself.

To read therefore habitually by hurried instalments has this bad tendency—that it is likely to found a taste for modes of composition too artificially irritating, and to disturb the equilibrium of the judgment in relation to the colourings of style. Lamb, however, whose constitution of mind was even ideally sound in reference to the natural, the simple, the genuine, might seem of all men least liable to a taint in this direction. And undoubtedly he *was* so as regarded those modes of beauty which nature had specially qualified him for apprehending. Else, and in relation to other modes of beauty, where his sense of the true, and of its distinction from the spurious, had been an acquired sense, it is impossible for us to hide from ourselves that, not through habits only, not through stress of injurious accidents only, but by original structure and temperament of mind, Lamb had a bias towards those very defects on which rested the startling characteristics of style which we have been noticing. He himself, we fear, not bribed by indulgent feelings to another, not moved by friendship, but by native tendency, shrank from the continuous, from the sustained, from the elaborate.

The elaborate, indeed, without which much truth and beauty must perish in germ, was by name the object of his invectives. The instances are many, in his own beautiful essays, where he literally collapses, literally sinks away from openings suddenly offering themselves to flights of pathos or solemnity in direct prosecution of his own theme. On any such summons, where an ascending impulse and an untired pinion were required, he *refuses* himself (to use military language) invariably. The least observing reader of *Elia* cannot have failed to notice that the most felicitous passages always accomplish their circuit in a few sentences. The gyration within which his sentiment wheels, no matter of what kind it may be, is always the shortest possible. It does not prolong itself—it does not repeat itself—it does not propagate itself. But, in fact, other features in Lamb's mind would have argued this feature by analogy, had we by accident been left unaware of it directly. It is not by chance, or without a deep ground in his nature, *common* to all his qualities, both affirmative and negative, that Lamb had an insensibility to music more absolute than can have been often shared by any human creature, or perhaps than was ever before acknowledged so candidly. The sense of music—as a pleasurable sense, or as any sense at all other than of certain unmeaning and impertinent differences in respect to high and low, sharp or flat—was utterly obliterated, as with a sponge, by nature herself from Lamb's organization. It was a corollary, from the same large *substratum* in his nature, that Lamb had no sense of the rhythmical in prose composition. Rhythmus, or pomp of cadence, or sonorous ascent of clauses, in the structure of sentences, were effects of art as much thrown away upon *him* as the voice of the charmer upon the deaf adder. We ourselves, occupying the very station of polar opposition to that of Lamb,— being as morbidly, perhaps, in the one excess as he in the other,—naturally detected this omission in Lamb's nature at an early stage of our acquaintance. Not the fabled Regulus, with his eyelids torn away, and his uncurtained eyeballs exposed to the noon-tide glare of a Carthaginian sun, could have shrieked with more anguish of recoil from torture than we from certain sentences and periods in which Lamb perceived no fault at all. *Pomp*, in our apprehension, was an idea of two categories: the *pompous* might be spurious, but it might also be genuine. It is well to love the simple—*we* love it; nor is there any opposition at all between *that* and the very glory of pomp. But, as we once put the case to Lamb, if, as a musician, as the leader of a mighty orchestra, you had this theme offered to you—'Belshazzar the King, gave a great feast to a thousand of his lords'—or this, 'And, on a certain day, Marcus Cicero stood up, and in a set speech rendered solemn thanks to Caius Cæsar for Quintus Ligarius pardoned, and for Marcus Marcellus restored'—surely no man would deny that, in such a case, simplicity, though in a passive sense not lawfully absent, must stand aside as totally insufficient for the *positive* part. Simplicity might guide even here, but could not furnish the power; a rudder it might be, but not an oar or a sail. This Lamb was ready to allow; as an intellectual *quiddity*, he recognized pomp in the character of a privileged thing; he was obliged to do so; for take away from great ceremonial festivals, such as the solemn rendering of thanks, the celebration of national anniversaries, the commemoration of public benefactors, &c., the element of pomp, and you take away their very meaning and life. But, whilst allowing a place for it in the rubric of the logician, it is certain that *sensuously* Lamb would not have sympathized with it, nor have *felt* its justification in any concrete instance. We find a difficulty in pursuing this subject without greatly exceeding the just limits. We pause, therefore, and add only this one suggestion as partly explanatory of the case. Lamb had the dramatic intellect and taste, perhaps in perfection; of the epic he had none at all. Here, as happens sometimes to men of genius preternaturally endowed in one direction, he might be considered as almost starved. A favourite of nature, so eminent in some directions, by what right could be complain that her bounties were not indiscriminate? From this defect in his nature it arose that, except by culture and by reflection, Lamb had no genial appreciation of Milton. The solemn planetary wheelings of the *Paradise Lost* were not to his taste. What he *did* comprehend were the motions like those of lightning, the fierce angular coruscations of that wild agency which comes forward so vividly in the sudden περιπέτεια, in the revolutionary catastrophe, and in the tumultuous conflicts, through persons or through situations, of the tragic drama.

There is another vice in Mr. Hazlitt's mode of composition, viz. the habit of trite quotation, too common to have challenged much notice, were it not for these reasons:—1st, That Sergeant Talfourd speaks of it in equivocal terms, as a fault perhaps, but as a 'felicitous fault, 'trailing after it a line of golden associations'; 2dly, Because sometimes it involves a dishonesty. On occasion of No. 1, we must profess our belief that a more ample explanation from the Sergeant would have left him in substantial harmony with ourselves. We cannot conceive the author of *Ion*, and the friend of Wordsworth, seriously to countenance that paralytic 'mouth-diarrhœa' (to borrow a phrase of Coleridge's)—that *fluxe de bouche* (to borrow an earlier phrase of Archbishop Huet's)—which places the reader at the mercy of a man's tritest remembrances from his most school-boy reading. To have the verbal memory infested with tags of verse and 'cues' of rhyme is in itself an infirmity as vulgar and as morbid as the stable-boy's habit of whistling slang airs upon the mere mechanical excitement of a bar or two whistled by some other blockhead in some other stable. The very stage has grown weary of ridiculing a folly that, having been long since expelled from decent society, has taken refuge amongst the most imbecile of authors. Was Mr. Hazlitt, then, of that class? No; he was a man of splendid talents, and of capacity for greater things than he ever attempted, though without known pretensions of the philosophic kind ascribed to him by the Sergeant. Meantime the reason for resisting the example and practice of Hazlitt lies in this—that essentially it is at war with sincerity, the foundation of all good writing, to express one's own thoughts by another man's words. This dilemma arises. The thought is, or it is not, worthy of that emphasis, which belongs to a metrical expression of it. If it is *not*, then we shall be guilty of a mere folly in pushing into strong relief that which confessedly cannot support it. If it *is*, then how incredible that a thought strongly conceived, and bearing upon it the impress of one's own individuality, should naturally, and without dissimulation or falsehood, bend to another man's expression of it! Simply to back one's own view by similar view derived from another may be useful; a quotation that repeats one's own sentiment, but in a varied form, has the grace which belongs to the *idem in alio*, the same radical idea expressed with a difference—similarity in dissimilarity; but to throw one's own thoughts, matter and form, through alien organs so absolutely as to make another man one's interpreter for evil and good, is either to confess a singular laxity of thinking that can so flexibly adapt itself to any casual form of words, or else to confess that sort of carelessness about the expression which draws its real origin from a sense of indifference about the things to be expressed. Utterly at war this distressing practice is with all simplicity and earnestness of writing; it argues a state of indolent ease inconsistent with the pressure and coercion of strong fermenting thoughts before we can be at leisure for idle or chance quotations. But, lastly, in reference to No. 2, we must add that the practice is sometimes dishonest. It 'trails after it a line of golden associations.' Yes, and the burglar, who leaves an army-tailor's after a midnight visit, trails after him perhaps a long roll of gold bullion epaulettes which may look pretty by lamp-light. But *that*, in the present condition of moral philosophy amongst the police, is accounted robbery; and to benefit too much by quotations is little less. At this moment we have in our eye a biographical work, at one time not without celebrity, which is one continued *cento* of splendid passages from other people. The natural effect from so much fine writing is that the reader rises with the impression of having been engaged upon a most eloquent work. Meantime the whole is a series of mosaics, a tessellation made up from borrowed fragments; and, first when the reader's attention is expressly directed upon the fact, he becomes aware that the nominal author has contributed nothing more to the book than a few passages of transition or brief clauses of connexion.

'Charles Lamb', *North British Review*, Nov. 1848; Masson V.

The Literature of Knowledge and the Literature of Power

Books, therefore, do not suggest an idea coextensive and interchangeable with the idea of Literature; since much literature, scenic, forensic, or didactic (as from lecturers and public orators), may never come into books, and much that *does* come into books may connect itself with no literary interest.[1] But a far

[1] What are called *The Blue Books*,—by which title are understood the folio Reports issued every session of Parliament by committees of the two Houses, and

more important correction, applicable to the common vague idea of literature, is to be sought not so much in a better definition of literature as in a sharper distinction of the two functions which it fulfils. In that great social organ which, collectively, we call literature, there may be distinguished two separate offices that may blend and often *do* so, but capable, severally, of a severe insulation, and naturally fitted for reciprocal repulsion. There is, first, the literature of *knowledge*; and, secondly, the literature of *power*. The function of the first is—to *teach*; the function of the second is—to *move*: the first is a rudder; the second, an oar or a sail. The first speaks to the *mere* discursive understanding; the second speaks ultimately, it may happen, to the higher understanding or reason, but always *through* affections of pleasure and sympathy. Remotely, it may travel towards an object seated in what Lord Bacon calls *dry* light[1]; but, proximately, it does and must operate,—else it ceases to be a literature of *power*,—on and through that *humid* light which clothes itself in the mists and glittering *iris* of human passions, desires, and genial emotions. Men have so little reflected on the higher functions of literature as to find it a paradox if one should describe it as a mean or subordinate purpose of books to give information. But this is a paradox only in the sense which makes it honourable to be paradoxical. Whenever we talk in ordinary language of seeking information or gaining knowledge, we understand the words as connected with something of absolute novelty. But it is the grandeur of all truth which *can* occupy a very high place in human interests that it is never absolutely novel to the meanest of minds: it exists eternally by way of germ or latent principle in the lowest as in the highest, needing to be developed, but never to be planted. To be capable of transplantation is the immediate criterion of a truth that ranges on a lower scale. Besides which, there is a rarer thing than truth,—namely, *power*, or deep sympathy with truth. What is the effect, for instance, upon society, of children? By the pity, by the tenderness, and by the peculiar modes of admiration, which connect themselves with the helplessness, with the innocence, and with the simplicity of children, not only are the primal affections strengthened and continually renewed, but the qualities which are dearest in the sight of heaven, —the frailty, for instance, which appeals to forbearance, the innocence which symbolises the heavenly, and the simplicity which is most alien from the world-

[1] *Bacon's Essay on Friendship.*

stitched into blue covers,—though often sneered at by the ignorant as so much waste paper, will be acknowledged gratefully by those who have used them diligently as the main wellheads of all accurate information as to the Great Britain of this day. As an immense depository of faithful (*and not superannuated*) statistics, they are indispensable to the honest student. But no man would therefore class the *Blue Books* as literature.

ly,—are kept up in perpetual remembrance, and their ideals are continually refreshed. A purpose of the same nature is answered by the higher literature, viz., the literature of power. What do you learn from 'Paradise Lost'? Nothing at all. What do you learn from a cookery-book? Something new, something that you did not know before, in every paragraph. But would you therefore put the wretched cookery-book on a higher level of estimation than the divine poem? What you owe to Milton is not any knowledge, of which a million separate items are still but a million of advancing steps on the same earthly level; what you owe is *power*,—that is, exercise and expansion to your own latent capacity of sympathy with the infinite, where every pulse and each separate influx is a step upwards, a step ascending as upon a Jacob's ladder from earth to mysterious altitudes above the earth. *All* the steps of knowledge, from first to last, carry you further on the same plane, but could never raise you one foot above your ancient level of earth: whereas the very *first* step in power is a flight—is an ascending movement into another element where earth is forgotten.

Were it not that human sensibilities are ventilated and continually called out into exercise by the great phenomena of infancy, or of real life as it moves through chance and change, or of literature as it recombines these elements in the mimicries of poetry, romance, &c., it is certain that, like any animal power or muscular energy falling into disuse, all such sensibilities would gradually droop and dwindle. It is in relation to these great *moral* capacities of man that the literature of power, as contradistinguished from that of knowledge, lives and has its field of action. It is concerned with what is highest in man; for the Scriptures themselves never condescended to deal by suggestion or co-operation with the mere discursive understanding: when speaking of man in his intellectual capacity, the Scriptures speak not of the understanding, but of '*the understanding heart*,'—making the heart, *i.e.* the great *intuitive* (or non-discursive) organ, to be the interchangeable formula for man in his highest state of capacity for the infinite. Tragedy, romance, fairy tale, or epopee, all alike restore to man's mind the ideals of justice, of hope, of truth, of mercy, of retribution, which else (left to the support of daily life in its realities) would languish for want of sufficient illustration. What is meant, for instance, by *poetic justice*?—It does not mean a justice that differs by its object from the ordinary justice of human jurisprudence; for then it must be confessedly a very bad kind of justice; but it means a justice that differs from common forensic justice by the degree in which it *attains* its object, a justice that is more omnipotent over its own ends, as dealing—not with the refractory elements of earthly life, but with the elements of its own creation, and with materials flexible to its own purest preconceptions. It is certain that, were it not for the Literature of Power, these ideals would often remain amongst us as mere arid notional forms; whereas, by the creative forces of man put forth in literature, they gain a vernal life of restoration, and germinate into vital activities. The commonest novel, by moving in alliance with human fears and hopes, with human instincts of wrong and right, sustains and quickens those affections. Calling them into action, it rescues them from torpor. And hence the pre-eminency over all authors that merely *teach* of the meanest that *moves*, or that teaches, if at all, indirectly *by* moving. The very highest work that has ever existed in the Literature of Knowledge is but a *provisional* work: a book upon trial and sufferance, and *quamdiu bene se gesserit*. Let its teaching be even partially revised, let it be but expanded,—nay, even let its teaching be but placed in a better order,—and instantly it is superseded. Whereas the feeblest works in the Literature of Power, surviving at all, survive as finished and unalterable amongst men. For instance, the *Principia* of Sir Isaac Newton was a book *militant* on earth from the first. In all stages of its progress it would have to fight for its existence: 1st, as regards absolute truth; 2dly, when that combat was over, as regards its form or mode of presenting the truth. And as soon as a La Place, or anybody else, builds higher upon the foundations laid by this book, effectually he throws it out of the sunshine into decay and darkness; by weapons won from this book he superannuates and destroys this book, so that soon the name of Newton remains as a mere *nominis umbra*, but his book, as a living power, has transmigrated into other forms. Now, on the contrary, the Iliad, the Prometheus of Æschylus, the Othello or King Lear, the Hamlet or Macbeth, and the Paradise Lost, are not militant, but triumphant for ever as long as the languages exist in which they speak or can be taught to speak. They never *can* transmigrate into new incarnations. To reproduce *these* in new forms, or variation, even if in some things they should be improved, would be to plagiarise. A good steam-engine is properly superseded by a better. But one lovely pastoral valley is not superseded by another, nor a statue of Praxiteles by a statue of Michael Angelo. These things are separated not by imparity, but by disparity. They are not thought of as unequal under the same standard, but as different in *kind*, and, if otherwise equal, as equal under a different standard. Human works of immortal beauty and works of nature in one respect stand on the same footing: they never absolutely repeat each other, never approach so near as not to differ; and they differ not as better and worse, or simply by more and less: they differ by undecipherable and incommunicable differences, that cannot be caught by mimicries, that cannot be reflected in the mirror of copies, that cannot become ponderable in the scales of vulgar comparison.

Applying these principles to Pope as a representative of fine literature in general, we would wish to remark the claim which he has, or which any equal writer has, to the attention and jealous winnowing of those critics in particular who watch over public morals. Clergymen, and all organs of public criticism put in motion by clergymen, are more especially concerned in the just appreciation of such writers, if the two canons are remembered which we have endeavoured to illustrate, viz. that all works in this class, as opposed to those in the literature of knowledge, 1st, work by far deeper agencies, and, 2dly, are more permanent; in the strictest sense they are κτήματα ἐς ἀεɩ: and what evil they do, or what good they do, is commensurate with the national language, sometimes long after the nation has departed. At this hour, five hundred years since their creation, the tales of Chaucer never equalled on this earth for their tenderness, and for life of picturesqueness, are read familiarly by many in the charming language of their natal day, and by others in the modernisations of Dryden, of Pope, and Wordsworth. At this hour, one thousand eight hundred years since their creation, the Pagan tales of Ovid, never equalled on this earth for the gaiety of their movement and the capricious graces of their narrative, are read by all Christendom. This man's people and their monuments are dust; but *he* is alive: he has survived them, as he told us that he had it in his commission to do, by a thousand years; 'and *shall* a thousand more.'

All the literature of knowledge builds only ground-nests, that are swept away by floods, or confounded by the plough; but the literature of power builds nests in aerial altitudes of temples sacred from violation, or of forests inaccessible to fraud. *This* is a great prerogative of the *power* literature; and it is a greater which lies in the mode of its influence. The *knowledge* literature, like the fashion of this world, passeth away. An Encyclopædia is its abstract; and, in this respect, it may be taken for its speaking symbol—that before one generation has passed an Encyclopædia is superannuated; for it speaks through the dead memory and unimpassioned understanding, which have not the repose of higher faculties, but are continually enlarging and varying their phylacteries. But all literature properly so called—literature κατ᾽ ἐξοχὴν,—for the very same reason that it is so much more durable than the literature of knowledge, is (and by the very same proportion it is) more intense and electrically searching in its impressions. The directions in which the tragedy of this planet has trained our human feelings to play, and the combinations into which the poetry of this planet has thrown our human passions of love and hatred, of admiration and contempt, exercise a power for bad or good over human life that cannot be contemplated, when stretching through many generations, without a sentiment allied to awe.[1] And of this let every one be assured—that he owes to the

---

[1] The reason why the broad distinctions between the two literatures of power and knowledge so little fix the attention lies in the fact that a vast proportion of books,—history, biography, travels, miscellaneous essays, &c.,—lying in a middle zone, confound these distinctions by interblending them. All that we call

impassioned books which he has read many a thousand more of emotions than he can consciously trace back to them. Dim by their origination, these emotions yet arise in him, and mould him through life, like forgotten incidents of his childhood.

'The Poetry of Pope', *North British Review*, Aug. 1848; Masson XI.

Letter to a Young Man whose Education has been Neglected

Here, however, to prevent all mistakes, let me establish one necessary distinction. The word *literature* is a perpetual source of confusion, because it is used in two senses, and those senses liable to be confounded with each other. In a philosophical use of the word, Literature is the direct and adequate antithesis of Books of Knowledge. But, in a popular use, it is a mere term of convenience for expressing inclusively the total books of a language. In this latter sense, a dictionary, a grammar, a spelling-book, an almanac, a pharmacopœia, a Parliamentary report, a system of farriery, a treatise on billiards, the Court Calendar, &c., belong to the literature. But, in the philosophical sense, not only would it be ludicrous to reckon these as part of the literature, but even books of much higher pretensions must be excluded—as, for instance, books of voyages and travels, and generally all books in which the matter to be communicated is paramount to the manner or form of its communication ('ornari res ipsa negat, contenta doceri'). It is difficult to construct the idea of 'literature' with severe accuracy; for it is a fine art—the supreme fine art, and liable to the difficulties which attend such a subtle notion; in fact, a severe construction of the idea must be the *result* of a philosophical investigation into this subject, and cannot precede it. But, for the sake of obtaining some expression for literature that may answer our present purpose, let us throw the question into another form. I have said that the antithesis of Literature is Books of Knowledge. Now, what is that antithesis to *knowledge* which is here implicitly latent in the word literature? The vulgar antithesis is *pleasure* ('aut prodesse volunt, aut delectare poetæ').

'amusement' or 'entertainment' is a diluted form of the power belonging to passion, and also a mixed form; and, where threads of direct *instruction* intermingle in the texture with these threads of *power*, this absorption of the duality into one representative *nuance* neutralises the separate perception of either. Fused into a *tertium quid*, or neutral state, they disappear to the popular eye as the repelling forces, which, in fact, they are.

Books, we are told, propose to *instruct* or to *amuse*. Indeed! However, not to spend any words upon it, I suppose you will admit that this wretched antithesis will be of no service to us. And, by the way, let me remark to you, in this, as in other cases, how men by their own errors of understanding, by feeble thinking, and inadequate distinctions, forge chains of meanness and servility for themselves. For, this miserable alternative being once admitted, observe what follows. In which class of books does the Paradise Lost stand? Among those which instruct, or those which *amuse*? Now, if a man answers among those which instruct, he lies; for there is no instruction in it, nor could be in any great poem, according to the meaning which the word must bear in this distinction, unless it is meant that it should involve its own antithesis. But, if he says, 'No; amongst those which amuse,' then what a beast must he be to degrade, and in this way, what has done the most of any human work to raise and dignify human nature. But the truth is, you see that the idiot does not wish to degrade it; on the contrary, he would willingly tell a lie in its favour, if that would be admitted; but such is the miserable state of slavery to which he has reduced himself by his own puny distinction; for, as soon as he hops out of one of his little cells, he is under a necessity of hopping into the other. The true antithesis[1] to knowledge, in this case, is not *pleasure*, but *power*. All that is literature seeks to communicate power; all that is not literature, to communicate knowledge. Now, if it be asked what is meant by communicating power, I, in my turn, would ask by what name a man would designate the case in which I should be made to feel vividly, and with a vital consciousness, emotions which ordinary life rarely or never supplies occasions for exciting, and which had previously lain unawakened, and hardly within the dawn of consciousness—as myriads of modes of feeling are at

---

[1] For which distinction, as for most of the sound criticism on poetry, or any subject connected with it that I have ever met with, I must acknowledge my obligations to many years' conversation with Mr. Wordsworth. Upon this occasion it may be useful to notice that there is a rhetorical use of the word 'power,' very different from the analytic one here introduced, which, also, is due originally to Mr. Wordsworth, and will be found in no book before 1798; this is now become a regular slang term in London conversation. In reference to which, it is worth notice that a critic, speaking of the late Mr. Shelley, a year or two ago, in the most popular literary journal of the day, said 'It is alleged that there is power in Mr. Shelley's poetry; now, there can be no power shown in poetry, except by writing good poems' (or words to that effect). Waiving, however, the question of Mr. Shelley's merits, so far is this remark from being true that the word was originally introduced expressly to provide for the case where, though the poem was *not* good, from defect in the *composition*, or from other causes, the stamina and *matériel* of good poetry, as fine thinking and passionate conceptions, could not be denied to exist.

this moment in every human mind for want of a poet to organize them? I say, when these inert and sleeping forms *are* organized, when these possibilities *are* actualized, is this conscious and living possession of mine *power*, or what is it?

When, in King Lear, the height, and depth, and breadth, of human passion is revealed to us, and, for the purpose of a sublime antagonism, is revealed in the weakness of an old man's nature, and in one night two worlds of storm are brought face to face—the human world, and the world of physical nature—mirrors of each other, semichoral antiphonies, strophe and antistrophe heaving with rival convulsions, and with the double darkness of night and madness,—when I am thus suddenly startled into a feeling of the infinity of the world within me, is this power, or what may I call it? Space, again, what is it in most men's minds? The lifeless form of the world without us, a postulate of the geometrician, with no more vitality or real existence to their feelings than the square root of two. But, if Milton has been able to *inform* this empty theatre, peopling it with Titanic shadows, forms that sat at the eldest counsels of the infant world, chaos and original night,—

> 'Ghostly shapes,
> To meet at noontide, Fear and trembling Hope,
> Death the Skeleton,
> And Time the Shadow,'—

so that, from being a thing to inscribe with diagrams, it has become under his hands a vital agent on the human mind,—I presume that I may justly express the tendency of the Paradise Lost by saying that it communicates power; a pretension far above all communication of knowledge. Henceforth, therefore, I shall use the antithesis power and knowledge as the most philosophical expression for literature (that is, Literæ Humaniores) and anti-literature (that is, Literæ didacticæ—Παιδεῖα).

London Magazine, 1823; Masson X.

Style

If you could look anywhere with a right to expect continual illustrations of what is good in the manifold qualities of style, it should reasonably be amongst our professional authors; but, as a body, they are distinguished by the most absolute carelessness in this respect. Whether in the choice of words and idioms, or in the construction of their sentences, it is not possible to conceive the principle of lazy indifference carried to a more revolting extremity. Proof lies before you, spread out upon every page, that no excess of awkwardness, or of inelegance, or of unrhythmical cadence, is so rated in the tariff of faults as to balance in the writer's estimate the trouble of remoulding a clause, of interpolating a phrase, or even of striking the pen through a superfluous word. In our own experience it has happened that we have known an author so laudably fastidious in this subtle art as to have recast one chapter of a series no less than seventeen times[1]: so difficult was the ideal or model of excellence which he kept before his mind; so indefatigable was his labour for mounting to the level of that ideal. Whereas, on the other hand, with regard to a large majority of the writers now carrying forward the literature of the country from the last generation to the next, the evidence is perpetual not so much that they rest satisfied with their own random preconceptions of each clause or sentence as that they never trouble themselves to form any such preconceptions. Whatever words tumble out under the blindest accidents of the moment, those are the words retained; whatever sweep is impressed by chance upon the motion of a period, that is the arrangement ratified. To fancy that men thus determinately careless as to the grosser elements of style would pause to survey distant proportions, or to adjust any more delicate symmetries of good composition, would be visionary. As to the links of connexion, the transitions, and the many other functions of logic in good writings, things are come to such a pass that what was held true of Rome in two separate ages by two great rhetoricians, and of Constantinople in an age long posterior, may now be affirmed of England: the idiom of our language, the mother tongue, survives only amongst our women and children; not, Heaven knows, amongst our women who write books—they are often painfully conspicuous for all that disfigures authorship—but amongst well-educated women not professionally given to literature. . . .

So far as concerns idiomatic English, we are satisfied, from the many beautiful female letters which we have heard upon chance occasions from every quarter of the empire, that they, the educated women of Great Britain—above all, the interesting class of women unmarried upon scruples of sexual honour—and also (as in Constantinople of old) the nurseries of Great Britain,—are the true and best depositaries of the old mother idiom. But we must not forget that, though this is another term for what is good in English when we are talking of a human and a popular interest, there is a separate use of the language, as in the higher forms of history or philosophy, which ought *not* to be idiomatic. As respects that which *is*, it is remarkable that the same orders cling to the ancient purity of diction amongst ourselves who did so in Pagan Rome: viz. *women*, for the reasons just noticed, *and people of rank*. So much has this been the tendency in

---

[1] Gibbon. The first chapter of *The Decline and Fall.*—B.D.

England that we know a person of great powers, but who has in all things a one-sided taste, and is so much a lover of idiomatic English as to endure none else, who professes to read no writer since Lord Chesterfield. It is certain that this accomplished nobleman, who has been most unjustly treated from his unfortunate collision with a national favourite, and in part also from the laxity of his moral principles,—where, however, he spoke worse than he thought— wrote with the ease and careless grace of a high-bred gentleman. But his style is not peculiar: it has always been the style of his order. After making the proper allowance for the continual new infusions into our peerage from the bookish class of lawyers, and for some modifications derived from the learned class of spiritual peers, the tone of Lord Chesterfield has always been the tone of our old aristocracy,—a tone of elegance and propriety, above all things free from the stiffness of pedantry or academic rigour, and obeying Cæsar's rule of shunning *tanquam scopulum* any *insolens verbum*. It is, indeed, through this channel that the solicitudes of our British nobility have always flowed; other qualities might come and go according to the temperament of the individual; but what in all generations constituted an object of horror for that class was bookish precision and professional peculiarity. From the free popular form of our great public schools, to which nine out of ten amongst our old nobility resorted, it happened unavoidably that they were not equally clear of popular vulgarities; indeed, from another cause, *that* could not have been avoided: for it is remarkable that a connexion, as close as through an umbilical cord, has always been maintained between the very highest orders of our aristocracy and the lowest of our demo- cracy, by means of nurses. The nurses and immediate personal attendants of all classes come from the same source, most commonly from the peasantry of the land; they import into all families alike, into the highest and lowest, the coarsest expressions from the vernacular language of anger and contempt. Whence, for example, it was that about five or six years ago, when a new novel circulated in London, with a private understanding that it was a juvenile effort from two very young ladies, daughters of a ducal house, nobody who reflected at all could feel much surprise that one of the characters should express her self- esteem by the popular phrase that she did not 'think small beer of herself.' Naturally, papa, the duke, had not so much modified the diction of the two young ladies as Nurse Bridget. Equally in its faults and its merits, the language of high life has always tended to simplicity and the vernacular ideal, recoiling from every mode of bookishness.

Blackwood's Magazine, July 1840; Masson X.

Didactic Poetry

What *is* didactic poetry? What does 'didactic' mean when applied as a distinguishing epithet to such an idea as a poem? The predicate destroys the subject: it is a case of what logicians call *contradictio in adjecto*—the unsaying by means of an attribute the very thing which is the subject of that attribute you have just affirmed. No poetry can have the function of teaching. It is impossible that a variety of species should contradict the very purpose which contradistinguishes its *genus*. The several species differ partially, but not by the whole idea which differentiates their class. Poetry, or any one of the fine arts (all of which alike speak through the genial nature of man and his excited sensibilities), can teach only as nature teaches, as forests teach, as the sea teaches, as infancy teaches,— viz. by deep impulse, by hieroglyphic suggestion. Their teaching is not direct or explicit, but lurking, implicit, masked in deep incarnations. To teach formally, and professedly is to abandon the very differential character and principle of poetry. If poetry could condescend to teach anything, it would be truths moral or religious. But even these it can utter only through symbols and actions. The great moral, for instance, the last result, of the Paradise Lost is once formally announced,—viz. *to justify the ways of God to man*; but it teaches itself only by diffusing its lesson through the entire poem in the total succession of events and purposes: and even this succession teaches it only when the whole is gathered into unity by a reflex act of meditation, just as the pulsation of the physical heart can exist only when all the parts in an animal system are locked into one organisation.

To address the *insulated* understanding is to lay aside the Prospero's robe of poetry. The objection, therefore, to didactic poetry, as vulgarly understood, would be fatal even if there were none but this logical objection derived from its definition. To be in self-contradiction is, for any idea whatever, sufficiently to destroy itself. But it betrays a more obvious and practical contradiction when a little searched. If the true purpose of a man's writing a didactic poem were to teach, by what suggestion of idiocy should he choose to begin by putting on fetters? wherefore should the simple man volunteer to handcuff and manacle himself, were it only by the encumbrances of metre, and perhaps of rhyme? But these he will find the very least of his encumbrances. A far greater exists in the sheer necessity of omitting in any poem a vast variety of details, and even capital sections of the subject, unless they will bend to purposes of ornament. Now this collision between two purposes,—the purpose of use in mere teaching, and the purpose of poetic delight,—shows, by the uniformity of its solution, which of the two is the true purpose, and which the merely ostensible purpose. Had the true purpose been instruction, the moment that this was found incompatible with a poetic treatment, as soon as it was seen that the sound education of the reader-pupil could not make way without loitering to gather poetic flowers, the stern cry of 'duty' would oblige the poet to remember that he had dedicated himself to a didactic mission, and that he differed from other poets, as a monk from other men, by his vows of self-surrender to harsh ascetic functions. But, on the contrary, in the very teeth of this rule, wherever such a collision does really take place, and one or other of the supposed objects must give way, it is always the vulgar object of *teaching* (the pedagogue's object) which goes to the rear, whilst the higher object of poetic emotion moves on triumphantly. In reality not one didactic poet has ever yet attempted to use any parts or processes of the particular art which he made his theme, unless in so far as they seemed susceptible of poetic treatment, and only *because* they seemed so. Look at the poem of *Cyder* by Philips, of the *Fleece* by Dyer, or (which is a still weightier example) at the *Georgics* of Virgil,—does any of these poets show the least anxiety for the correctness of your principles, or the delicacy of your manipulations, in the worshipful arts they affect to teach? No; but they pursue these arts through every stage that offers any attractions of beauty. And, in the very teeth of all anxiety for teaching, if there existed traditionally any very absurd way of doing a thing which happened to be eminently picturesque, and if, opposed to this, there were some improved mode that had recommended itself to poetic hatred by being dirty and ugly, the poet (if a good one) would pretend never to have heard of this disagreeable improvement. Or, if obliged, by some rival poet, not absolutely to ignore it, he would allow that such a thing could be done, but hint that it was hateful to the Muses or Graces, and very likely to breed a pestilence.

This subordination of the properly didactic function to the poetic,—which leaves the old essential distinction of poetry (viz. its sympathy with the genial motions of man's heart) to override all accidents of special variation, and shows that the essence of poetry never *can* be set aside by its casual modifications,— will be compromised by some loose thinkers, under the idea that in didactic poetry the element of instruction is, in fact, one element, though subordinate and secondary. Not at all. What we are denying is that the element of instruction enters *at all* into didactic poetry. The subject of the Georgics, for instance, is Rural Economy as practised by Italian farmers; but Virgil not only *omits* altogether innumerable points of instruction insisted on as articles of religious necessity by Varro, Cato, Columella, &c., but, even as to those instructions which he *does* communicate, he is careless whether they are made technically intelligible or not. He takes very little pains to keep you from capital mistakes in *practising* his instructions; but he takes good care that you shall not miss any strong impression for the eye or the heart to which the rural process, or rural scene, may naturally lead. He pretends to give you a lecture on farming, in order to have an excuse for carrying you all round the beautiful farm. He pretends to show you a good plan for a farm-house, as the readiest means of veiling his impertinence in showing you the farmer's wife and her rosy children. It is an excellent plea for getting a peep at the bonny milkmaids to propose an inspection of a model dairy. You pass through the poultry-yard, under whatever pretence, in reality to see the peacock and his harem. And so, on to the very end, the pretended instruction is but in secret the connecting tie which holds together the laughing flowers going off from it to the right and to the left; whilst, if ever at intervals this prosy thread of pure didactics is brought forward more obtrusively, it is so by way of foil, to make more effective upon the eye the prodigality of the floral magnificence.

We affirm, therefore, that the didactic poet is so far from seeking even a secondary or remote object in the particular points of information which he may happen to communicate, that much rather he would prefer the having communicated none at all. We will explain ourselves by means of a little illustration from Pope, which will at the same time furnish us with a miniature type of what we ourselves mean by a didactic poem, both in reference to what it *is* and to what it is *not*. In the Rape of the Lock there is a game of cards played, and played with a brilliancy of effect and felicity of selection, applied to the circumstances, which make it a sort of gem within a gem. This game was not in the first edition of the poem, but was an afterthought of Pope's, laboured therefore with more than usual care. We regret that *ombre*, the game described, is no longer played, so that the entire skill with which the mimic battle is fought cannot be so fully appreciated as in Pope's days. The strategics have partly perished; which really Pope ought not to complain of, since he suffers only as Hannibal, Marius, Sertorius, suffered before him. Enough, however, survives of what will tell its own story. For what is it, let us ask, that a poet has to do in such a case, supposing that he were disposed to weave a didactic poem out of a pack of cards, as Vida has out of the chess-board?[1] In describing any particular game he does not seek to *teach* you that game—he postulates it as *already* known to you; but he relies upon separate resources. 1st, He will revive in the reader's eye, for picturesque effect, the well-known personal distinctions of the several kings, knaves, &c., their appearances and their powers. 2dly, He will choose some game in which he may display a happy selection applied to the chances and turns of fortune, to the manœuvres, to the situations of doubt, of brighten-

[1] Marco Girolamo Vida, of Cremona (1490–1566), author of a Latin poem on the Game of Chess, and of other Latin poems; of one of which, *The Christiad*, Milton says, in his juvenile poem on The Passion,—

'Loud o'er the rest Cremona's trump doth sound.'—M.

ing expectation, of sudden danger, of critical deliverance, or of final defeat. The interest of a war will be rehearsed: *lis est de paupere regno*—that is true; but the depth of the agitation on such occasions, whether at chess, at draughts, or at cards, is not measured of necessity by the grandeur of the stake; he selects, in short, whatever fascinates the eye or agitates the heart by mimicry of life; but, so far from *teaching*, he presupposes the reader already *taught*, in order that he may go along with the movement of the descriptions.

'The Poetry of Pope', *North British Review*, Aug. 1848; Masson XI.

Poetic Diction

One original obstacle to the favourable impression of the Wordsworthian poetry, and an obstacle purely self-created, was his theory of Poetic Diction. The diction itself, without the theory, was of less consequence; for the mass of readers would have been too blind or too careless to notice it. But the preface to the second edition of his Poems (2 vols. 1799-1800) compelled all readers to notice it. Nothing more injudicious was ever done by man. An unpopular truth would, at any rate, have been a bad inauguration for what, on *other* accounts, the author had announced as 'an experiment.' His poetry was already, and confessedly, an experiment as regarded the quality of the subjects selected, and as regarded the mode of treating them. That was surely trial enough for the reader's untrained sensibilities, without the unpopular novelty besides as to the quality of the diction. But, in the meantime, this novelty, besides being unpopular, was also in part false; it was true, and it was *not* true. And it was not true in a double way. Stating broadly, and allowing it to be taken for his meaning, that the diction of ordinary life (in his own words, 'the very language of men') was the proper diction for poetry, the writer meant no such thing; for only a *part* of this diction, according to his own subsequent restriction, was available for such a use. And, secondly, as his own subsequent practice showed, even this part was available only for peculiar classes of poetry. In his own exquisite 'Laodamia,' in his 'Sonnets,' in his 'Excursion,' few are his obligations to the idiomatic language of life, as distinguished from that of books, or of prescriptive usage. Coleridge remarked, justly, that the 'Excursion' bristles beyond most poems with what are called 'dictionary' words,—that is, polysyllabic words of Latin or Greek origin. And so it must ever be in meditative poetry upon solemn philosophic themes. The gamut of ideas needs a corresponding gamut of expressions; the scale of the thinking which ranges through *every* key exacts, for the artist, an unlimited command over the entire scale of the instrument which he employs. Never, in fact, was there a more erroneous direction—one falser in its grounds, or more ruinous in its tendency—than that given by a modern Rector[1] of the Glasgow University to the students—viz. that they should cultivate the Saxon part of our language rather than the Latin part. Nonsense. Both are indispensable; and, speaking generally, without stopping to distinguish as to subjects, both are *equally* indispensable. Pathos, in situations which are homely, or at all connected with domestic affections, naturally moves by Saxon words. Lyrical emotion of every kind, which (to merit the name *lyrical*) must be in the state of flux and reflux, or, generally, of agitation, also requires the Saxon element of our language. And why? Because the Saxon is the aboriginal element,—the basis, and not the superstructure; consequently it comprehends all the ideas which are natural to the heart of man, and to the *elementary* situations of life. And, although the Latin often furnishes us with duplicates of these ideas, yet the Saxon, or monosyllabic part, has the advantage of precedency in our use and knowledge; for it is the language of the NURSERY, whether for rich or poor,—in which great philological academy no toleration is given to words in '*osity*' or '*ation*'. There is, therefore, a great advantage, as regards the consecration to our feelings, settled, by usage and custom, upon the Saxon strands in the mixed yarn of our native tongue. And, universally, this may be remarked—that, wherever the passion of a poem is of that sort which *uses*, *presumes*, or *postulates* the ideas, without seeking to extend them, Saxon will be the 'cocoon' (to speak by the language applied to silkworms) which the poem spins for itself. But, on the other hand, where the motion of the feeling is *by* and *through* the ideas, where (as in religious or meditative poetry—Young's, for instance, or Cowper's) the sentiment creeps and kindles underneath the very tissues of the thinking, there the Latin will predominate; and so much so that, whilst the flesh, the blood, and the muscle, will be often almost exclusively Latin, the articulations or hinges of connexion and transition will be Anglo-Saxon.

But a blunder, more perhaps from thoughtlessness and careless reading than from malice, on the part of the professional critics ought to have roused Wordsworth into a firmer feeling of the entire question. These critics had fancied that, in Wordsworth's estimate, whatsoever was plebeian was also poetically just in diction—not as though the impassioned phrase were sometimes the vernacular phrase, but as though the vernacular phrase were universally the impassioned. They naturally went on to suggest, as a corollary which Wordsworth (as they fancied) could not refuse, that Dryden and Pope must be translated into the flash diction of prisons and the slang of streets before they could be regarded as poetically costumed. Now, so far as these critics were concerned, the answer

---

[1] '*Modern Rector*': viz., Lord Brougham.

would have been simply to say that much in the poets mentioned, but especially of the racy Dryden, actually *is* in that vernacular diction for which Words-worth contended, and, for the other part, which is *not*, frequently it *does* require the very purgation (if *that* were possible) which the critics were presuming to be so absurd. In Pope, and sometimes in Dryden, there is much of the unfeeling and the prescriptive diction which Wordsworth denounced. During the eighty years between 1660 and 1740 grew up that scrofulous taint in our diction which was denounced by Wordsworth as technically received for 'poetic language'; and, if Dryden and Pope were less infected than others, this was merely because their understandings were finer. Much there is in both poets, as regards diction, which *does* require correction, and correction of the kind presumed by the Wordsworth theory. And, if, *so* far, the critics should resist Wordsworth's principle of reform, not he, but they, would have been found the patrons of deformity. This course would soon have turned the tables upon the critics. For the poets, or the class of poets, whom they unwisely selected as models suscept-ible of no correction, happen to be those who chiefly require it. But their foolish selection ought not to have intercepted or clouded the true question when put in another shape, since in this shape it opens into a very troublesome dilemma. Spenser, Shakspere, the Bible of 1611, and Milton—how say you, William Wordsworth—are these sound and true as to diction, or are they not? If you say they *are*, then what is it that you are proposing to change? What room for a revolution? Would you, as Sancho says, have 'better bread than is made of wheat'? But, if you say *No*, they are *not* sound, then, indeed, you open a fear-ful range to your own artillery, but in a war greater than you could, by possibility, have contemplated. In the first case,—that is, if the leading classics of the English literature are, in quality of diction and style, loyal to the canons of sound taste,—then you cut away the *locus standi* for yourself as a reformer: the reformation applies only to secondary and recent abuses. In the second case, if they also are faulty, you undertake an *onus* of hostility so vast that you will be found fighting against stars.

'On Wordsworth's Poetry', *Tait's Magazine*, Sept. 1845; Masson XI.

Johnson on Milton

But in writing *The Lives of the Poet*, one of the Doctor's latest works, he had learned caution. Malice, he found, was not always safe; and it might sometimes be costly. Still, there was plenty of game to be had without too much risk. And the Doctor, prompted by the fiend, resolved to 'take a shy', before parting, at the most consecrated of Milton's creations. It really vexes me to notice this second case at all in a situation where I have left myself so little room for unmasking its hollowness. But a whisper is enough if it reaches a watchful ear. What, then, is the supreme jewel which Milton has bequeathed to us? Nobody can doubt that it is *Paradise Lost.*[1]

Into this great *chef-d'œuvre* of Milton it was no doubt Johnson's secret determination to send a telling shot at parting. He would lodge a little *gage d'amitié*, a farewell pledge of hatred, a trifling token (trifling, but such things are not estimated in money) of his eternal malice. Milton's admirers might divide it among themselves; and, if it should happen to fester and rankle in their hearts, so much the better; they were heartily welcome to the poison: not a jot would he deduct for himself if a thousand times greater. O Sam! kill us not with munificence. But now, as I must close within a minute or so, what *is* that pretty

[1] Not meaning, however, as so many people do, insolently to gainsay the verdict of Milton himself, with whom, for my own part, making the distinctions that *he* would make, I have always coincided. The poet himself is often the best critic on his own works; and in this case Milton expressed with some warmth, and perhaps scorn, his preference of the *Paradise Regained*. Doubtless what disgusted him naturally enough was that too often he found the disparagers of the one Paradise quite as guiltless of all real acquaintance with it as were the *proneurs* of the other. Else the distribution of merits is apparently this: in the later poem the execution is more highly finished; or, at least, partially so. In the elder and larger poem, the scenical opportunities are more colossal and more various. Heaven opening to eject her rebellious children; the unvoyageable depths of ancient Chaos, with its 'anarch old' and its eternal war of wrecks; these traversed by that great leading Angel that drew after him the third part of the heavenly host; earliest Paradise dawning upon the warrior-angel out of this far-distant 'sea without shore' of chaos; the dreadful phantoms of Sin and Death, prompted by secret sympathy, and snuffing the distant scent of mortal 'change on earth,' chasing the steps of their great progenitor and sultan; finally the heart-freezing visions, shown and narrated to Adam, of human misery through vast successions of shadowy generations: all these scenical opportunities offered in the *Paradise Lost* become in the hands of the mighty artist elements of undying grandeur not matched on earth. The compass being so much narrower in the *Paradise Regained*, if no other reason operated, inevitably the splendours are sown more thinly. But the great vision of the temptation, the banquet in the wilderness, the wilderness itself, the terrific pathos of the ruined archangel's speech—'*Tis true I am that spirit unfortunate,* &c. (the effect of which, when connected with the stern unpitying answer, is painfully to shock the reader), all these proclaim the ancient skill and the ancient power. And, as regards the skill naturally brightened by long practice, that succession of great friezes which the archangel unrolls in the pictures of Athens, Rome, and Parthia, besides their native and intrinsic beauty, have an unrivalled beauty of position through the reflex illustration which reciprocally they give and receive.

souvenir of gracious detestation with which our friend took his leave? The
Paradise Lost, said he, in effect, is a wonderful work; wonderful; grand beyond
all estimate; sublime to a fault. But—well, go on; we are all listening. But—I
grieve to say it, wearisome. It creates a world of admiration (*one* world, take
notice); but—oh, that I, senior offshoot from the house of Malagrowthers,
should live to say it!—ten worlds of *ennui*; one world of astonishment; ten
worlds of *tædium vitæ*. Half and half might be tolerated—it is often tolerated by
the bibulous and others; but one against ten? No, no!

This, then, was the farewell blessing which Dr. Johnson bestowed upon the
Paradise Lost! What is my reply? The poem, it seems, is wearisome; Edmund
Waller called it *dull*. A man, it is alleged by Dr. Johnson, opens the volume;
reads a page or two with feelings allied to awe: next he finds himself rather
jaded; then sleepy; naturally shuts up the book; and forgets ever to take it down
again. Now, when any work of human art is impeached as wearisome, the first
reply is—wearisome to *whom*? For it so happens that nothing exists, absolutely
nothing, which is not at some time, and to some person, wearisome or even
potentially disgusting. There is no exception for the works of God. 'Man
delights not me, nor woman either,' is the sigh which breathes from the morbid
misanthropy of the gloomy but philosophic Hamlet. Weariness, moreover, and
even sleepiness, is the natural reaction of awe or of feelings too highly strung;
and this reaction in some degree proves the sincerity of the previous awe. In
cases of that class, where the impressions of sympathetic veneration have been
really unaffected, but carried too far, the mistake is—to have read too much at a
time. But these are exceptional cases: to the great majority of readers the poem
is wearisome through mere vulgarity and helpless imbecility of mind; not from
overstrained excitement, but from pure defect in the *capacity* for excitement.
And a moment's reflection at this point lays bare to us the malignity of Dr.
Johnson. The logic of that malignity is simply this: that he applies to Milton, as
if separately and specially true of *him*, a rule abstracted from human experience
spread over the total field of civilisation. All nations are here on a level. Not a
hundredth part of their populations is capable of any unaffected sympathy with
what is truly great in sculpture, in painting, in music, and by a transcendent
necessity in the supreme of Fine Arts—Poetry. To be popular in any but a meagre
comparative sense as an artist of whatsoever class is to be *confessedly* a condes-
cender to human infirmities. And, as to the test which Dr. Johnson, by implica-
tion, proposes as trying the merits of Milton in his greatest work, viz. the degree
in which it was read, the Doctor knew pretty well, and when by accident he did
not was inexcusable for neglecting to inquire,—that by the same test all the great
classical works of past ages, Pagan or Christian, might be branded with the
mark of suspicion as works that had failed of their paramount purpose, viz. a

deep control over the modes of thinking and feeling in each successive generation. Were it not for the continued succession of academic students having a contingent *mercenary* interest in many of the great authors surviving from the wrecks of time, scarcely one edition of fresh copies would be called for in each period of fifty years. And, as to the arts of sculpture and painting, were the great monuments in the former art, those, I mean, inherited from Greece, such as the groups, &c., scattered through Italian mansions,—the Venus, the Apollo, the Hercules, the Faun, the Gladiator, and the marbles in the British Museum, purchased by the Government from the late Lord Elgin,—stripped of their metropolitan advantages, and left to their own unaided attraction in some provincial town, they would not avail to keep the requisite officers of any establishment for housing them in salt and tobacco. We may judge of this by the records left behind by Benjamin Haydon of the difficulty which *he* found in simply upholding their value as wrecks of the Phidian æra. The same law asserts itself everywhere. What is *ideally* grand lies beyond the region of ordinary human sympathies; which must, by a mere instinct of good sense, seek out objects more congenial and upon their own level. One answer to Johnson's killing shot, as he kindly meant it, is that our brother is not dead but sleeping. Regularly as the coming generations unfold their vast processions, regularly as these processions move forward upon the impulse and summons of a nobler music, regularly as the dormant powers and sensibilities of the intellect in the working man are more and more developed, the *Paradise Lost* will be called for more and more: less and less continually will there be any reason to complain that the immortal book, being once restored to its place, is left to slumber for a generation. So far as regards the Time which is coming; but Dr. Johnson's insulting farewell was an arrow feathered to meet the Past and Present. We may be glad at any rate that the supposed neglect is not a wrong which Milton does, but which Milton suffers. Yet that Dr. Johnson should have pretended to think the case in any special way affecting the reputation or latent powers of Milton,—Dr. Johnson, that knew the fates of Books, and had seen by moonlight in the Bodleian, the ghostly array of innumerable books long since departed as regards all human interest or knowledge—a review like that in Béranger's Dream of the First Napoleon at St. Helena, reviewing the buried forms from Austerlitz or Borodino, horses and men, trumpets and eagles, all phantom delusions, vanishing as the eternal dawn returned,—might have seemed incredible except to one who knew the immortality of malice,—that for a moment Dr. Johnson supposed himself seated on the tribunal in the character of judge, and that Milton was in fancy placed before him at the bar,—

'*Quem si non aliquâ nocuisset, mortuus esset.*'

'Johnson's Life of Milton', De Quincey's Collected Edition, 1859; Masson IV.

Bentley

Dealing much in cattle, a man's talk is of oxen; and living in this Eldorado of books, it was natural that a man should think of writing one. Golden schemes floated in Bentley's mind; for he was a golden scholar, and these were the golden hours of his early manhood. Amongst other works, he projected at this period an entire edition of the Fragments of the Greek Poets, and also a Corpus of the Greek Lexicographers (Hesychius, Suidas, Pollux, &c.). To the irreparable loss of Grecian literature, neither scheme was accomplished. Already in his 'Epist. ad Mill.' he speaks of the first as abandoned,—'*Sed hæc fuerunt*' is the emphatic expression. It was in the fates that Bentley's maiden performances as an author should be in other and more obscure society. Amongst the manuscript riches of the Bodleian there was a copy—the one sole[1] copy in this world—of a certain old chronicler, about whose very name there had been a considerable amount of learned dust kicked up. Properly speaking, he ought to be called *Joannes Malĕlas Antiochenus*: but, if you are not particular about your Greek, you may call him *Malela*, without an *s*. This old gentleman, a fellow of infinite dulness, wrote a chronicle beginning with Adam, and coming down to the 35th year of Justinian. And here lies the necessity of calling him either *Malela* or *Malelas*; for, strange to say, as there were two Alexander Cunninghams, who at this very time were going about the world mere echoes or mocking-birds of each other, so there were two Johns, both of Antioch, both chroniclers, both asses (no distinction there), and both choosing to start from Adam. The publication of this chronicle had been twice meditated before, but interrupted by accidents. At length, in 1690, it was resumed under the superintendence of Mill, who claimed from Bentley a promise he had made to throw together any notes which might occur to him upon the proof-sheets, as they came reeking from the press. These notes took the shape of an 'Epistola ad Millium': and thus the worthy old jackass of Antioch had the honour of coming forth to the world with the notes of Chilmead (one of the two early projectors of an edition), *Prolegomena* by Hody, a learned chaplain of Bishop Stillingfleet's, and with this

[1] By the way, it should be borne in mind that, over and above the translations which yet survive into the Arabic (a resource obviously of little hope, except in the case of scientific books), there are first and last four avenues by which we may have a chance for recovering any of the lost classics: 1. The Palimpsests, as in repeated instances of late in the Ambrosian Library at Milan; 2. The Pompeii MSS. (for the sensible way of dealing with which see a letter of Lord Holland to Dr. Parr); 3. *The great chests of Greek MSS. in the Sultan's Library at Constantinople*, packed up ever since the triumph of the Crescent in 1453; and, finally, the MSS. lurking in the Christian monasteries of Mount Athos.

very masterly collection of disquisitions by Bentley upon topics either closely connected with the work or remotely suggested by it.

Blackwood's Magazine, Sept. 1830; Masson IV.

Shelley

Shelley, it must be remembered, carried his irreligion to a point beyond all others. Of the darkest beings we are told that they 'believe and tremble'; but Shelley believed and *hated*, and his defiances were meant to show that he did *not* tremble. Yet, has he not the excuse of something like *monomania* upon this subject? I firmly believe it. But a superstition, old as the world, clings to the notion that words of deep meaning, uttered even by lunatics or by idiots, execute themselves, and that also, when uttered in presumption, they bring round their own retributive chastisements.

On the other hand, however shocked at Shelley's obstinate revolt from all religious sympathies with his fellow-men, no man is entitled to deny the admirable qualities of his moral nature, which were as striking as his genius. Many people remarked something seraphic in the expression of his features; and something seraphic there was in his nature. No man was better qualified to have loved Christianity; and to no man, resting under the shadow of that one darkness, would Christianity have said more gladly—*talis cum sis, utinam noster esses!*[1] Shelley would, from his earliest manhood, have sacrificed all that he possessed to any comprehensive purpose of good for the race of man. He dismissed all injuries and insults from his memory. He was the sincerest and the most truthful of human creatures. He was also the purest. If he denounced marriage as a vicious institution, *that* was but another phasis of the partial lunacy which affected him; for to no man were purity and fidelity more essential elements in his idea of real love. I agree, therefore, heartily with Mr. Gilfillan, in protesting against the thoughtless assertion of some writer in the 'Edinburgh Review' that Shelley at all selected the story of his 'Cenci' on account of its horrors, or that he has found pleasure in dwelling on those horrors. Far from it! Indeed, he has retreated so entirely from the most shocking feature of the story—viz. the incestuous violence of Cenci the father—as actually to leave it doubtful whether the murder were in punishment of the last outrage committed or in repulsion of a menace continually repeated. The true motive of the selection of such a story was—not its darkness, but (as Mr. Gilfillan, with so much penetration, perceives)

---

[1] *Such when thou art, would to God thou wert ours.*

the light which fights with the darkness: Shelley found the whole attraction of this dreadful tale in the angelic nature of Beatrice, as revealed in local traditions and in the portrait of her by Guido. Everybody who has read with understanding the 'Wallenstein' of Schiller is aware of the repose and the divine relief arising upon a background of so much darkness, such a tumult of ruffians, bloody intriguers, and assassins, from the situation of the two lovers, Max. Piccolomini and the Princess Thelka, both yearning so profoundly after peace, both so noble, both so young, and both destined to be so unhappy. The same fine relief, the same light shining in darkness, arises here from the touching beauty of Beatrice, from her noble aspirations after deliverance, from the remorse which reaches her in the midst of real innocence, from her meekness, and from the depth of her inexpressible affliction. Even the murder, even the parricide, though proceeding from herself, do but deepen that background of darkness which throws into fuller revelation the glory of that suffering face immortalised by Guido.

Something of a similar effect arises to myself when reviewing the general abstract of Shelley's life—so brief, so full of agitation, so full of strife. When one thinks of the early misery which he suffered, and of the insolent infidelity which, being yet so young, he wooed with a lover's passion, then the darkness of midnight begins to form a deep, impenetrable background, upon which the phantasmagoria of all that is to come may arrange itself in troubled phosphoric streams, and in sweeping processions of woe. Yet, again, when one recurs to his gracious nature, his fearlessness, his truth, his purity from all fleshliness of appetite, his freedom from vanity, his diffusive love and tenderness, suddenly out of the darkness reveals itself a morning of May, forests and thickets or roses advance to the foreground, and from the midst of them looks out 'the eternal child,' cleansed from his sorrow, radiant with joy, having power given him to forget the misery which he suffered, power given him to forget the misery which he caused, and leaning with his heart upon that dove-like faith against which his erring intellect had rebelled.

Tait's Magazine, Dec. 1845; Masson XI.

Lessing's Laocoon

I have argued that the sculptor, in setting limits to the expression of pain in the Laocoon, proceeded upon principle. On looking over the reasons by which this has been maintained, I find that they all resolve themselves into the peculiar constitution of his art, and its original and natural necessities. This being the

case, it is scarcely possible that any one of these arguments should be applicable
to the art of Poetry.

Without stopping to examine how far the poet can succeed in representing
personal beauty, thus much is indisputable—that, since the whole immeasurable field of perfection in every mode is open to his art, that particular mani-
festation, or (to speak learnedly) that incarnation of the perfect which is called
Beauty, can never be more than one amongst many resources (and those the
slightest) by which he has it in his power to engage our interest for his characters. Least of all is it necessary in any single trait of description, not expressly
designed for the sight, that the poet should address himself to that sense. When
Virgil's Laocoon shrieks, who thinks of the wide opening of the mouth that
takes place in that act, and of its ugliness? Enough that the expression *Clamores
horrendos ad sidera tollit'* is a grand trait for the ear, be it what it may for the sight.
And he that looks for a beautiful image in this place has wholly missed the true
effect designed by the poet.

In the next place, nothing obliges the poet (like the painter) to concentrate his
picture into one punctual instant of time. Any action whatsoever he is at liberty
to take up from its origin, and to conduct it through every stage to the conclusion. Each one of these stages, which would cost the painter a separate picture,
is despatched by *him* in a single trait of description; and, supposing this trait,
separately considered, to be offensive, yet, by skilful position in respect to what
precedes and follows, it may be so *medicated* (as it were) by the preparation of
the one, and the reaction of the other, as to merge its peculiar and separate
effect in the general impression.

Virgil, therefore, may be justified for departing from the sculptor in his treatment of the Laocoon. But Virgil is a narrative poet: how far, then, will the
benefit of *his* justification extend to the dramatic poet? It is one thing to tell us of
a shriek, and another thing actually to reproduce the shriek in a mimic representation: and possibly it may be the duty of Drama, as a sort of living art of
Painting by means of actors, to bind itself more severely than other kinds of
poetry to the laws of that art. In the representation of the theatre it will be urged
that we no longer *fancy* that we are seeing and hearing a shrieking Philoctetes;
we do actually see and hear him; and, the nearer to the truth of nature that the
mimetic art of the actor is in this instance carried, so much the more sensibly
should our eyes and ears be offended,—for it is undeniable that they are so, in
the realities of nature, by all violent expressions of pain. Bodily pain above all is,
in general, ill adapted to call forth the sympathy which is given to other modes
of suffering. It presents to our imagination too little of distinct features for the
mere sight of it to impress us with a proportionate feeling. *Prima facie*, therefore,
it is not absolutely impossible that Sophocles, in representing his suffering

heroes as weeping and wailing, may have violated a law of decorum, not arbitrary or fantastic, but grounded in the very nature of humane motions. The bystanders, it is clear, cannot possibly take as much interest in their sufferings as this clamorous uproar of ejaculation seems to call for. They will, therefore, appear to us, the spectators, comparatively cold; and yet we cannot possibly regard their sympathy as other than the fit measure for our own. Add to this, that the actor can with great difficulty, if at all, carry the expression of pain to the necessary point of illusion.

How plausible, how irrefragable, would many an objection drawn from theory appear, had not genius succeeded in demonstrating its falsehood by mere blank argument of fact. None of the considerations alleged seems to be without some foundation; yet, for all that, the Philoctetes remains a *chef-d'œuvre* of the stage. The truth is that one part of the objections glances wide of Sophocles; and, with respect to the other, simply by managing the subject so as to throw it out of the level of their range, the poet has achieved beauties which the timid connoisseur, in the absence of such a model, could never have imagined to be possible.

Marvellously, indeed, has the poet succeeded in strengthening and exalting the idea of bodily pain. First of all, he selected for the ground of his interest a wound rather than an internal malady, however painful, as judging the former to be susceptible of a more impressive representation. On this principle the internal fire which consumes Meleager, in fatal sympathy with the brand which his mother throws into the fire as a sacrifice to her sisterly wrath, would be less adapted to the illusions of the scene than a wound. Secondly, the wound of Philoctetes was a judgment from Heaven. A poison in which was more than a natural malignity gnawed within the wound for ever; intervals there were none, except as regarded the extreme paroxysms; these had their stated periods, after which the miserable man regularly sank into a comatose sleep, in which nature rested from her agonies to restore him strength for treading the same round of torment again.

Dreadful, however, as were the bodily sufferings of his hero, Sophocles was sensible that these alone were not sufficient to sustain any remarkable degree of pity. With pain, therefore, he connected other evils; and these also taken separately might not have been particularly moving; but, connected as they were, they lent to the bodily torments a sad and touching interest, which again was reflected back upon themselves. These evils consist in hunger, in the inclemency of a raw ungenial climate, in utter solitude, in the want of any σύντροφον ὄμμα(*i.e.* any household sympathising eye), together with the naked and calamitous condition of life to which a human being is exposed under circumstances of such perfect destitution. When the Chorus is reflecting on the miserable condition of Philoctetes, the helpless solitude of it is the circumstance to which they direct their chief regard. In every word of this we recognise the social Grecian. For, represent a man as oppressed by the most painful and incurable complaint, but at the same time as surrounded by affectionate friends who suffer him to want for no alleviation of his sufferings, and fail in no offices of consolation,—undoubtedly we grant him our sympathy, but not of a deep or an enduring character. Figure him, on the other hand, under the double calamity of sickness and of solitude; figure him mastered as by a demoniacal possession, incapable of giving help to himself through disease, incapable of receiving it through this situation; imagine him throwing out his complaints upon the desert air, expostulating with the very rocks and the sea, and pouring forth his wild litanies of anguish to the heavens, we then behold our human nature under the uttermost burden of wretchedness that it can support; we clasp our hands over the poor suffering creature; and, if ever an image crosses our fancy of ourselves as standing in the same situation, we dismiss it with a shuddering horror.

Blackwood's Magazine, 1826–7; Masson XI.

General

Miracles as Testimony

Hume's argument against miracles is simply this: Every possible event, however various in its degree of credibility, must of necessity be more credible when it rests upon a sufficient cause lying within the field of what is called *nature* than when it does not,—more credible when it obeys some mechanical cause than when it transcends such a cause and is miraculous.

Therefore, assume the resistance to credibility in any preternatural occurrence as equal to x, and the very ideal or possible value of human testimony as no more than x: in that case, under the most favourable circumstances conceivable, the argument for and against a miracle, $+x$ and $-x$, will be equal; the two values will destroy each other; and the result will be $=0$.

But, inasmuch as this expresses the value of human testimony in its highest or ideal form,—a form which is seldom realized in experience,—the true result will be different: there will always be a negative result, much or little according to circumstances, but in any case enough to turn the balance *against* believing a miracle.

'Or, in other words,' said Hume, popularizing his argument, 'it will always be more credible that the reporter of a miracle should have told a falsehood, or should himself have been the dupe of appearances, than that a miracle should have actually occurred,—that is, an infraction of those natural laws (any or all) which limit what we call experience. For, assume the utmost disinterestedness, veracity, and sound judgement in the witness, with the utmost advantage in the circumstances for giving full play to those qualities; even in such a case the value of affirmative testimony could, at the very utmost, be equal to the negative value on the other side of the equation: and the result would be to keep my faith suspended *in equilibrio*. But, in any real case ever likely to come before us, the result will be worse; for the affirmative testimony will be sure to fall in many ways below its ideal maximum,—leaving, therefore, for the final result some excess, much or little, to the negative side of the equation.'[1]

SECTION II

Of the Argument as affected by the Covert Limitations under which it is presented

Such is the argument; and, as the first step towards investigating its sanity and its strength, its kind of force and its quantity of force, we must direct our

[1] This paragraph, though printed within quotation-marks, is not an actual quotation from Hume, but only an expression of Hume's argument in De Quincey's own words.—M.

attention to the following fact: viz. that, amongst three separate conditions under which a miracle (or any event whatever) might become known to us, Hume's argument is applied only to one. Assuming a miracle to happen (for the possibility of a miracle is of course left open throughout the discussion, since any argument against *that* would at once foreclose every question about its communicability), then it might happen under three several sets of circumstances, in relation to our consciousness. 1. It might happen in the presence of a single witness,—that witness not being ourselves. This case let us call *Alpha*. 2. It might happen in the presence of many witnesses,—witnesses to a variable amount, but still (as before) ourselves not being amongst that multitude. This case let us call *Beta*. 3. It might happen in our presence, and fall within the direct light of our own consciousness. This case let us call *Gamma*.

Now, these distinctions are important to the whole extent of the question. For the second case, which is the actual case of many miracles recorded in the New Testament, at once cuts away a large body of sources in which either error or deceit could lurk. Hume's argument supposes the reporter of the miracle to be a dupe, or the maker of dupes—himself deluded, or wishing to delude others. But, in the case of the thousands fed from a few loaves and small fishes, the chances of error, wilful or not wilful, are diminished in proportion to the number of observers,[1] and Hume's inference as to the declension of the affirmative x, in relation to the negative x, no longer applies, or, if at all, with vastly diminished force. With respect to the third case, it cuts away the whole argument at once in its very radix. For Hume's argument applies to the *communication* of a miracle, and therefore to a case of testimony. But, wherever the miracle falls within direct personal cognisance, there it follows that no question can arise about the value of human testimony. The affirmative x, expressing the value of testimony, disappears altogether; and that side of the equation is possessed by a new quantity (viz. a quantity representing ourselves—our own consciousness), not at all concerned in Hume's arguments.

Hence it results that, of three possible conditions under which a miracle may be supposed to offer itself to our knowledge, two are excluded from the view of Hume's argument.

Blackwood's Magazine, July 1839; Masson VIII.

---

[1] '*In proportion to the number of observers*': Perhaps, however, on the part of Hume, some critical apologist will say, 'Doubtless he was aware of that; but still the reporters of the miracle were few. No matter how many were present, the witnesses for us are but the Evangelists.' Yes, certainly, the Evangelists; and, let us add, all those contemporaries to whom the Evangelists silently appealed. These make up the 'multitude' contemplated in the case *Beta*.

Casuistry

LAWS OF HOSPITALITY IN COLLISION WITH CIVIC DUTIES

Suppose the case that, taking shelter from a shower of rain in a stranger's house, you discover proofs of a connexion with smugglers. Take this for one pole of such case, the trivial extreme; then, for the other pole, the greater extreme, suppose the case that, being hospitably entertained, and happening to pass the night in a stranger's house, you are so unfortunate as to detect unquestionable proofs of some dreadful crime, say murder, perpetrated in past times by one of the family. The principle at issue is the same in both cases—viz. the command resting upon the conscience to forget private considerations and personal feelings in the presence of any solemn duty; yet merely the difference of degree, and not any at all in the kind of duty, would lead pretty generally to a separate practical decision for the several cases. In the last of the two, whatever might be the pain to a person's feelings, he would feel himself to have no discretion or choice left. Reveal he must; not only, if otherwise revealed, he must come forward as a witness, but, if not revealed, he must denounce—he must lodge an information, and that instantly; else even in law, without question of morality, he makes himself a party to the crime—an accomplice after the act. That single consideration would with most men at once cut short all deliberation. And yet, even in such a situation, there is a possible variety of the case that might alter its complexion. If the crime had been committed many years before, and under circumstances which precluded all fear that the same temptation or the same provocation should arise again, and with no lurking chance that an innocent person should fall under suspicion, most reflecting people would think it the better course to leave the criminal to his conscience. Often in such denunciations it is certain that human impertinence, and the spirit which sustains the habit of gossip, and mere incontinence of secrets, and vulgar craving for being the author of a sensation, have far more often led to the publication of the offence than any concern for the interests of morality.[1]

On the other hand, with respect to the slighter extreme—viz. in a case where the offence is entirely created by the law, with no natural turpitude about it, and besides (which is a strong argument in the case) enjoying no special facilities of escaping justice—no man in the circumstances supposed would have a reason for hesitating. The laws of hospitality are of everlasting obligation; they

---

[1] Most confessions in prison fall within this category. They are special luxuries to all parties, especially to the criminal, whose only vexation is that he cannot make ten confessions; since ever after he becomes a pet, and is regularly fattened up for the scaffold.

are equally binding on the host and on the guest. Coming under a man's roof for one moment, in the clear character of guest, creates an absolute sanctity in the consequent relations which connect the parties. That is the popular feeling. The king in the old ballads is always represented as feeling that it would be damnable to make a legal offence out of his own venison which he had eaten as a guest. There is a cleaving pollution, like that of the Syrian leprosy, in the act of abusing your privileges as a guest, or in any way profiting by your opportunities as a guest to the injury of your confiding host. Henry VII, though a prince, was no gentleman; and in the famous case of his dining with Lord Oxford, and saying at his departure, with reference to an infraction of his recent statute, 'My lord, I thank you for my good cheer, but my attorney must speak with you,' Lord Oxford might have justly retorted, 'If he does, then posterity will speak pretty plainly with your grace'; for it was in the character of Lord Oxford's guest that he had learned the infraction of his law. Meantime, the general rule, and the *rationale* of the rule, in such cases, appears to be this; whenever there is, or can be imagined a sanctity in the obligations on one side, and only a benefit of expediency in the obligations upon the other, the latter must give way. For the detection of smuggling (the particular offence supposed in the case stated) society has an express and separate machinery maintained. If their activity droops, that is the business of government. In such a case government is entitled to no aid from private citizens; on the express understanding that no aid must be expected has so expensive an establishment been submitted to. Each individual refuses to participate in exposure of such offences, for the same reason that in some towns he refuses to keep the street clean even before his own door: he has already paid for having such work discharged by proxy.

Blackwood's Magazine, Oct. 1839; Masson VIII.

Christianity

As there are some important truths, dimly perceived or not at all, lurking in the idea of God—an idea too vast to be navigable as yet by the human understanding, yet here and there to be coasted—I wish at this point to direct the reader's attention upon a passage which he may happen to remember in Sir Isaac Newton. The passage occurs at the end of the *Optics*, and the exact expressions I do not remember; but the sense is what I am going to state:—Sir Isaac is speaking of God; and he takes occasion to say that God is not good, but goodness; is not holy, but holiness; is not infinite, but infinity. This, I apprehend, will have struck many readers as merely a rhetorical *bravura*; sublime, perhaps, and fitted to exalt the feeling of awe connected with so unapproachable a mystery, but otherwise not throwing any new light upon the darkness of the idea as a problem before the intellect. Yet indirectly perhaps it *does*, when brought out into its latent sense by placing it in juxtaposition with Paganism. If a philosophic theist who is also a Christian, or who (*not* being a Christian) has yet by his birth and breeding become saturated with Christian ideas and feelings,[1] attempts to realise the idea of supreme Deity, he becomes aware of a double and contradictory movement in his own mind whilst striving towards that result. He demands, in the first place, something in the highest degree generic, and yet again, in the opposite direction, something in the highest degree individual; he demands on the one path a vast ideality, and yet on the other in union with a determinate personality. He must not surrender himself to the first impulse, else he is betrayed into a mere *anima mundi*; he must not surrender himself to the second, else he is betrayed into something merely human. This difficult antagonism of what is most and what is least generic must be maintained; otherwise the idea, the possible idea, of that august unveiling which takes place in the Judaico-Christian God is absolutely in clouds. Now, this antagonism utterly collapses in Paganism. And to a philosophic apprehension this peculiarity of the heathen gods is more shocking and fearful than what at first sight had seemed most so. When a man pauses for the purpose of attentively reviewing the Pantheon of Greece and Rome, what strikes him at the first with most depth of impression and with most horror is the *wickedness* of this Pantheon. And he observes with surprise that this wickedness, which is at a furnace-heat in the superior gods, becomes fainter and paler as you descend. Amongst the semi-deities, such as the Oreads or Dryads, the Nereids or Naiads, he feels not at all offended. The odour of corruption, the *sæva mephitis*, has by this time exhaled. The uproar of eternal outrage has ceased. And these gentle divinities, if too human and too beset with infirmities, are not impure, and not vexed with ugly appetites, nor instinct of quarrel: they are tranquil as are the hills and the forests; passionless as are the seas and the fountains which they tenant. But, when he ascends to the *dii*

---

[1] '*Not being a Christian, has yet become saturated with Christian ideas*': This case is far from uncommon; and undoubtedly, from having too much escaped observation, it has been the cause of much error. Poets I could mention, if it were not invidious to do so, who, whilst composing in a spirit of burning enmity to the Christian faith, yet rested for the very sting of their pathos upon ideas that but for Christianity could never have existed. Translators there have been, English, French, German, of Mohammedan books, who have so coloured the whole vein of thinking with sentiments peculiar to Christianity as to draw from a reflecting reader the exclamation, 'If this can be indeed the product of Islamism, wherefore should Christianity exist? If thoughts so divine can indeed belong to a false religion, what more could we gain from a true one?'

majorum gentium, to those twelve gods of the supreme house who may be called, in respect of rank, the Paladins of the classical Pantheon, secret horror comes over him at the thought that demons, reflecting the worst aspects of brutal races, ever *could* have levied worship from his own. It is true they do so no longer as regards *our* planet. But what *has* been apparently *may* be. God made the Greeks and Romans of one blood with himself; he cannot deny that *intellectually* the Greeks—he cannot deny that *morally* the Romans—were amongst the foremost of human races; and he trembles in thinking that abominations, whose smoke ascended through so many ages to the *supreme* heavens, may, or might, so far as human resistance is concerned, again become the law for the noblest of his species. A deep feeling, it is true, exists latently in human beings of something perishable in evil. Whatsoever is founded in wickedness, according to a deep misgiving dispersed amongst men, must be tainted with corruption. *There* might seem consolation; but a man who reflects is not quite so sure of *that*. As a commonplace resounding in schools, it may be justly current amongst us that what is evil by nature or by origin must be transient. But *that* may be because evil in all human things is partial, is heterogeneous,—evil mixed with good,—and the two natures, by their mutual enmity, must enter into a collision which may possibly guarantee the final destruction of the whole compound. Such a result may not threaten a nature that is purely and totally evil, that is *homogeneously* evil. Dark natures there may be whose *essence* is evil, that may have an abiding root in the system of the universe not less awfully exempt from change than the mysterious foundations of God.

Tait's Magazine, April 1846; Masson VIII.

War

Few people need be told that associations exist up and down Christendom having the ambitious object of abolishing war. Some go so far as to believe that this evil of war, so ancient, so ubiquitous, and apparently so inalienable from man's position upon earth, is already doomed: that not the private associations only, but the prevailing voice of races the most civilised, is tending to confederation against it; that sentence of extermination has virtually gone forth; and that all which remains is gradually to execute the sentence. Conscientiously, I find myself unable to join in these views. Of all romances, this seems to me the most romantic. Consequently, when asked to become a member of any such association, I have always thought it most respectful, because most sincere, to decline. Yet, as it is painful to refuse all marks of sympathy with persons whose motives one honours, I design at my death to bequeath half-a-crown as the foundation-stone of a fund for extinguishing war; the said half-crown to be improved in all time coming for the benefit of the aforesaid fund, under the trusteeship of Europe, Asia, and America, but not of Africa. I really dare not trust Africa with money, so little is she able as yet to take care of herself. This half-crown (a fund that will overshadow the earth before it comes to be wanted, under the provisions of my will) is to be improved at any interest whatever—no matter what; for the vast period of the accumulations will easily compensate any tardiness of advance, long before the time comes for its commencing payment; a point which will be readily understood by any gentleman that hopes to draw upon the fund, when he has read the following explanation.

Collected Edition, 1854; Masson VIII.